The Devil Who Walked The Earth

My Life as a Hospitalist

Glenn Allen

Bloomington, IN   Milton Keynes, UK

AuthorHouse™
1663 Liberty Drive, Suite 200
Bloomington, IN 47403
www.authorhouse.com
Phone: 1-800-839-8640

AuthorHouse™ UK Ltd.
500 Avebury Boulevard
Central Milton Keynes, MK9 2BE
www.authorhouse.co.uk
Phone: 08001974150

© 2007 Glenn Allen. All rights reserved.

No part of this book may be reproduced, stored in a retrieval system, or transmitted by any means without the written permission of the author.

First published by AuthorHouse   5/17/2007

ISBN: 978-1-4343-0488-9 (sc)

Library of Congress Control Number: 2007902364

Printed in the United States of America
Bloomington, Indiana

This book is printed on acid-free paper.

Front cover art work by Julee Gardner, rlj71@bellsouth.net

You may contact the author at: death_to_lawyers@yahoo.com

Acknowledgements

To my wife who put up with me while I was writing this book and who promises to return to the United States when the statute of limitations has run out.

And to all those lawyers who plan to sue me, remember, the last chapter's not been written.

"It's hard to care about others more than they care about themselves." An anonymous selfish doctor whom I neither confirm nor deny was me.

Author's Notes:

You'll notice that the tense keeps changing in this book without obvious cause or reason. This wasn't so much a literary ploy as a reflection of my incompetence and laziness. If you don't think you can stomach it, don't buy this book or **you can** volunteer to edit my next one. In any case, the flow of the story is only marginally affected and since it's all made up anyway, it really makes no difference.

Also, there are a number of literary allusions in this book which I've included as a tribute to the brilliance of the original thinkers who came up with them. I've ascribed authorship to them but have not asked for permission for their use. I hope that I will be granted ex post facto permission, if not, stand in line and sue me.

Although virtually everything in this book is a product of my own imagination and wishful thinking, almost everything depicted was inspired by actual events and in a number of circumstances were written down almost verbatim (as best as I could remember them after the heat of the battle). I am not saying that entering a nursing home is the death knell, but I am saying that anyone ending up in a nursing home is the result of both an economic and a social failure of planning. You weren't nice enough to have people love you so they'd be willing to take care of you at home and you failed to save enough money to buy home health care in the absence of willing volunteers. In some circumstances people insist on going to the nursing home because of an entitlement mentality, they think it's their right to be there. If even ten percent of what I've written in this book is true, they'll get what they deserve.

And don't even get me started on lawyers.

Hope you have a good read. Suspend your disbelief for a while and enjoy a romp in make believe. Or is it?

Prelude

"Summon Satan unto me!"

"I am here my lord."

"Satan, you bad boy, I have a job for you."

"As you wish, my lord."

Prologue

Hate. A powerful emotion. Perhaps an even more powerful motivation. Oh, there are various degrees of hate. I might hate this movie or hate this food, but that type of hate is ephemeral and of little consequence. Worse, I might hate this place, perhaps motivating me to some action: moving, cursing, drugs. I might even hate my ex-wife, but is acting on that worth a life on the run? Maybe. But the worst type of hate is a visceral loathing of an idea, in this case the idea that lawyers, and, now that I think of it, ex-wives too, are allowed to continue to walk the earth. Dante would be hard pressed to fathom the hell I envision for them, these blood sucking creatures spawned from all that is evil in this world. Perhaps they're even from another world whose horror is beyond the comprehension of mere mortal earthlings. In any case, now there's a call to arms, literally, that almost all of us can agree with. I often saw my defense as "no jury in the world would ever convict me, he was a lawyer", but no, it would never get that far. I'm too smart and clever to get caught. I even considered enlisting the help of others to carry out my plans, but again no, that would not be smart. If I'm the smart one, everyone else would be the weak links. I couldn't afford any weak links. I had no intention of being thwarted. So many lawyers, so little time. Thus I started the journey alone, never considering looking back.

Why lawyers you might ask? They're learned and good people. Sworn by oath to seek justice and right the wrongs befalling their clients. Fortunately for you I've not targeted mush headed lawyer apologists who clearly can't sustain a thought in their head long enough to consider it. I don't have nearly enough time to bring each unenlightened soul up to speed regarding lawyers. Suffice it to say the above premise on which you based your defense of lawyers is not only wrong but also in operation is the exact opposite of their motivation. The single most important thing to a lawyer is money. Your money, anyone's money, everyone's money. Any money they can get their hands on by any means possible short of being so egregiously illegal that they themselves might need the help of a lawyer. To this end, they are able to justify virtually every lie conceivable to man. There are quite a few who do themselves in by coming up with such whoppers that even their liars-in-arms can't keep a straight face and feel compelled to do something about it before the general population gets the right idea and wises up to their shenanigans. That would queer the deal for all and therefore couldn't be tolerated. The remedial action usually recommended is an ethics course. This doesn't teach the errant lawyers real ethics, right and wrong, ten commandment type stuff. No, it merely educates them what is permissible for the public to see and how to be cleverer in their deceit.

I myself am not a Ten Commandments type guy, a far right religious wacko. I don't even attend services and haven't since I was 18 and freed from my juvenile bonds. So where do I get the notion that liars, I mean lawyers, are so evil. Everyone lies and everyone knows it. What sets lawyers apart is they're so good at it and it is their modus operandi, almost their raison d'être except that that is really the pursuit of money. Power too, but that really boils down to money. In medicine, we'd call them pathological liars. That is, they'd lie even if telling the truth was in their best interest. If you need a glaring example, look at Bill and Hillary Clinton and how they kept it up with a straight face for eight years even after the rest of the country had stopped listening to them. So lawyers lie, what else is new? The problem is that since they're sworn to tell the truth they are believed where it counts, in court, and they can do you untold harm. And that undeserved harm can lead to a state of mind, an overwhelming, all encompassing, all pervasive state of mind – hate.

So I developed a master plan fairly early on to relieve the boiling tensions within me. A conflict between righting perceived wrongs and self-preservation. One just didn't mount a frontal assault on an entire class of SPOS's who were acknowledged to be quite powerful individually and almost overwhelmingly omnipotent as a group without some second thoughts and quite a bit of planning. So I decided that I would join a similarly powerful and even more respected group and become a physician. From within the framework of the medical establishment I would be both invisible as an agent of change and a subtle but formidable protagonist of that change I desire to bring about. It was during medical training that I first heard the name I could apply to the enemy that was both clever and recognized within the medical field as nothing more than a generally agreed upon name for those we don't like, therefore not raising any undesired questions: SPOS. Subhuman Piece of Shit. Generally, others applied it to undesirables of any ilk but I reserved it for lawyers.

Still, after all the above, what had a lawyer ever done to me? Don't ask. But, what the heck, I'll tell you anyway.

Chapter 1:
I'm So Naïve

When you look in the dictionary for the definition of middle class, there I am. You actually see a picture of my family and me. We didn't have what you might call a boring existence but perhaps somewhat dull. Suburbia par excellence. A nice ranch house, the required three progeny, a cheery, stay at home mom and a productive dad. The correct smattering of boyfriends and girlfriends. Overall, a truly pleasant albeit ordinary existence.

Until that day. A certified letter was delivered to the door. An unusual event in my household to be sure. Mom signed for it but put it aside in the place she would use to hide presents and other personal items from the kids until the proper moment.

Mom wasn't quite sure what to make of it. She did seem a little upset. I glimpsed a peak at the envelope as she hurried by. Jones and someone, Attorneys at Law. I hadn't met a lawyer in real life but I watched TV shows about them all the time. The only show I could think of about good attorneys was "The Bold Ones". I really liked that show. Good lawyers sticking up for the rights of a downtrodden individual and justice always prevailing. All the other shows made me want to cheer the demise of attorneys as we all did later on when that lawyer was snatched out of the toilet by a tyrannosaurus rex in "Jurassic Park". Anyway, at the time, I was a little concerned over the reaction of my mother to the letter. I didn't really know what such an innocent looking letter could hold that would cause my usually cheerful mom to be so concerned. My life seemed so secure. I was so blissfully ignorantly happy. I was so naive.

Dad finally came home at the usual time, in the usual way and hugged all the kids in the usual manner. We ate dinner and the kids sat to watch television in the usual way. However, mom and dad did not join us, as was their custom. Something was different, something was wrong. Looking back on it, that was the first time I ever associated lawyers with something going wrong personally. I couldn't possibly foresee the degree to which lawyers and evil would become so entwined in my mind so as to become synonymous.

So we sat and watched TV, my two sisters and me. They sensing nothing even though they were older by several years. But I did, even though only 10. An uneasiness crept over me, which, I must admit, frequently did. I guess I was just a sensitive kid. Mom finally came into the room and said it was time for bed. Too timid to question her about the letter, I dutifully followed my sisters down the hall to the bedrooms. We went to bed and slept fairly well.

I long since noticed that no matter what happens or what's on my mind, nothing prevents me from having a good sleep. In my professional career it's become clear what a blessing this quality is. Half of the people I talk to have trouble getting to sleep. They just ruminate all night long, sleeping fitfully at best. When morning finally comes, they feel just miserable for the rest of the day. Annoyed (and annoying) and irritated. In a word, perfect fodder for the attorney engine. One of my favorite cartoons was a Far Side panel depicting explorers landing on a tropical island. Out of the woods came a series of natives dressed in nothing but loin clothes and derby hats and carrying briefcases. The caption read: "The natives sent out their fiercest lawyers crying, 'Sue them! Sue them!'"

The next morning I awoke, feeling quite rested. Mom said nothing unusual, dad said nothing unusual and nothing unusual happened. I rode off to school on my bike in a most usual way.

I didn't have to ride my bike to school. School was five miles away and a bus would have gladly picked me up. But even at that tender age, I not only wanted to be different but also wanted to be able to tell stories of having to ride back and forth to school every day, rain or shine, snow or sleet, light or dark, uphill both ways. Abe Lincoln would have nothing on me.

What a jerk. That actually became my little name for myself as I proceeded through life, bouncing, sometime hurdling, from one embarrassing faux paux to the next.

School went through its usual uneventful course. I was oblivious to everything that happened that day. My main concern was having lunch and going home. I grew fond of a neologism I coined later on in life, oblivioma, to describe anyone who didn't have a clue. I was a prime example of one.

Arriving home did little to change my state of mind. Everything was as I left it and nothing seemed amiss. The next day continued as before. I was beginning to think that the letter meant nothing and I was lulled into a sense of complacency that suited me fine.

In fact, nothing happened as a direct result of that letter that I could see and it soon faded from my mind. Life went on as always and things remained pleasant. Until summer. Every summer I would go to summer camp. I didn't even know there were kids who didn't go to summer camp. Until I was 10. That summer my sisters and I stayed home. I asked mom "Why" but she only said "Because". Now that's annoying. I was getting my proper sleep, and as far as I could tell, mom was getting her proper sleep. But nevertheless, an answer of "Because", especially one not coming from me and especially one regarding a topic so significant to me as no summer camp, is annoying.

Being a clever little kid, having a very long memory and never getting over the strange foreboding I felt several months ago when "The Letter" came, I put two and two together and decided to investigate this issue further.

I went to that special hiding place mom has but found nothing. To a 10 year old that could have been a little frustrating but I was getting a little education in frustration and corrective action bit by bit which would stand me in good stead in later years. I regrouped, thought about where mom would hide an important letter and hit upon a brilliant idea. Look in her desk! The desk is usually off limits but every once in a while I would steal a peak when I needed some stamps. So I waited until everyone was out or busy and did a little search. Then a long search and finally a complete, exhaustive, spare no expense search. But there was no letter. Nothing that looked like a letter. No microdot (Secret Agent with Patrick McGoohan was my favorite TV show at the time and there was nothing he couldn't do or find and he was especially good with microdots). But I was either no secret agent or there was no letter there. I couldn't even contemplate the former so the latter had to be true.

I sat in my room and took stock of the issue. I wasn't in any big hurry as I had ALL SUMMER to figure it out, as that was the cause of the search in the first place. Then it struck me. The letter wasn't to mom, it was to dad. How could it be to mom anyway? She never did anything, never went out without the kids or dad, had nothing to offer or offend anyone with. This realization became the underlying premise for one of my most important principles: Why bother even acknowledging their existence, they're only commoners. A corollary is: If they have nothing to offer me, why deal with them?

So, with this great revelation, I snuck back into mom's room but this time went to The Other Desk, dad's! Like a treasure hunter upon first realizing the pirate's map is real and the treasure found, I stumbled upon not only The Letter but also a series of letters and other odd sized papers encompassing several large folders. I had never seen so many related papers in one spot except in my school textbooks nor had I ever seen the extra long papers that seemed to comprise the bulk of the trove.

There was too much to read in one sitting. I couldn't risk removing it from the room and I couldn't understand most of what was written on the one page I looked at. I needed a plan. First, I'd need a dictionary, except for a few words I could understand, such as my dad's name listed under defendant, which I couldn't understand, it looked like the words were a foreign language. Second, I needed uninterrupted time to be able to sort out the papers and try to understand what they meant. Therefore, mom and everyone had to be out of the house. The only time that happened without me was a shopping trip to the mall. Strangely enough, they hadn't gone to the mall for some time. Okay, initiate plan B. The only problem there was no plan B. No good plan B that is. Everyone was always home and they all seemed to be bouncing off the walls with boredom. There were no friends over, no meals out, no new toys, no nothing. What was going on?

Before I could proceed with the radical, dangerous, plan C – a direct frontal assault on The Other Desk and take my chances at being caught, there were moving men everywhere. Packing up everything. Well, not everything because we had a yard sale and sold almost everything. We were left with almost nothing except the shirts on our back when we moved into a two bedroom rental in a part of town mom warned us against ever going into. We weren't even allowed to mention the name if it ever came up which it rarely did. So you can imagine the confusion the kids had in finding ourselves living in an area whose name we weren't even allowed to say.

I never did find out firsthand what were in those papers. Mom never talked about it and dad never said goodbye. As years went by, I often ruminated what The Letter contained but I never knew. The only even glancing reference to The Letter was one time I overheard mom say to someone on the phone that lawyers and the system were so unfair and they had ruined her life. If those were the only pieces of information I was ever to learn of this episode, it must have meant they were real important. The realization that lawyers were unfair and they ruin lives was to become the very crux of meaning of my life and my byword for future action.

Chapter 2: The Plan

"So, have you decided on a major yet?" asked Biff. Biff was my best friend in high school but I called him Biff the chicken hearted because he was never there when it counted.

I would judge everybody's reliability on the Biff scale. There are many people in this world. Some would never let you down. Some would occasionally disappoint you. And some would be worthless, whom I'd refer to as Biff. Only my wife in later years knew this scale but it served as worthwhile shorthand.

"Actually, I have. Premed." I responded. "How about you?"

Biff hesitated. He smoked so much pot it was unclear as to whether or not he was stoned at any particular time or he just didn't know. A betting man would usually win if he put his money on stoned. "Yeah."

"Well?"

"Well what?" Pay the man who bet on stoned.

"Biff, focus. What are you going to be if you live long enough to grow up?"

"Oh. How about a lawyer?"

Cool, FVA. "You're asking me what you want to be? Doesn't that strike you as a little silly, if not a whole lot strange?"

Biff hesitated again. "Are you calling me silly and strange or lawyers?"

"Yes."

In his current state, two answers in a row that didn't compute would almost inevitably set Biff into a tailspin. He'd spend so much time trying to convert such answers to pothead language he would almost seem to be catatonic to a casual observer. Once, a school nurse thought he was dead and actually took his pulse.

In short order Biff would come around and we would have to start again. Sometimes it was so frustrating trying to put him back on tract when I really wanted something. Most of the time I'd just let him get started again as if nothing happened. I filed the episode away to ask my psychiatry professor what it meant.

"Are you going to college?" Biff fumbled his way back into the conversation.

Class was about to start and I didn't want to overload him again. "Yes."

"Cool. Maybe I should go to."

Seeing this is where I came in, I felt it would be better to review this line of reasoning (?) later. "Gotta go, see you after school." FVA, Future Victim of America, I thought to myself.

"So, what's your major?" asked Sonia.

Oh my God, I'm in a time warp! On the other hand, May of your senior year and everyone's future course already set, asking what you're going to do is probably a sane question. Also, Sonia, being one of my early girlfriends, held a special place in my heart. She'd since moved on to others but it's hard to let go completely.

"Premed. U. Of P. How about you?"

"Prelaw, Harvard."

Now I'm in trouble. Can you paint every member of a class, lawyers, with the same brush? Are they all enemies of civilization? Does not an old, special friend deserve special dispensation? I'll have to get back to you on that. "Great." Trumped my Penn. Strike two. "How much?"

"Full scholarship."

Such a nonchalant response for such an incredible achievement. But Sonia was like that. All brains, all girl. What a catch. If she'd only used her gifts for good instead of evil. Thank you, Maxwell Smart.

"Well, see you later, I'm late for class."

School in the last month of your senior year drags on. Let's get it over with already. Let's get to the real work of life. Biff would say that that would be partying and I dare say he'd win more than half the popular vote. I, on the other hand, wasn't in this for a popularity contest. Maybe partly because I couldn't win one even if I bribed everyone, was the only candidate and counted the ballots personally. My true work was already set in stone. I looked on it in a somewhat poetic light, best espoused by Shakespeare, was it in Henry VI? – "Let's kill all the lawyers." Nicely put, Will, my boy. We need to do lunch some day.

How did he plan to eliminate the lawyers? I need to read that book again. The problem is I don't remember who said it or when. I really couldn't stomach reading all those plays again. Shakespeare was difficult. If he'd only written in English. Would his plan from the Middle Ages be relevant to the twenty-first century anyway? Doubtful. I'd have to figure it out for myself. Details, details.

How does one go about the elimination of a widespread class of people? The Romans tried lions and gladiators but the Christians won out anyway. The Christians tried torture, medieval of course, but the Jews persevered. Hitler picked on the Jews again with gas chambers and other means but he apparently bit off more than he could chew in not being selective and pissing off the entire world. The Arabs are still trying but they seem to hate each other even more than they hate the Jews. The Turks took on the Armenians and were fairly successful in a regional sort of way. So apparently, organized government efforts weren't enough. This is probably because opponents could identify the enemy and rally support to thwart them. Guerilla groups like the Red Brigade and Direct Action were far less successful. Most being a mere pinprick in a dragon. So what could one person possibly hope to accomplish. Perhaps a meld of the best of both worlds, large-scale action carried out by a single person. Stealth yet power. Okay, that's a good plan. Kill millions but don't get caught. Who's best suited to do this? Why, a doctor, of course. He's usually above suspicion, except for the odd malpractice case. People let down their guard with him. And people do die naturally. There's the answer, make it look natural! How long will excess death of lawyers last without raising suspicion? We'll find out. The best way to start will probably be small to be able to become efficient – practice makes perfect. Then large disasters at large gathering of lawyers will be the most efficient way. Medical school will teach me how; civil engineering will make it possible. Let's go team! We'll give it the old college try!

Chapter 3: "I hate this fucking place" – Tom Clancy – "Red Storm Rising"

The University of Pennsylvania was steeped in Ivy League tradition. What I didn't know until I got there was that the Ivy League wasn't an academic designation, it was a sports league. And sports ruled the roost. Alumni donors didn't care what academic rank the school held, they only cared about the football team. In a good year they noticed the basketball team but that didn't bring in the bucks. No, football was king. Therefore, if you were a member of (a winning) football team, you could get away with anything.

I found this out personally my freshman year. My roommate in the quad turned out to be a reincarnated Teutonic warrior. Even his major was German. He was also the captain of the frosh football team. And they were winning. As average in height and looks as I was, he was outstanding in both categories and more. On the other hand, he wasn't all that bright, but hey, remember, the Ivy's were a sports league and full scholarships went to brawn, not brains. He also lacked most social graces and a sense of humor. I mean, what's not funny about calling him steisskauph?

Apparently he finally learned enough from his German classes to figure out what this meant. I, at least this one time, underestimated his intelligence if not his strength.

"You didn't think I'd figure out that you were calling me a shit head? I'm a German major for God's sake. Well, I've a special treat for you, you moron." Spat out steisskauph.

I've never been rolled in a rug before and stuffed head first in the toilet. It wasn't all that bad. I needed a bath anyway. Also, I read that there are fewer germs in a toilet than on the serving utensils of a salad bar. Still, I would have preferred a scuba tank and mask the next time I stay under water that long.

I blamed the ants crawling in through the window for the reason for my request for a room change. That request was turned down. It turns out that there is a real reason that they named it the Ivy League. That is, all the outside walls of virtually every building standing for more than a few years are actually covered with ivy. This must be a special ivy too because it seemed to secrete a special pheromone that attracts ants. Thus, virtually every room in every corner of campus is overrun with ants. They spend more money per year on exterminators than on professors' salaries. You'd think that an academic giant like Penn with over a dozen Nobel Laureates would be able to figure out that you'd save a whole lot of money if you only get rid of the ivy. But they probably thought ahead to alumni weekend and weighed the cost of exterminators against the gross from annual giving. They probably felt the alumni would be disappointed not to be able to have a synthenesia from their lost youth if they didn't see ivy-covered walls when they returned once a year to their alma mater. Without ivy they really couldn't consider themselves part of the Ivy League and without that there would be no reason for pride because, Lord knows, Penn wasn't an academic institution. So no, the ivy stayed, the alumni kept giving and the smell of exterminator sprays kept wafting throughout every nook and cranny of the institution. That's why I later, unaffectionately, kept referring to my alma mater as PU.

But this gave me an idea. How about a long weekend away and a lot, a really lot, of bug spray in the room. The problem with this is that bug spray smells. It more than smells, it reeks. Really, really bad with an unmistakable odor. Even my brain dead roommate had spinal level reflexes that wouldn't allow him to ignore the smell. On the other hand, he washed so infrequently and had such a god awful body odor that maybe he didn't have any sense of smell at all. It was worth a try. I bought a half dozens foggers and set them off just before leaving Friday evening. To remove the evidence, I tied them all together and pulled them out the door by the string without having to go in and expose myself to the toxic fumes. These were long lasting, lingering evil odors. Perfect. Now home for the weekend and back for the big surprise in two days.

The train home to New York is always an experience. For someone never having been subjected to public transportation before, riding with the masses is a joy to be wished only upon your worst enemies. I was surrounded by New Yorkers and developed an abiding dislike of them. A consolation was that there were so many New York lawyers that a good percent of those riding on the train were on my list anyway.

I frequently read about New York tag in the papers. Find an unsuspecting rider, usually an out of towner, standing near the edge of the platform, close to the trains, and give them a little push just before the train passes. I could just imagine the pusher saying, "Tag, you're it!" They themselves always won the game but the other participant would either fry on the third rail or be smushed by the oncoming train. In either case, they wouldn't be in the mood for fun and games ever again. In any case, spaces along the wall were always at a premium. Fortunately, I was always able to find one. They'd have to launch a frontal assault on me but I'd have time to see them coming and do something about it. If they were built like my hopefully soon to be ex-roommate, there'd be little I could do about it. My saving grace was that there were other, easier targets and there'd be no reason to single me out. So I kept taking the subway and kept taking chances. Heck, if something did happen, my estate could always hire a lawyer and sue the perp's broke, recidivist ass. Whoopee!

Is it true that New Yorkers are loud, obnoxious, boring and dangerous? In my experience, yes. Do they have any redeeming value? I believe there should be a good recipe for New Yorker soylent green.

If my trips home were generally unpleasant, my actual stay was even worse. By now, my sisters were on their own and mom had no one to talk to except me. What would we talk about? Nothing and everything. I wanted to talk about nothing so that anything was more than I cared for. Why'd I come home? Someone had to do the laundry. And Robin was there.

I had been going out with Robin for three years before college and I was quite fond of her. Unfortunately, absence does not make the heart grow fonder. Perhaps a better saying is when the cat's away, the mice will play and Robin was into playing. After several calls, I finally got her to answer.

"Go away."

"Robin, are you saying you don't want to see me anymore?"

"What part of 'go away' don't you understand?"

"Okay, I won't bother you anymore. I'm sorry. Just one thing before I go. What's your major?"

"You know quite well, prelaw."

Perfect. "Just checking, seeing if you've changed your mind. Bye."

You see in movies when somebody slams down the phone, the guy on the other line always cringes and grabs his ear in pain from the noise. In reality, it turns out that you never hear the slam because the electricity is cut off a fraction of a second before the receiver touches the rest of the phone. Thus the sound is cut off before the noise occurs.

Therefore the only person hearing the fury is the one creating it. All I heard was a soft "click". Bye again. Be seeing you.

"So, your girlfriend broke up with you?"

"Mom, you're the master of the rhetorical question. Now a sample of my own: You weren't listening on the other line were you?"

"I'm your mom, I care for you. Also, this is my house and I'll do what I want."

"Thanks for the fair warning. Have you finished the wash? I want to get back to school."

"Yes, but you rushed me and got me so nervous that I forgot to separate your red Penn shirts from your white underwear again. Ruined your sex life didn't it?"

Penn's colors were red and blue and almost all my shirts were red. "My new underwear?!" Pulling them from the dryer, I was faced with one of my recurring nightmares, pink underwear. Steisskauph was beginning to think I was either queer or weird because I never pranced around in my underwear. He spread that around and it was becoming a concern of mine on campus. I couldn't figure out which was worse, being queer in the sixties or having pink underwear. For the time being I decided it was pink underwear. Having just bought a new six pack, I thought I was finally free. Now they were pink again. Did mom really hate me or just liked playing warped tricks. I couldn't tell and didn't want to go there. I let it lie. I hate going home. But I really hate my roommate. Maybe I'll get lucky. I couldn't wait to find out.

Back to Philly on the train was relatively uneventful. The key as always was hug the wall until the train stops then run like hell to get a seat. Preferably a clean, dry, repaired one so the two hour trip would at least be bearable.

I put the key in the lock, turned it, opened the door and entered. No smell, no sound, nothing untoward. No ambulances but they wouldn't still be there for two days. So far so good. I dropped my bags and turned on the light. I felt a sudden jolt and when I awoke, I was on the floor rolled up in the same rug as before, looking up at steisskauph and three of his Hessian football buddies. He didn't need one let alone three buddies but I guess he wanted to share this with his friends.

My first instinct was to yell for help. But they're right. Duct tape can be used for just about anything. A tried and true use is to tape the mouth shut and now, as always, it was working admirably.

"So vat did you zink you ver doink wiz ze bug spray, cockroach?"

He knew I hated his German and used his fake accent whenever I was around. I assumed he knew he was doubly annoying with the use of the rhetorical question too. The rug was thick enough to blunt most of the kicks for not answering his question. Nevertheless, I gained a new respect for the skill of the frosh team's ace punter as he really could deliver a powerful blow with great precision.

"Ummpphh" muffled through duct tape is about as threatening as a newborn kitten's meow.

"You talking to me? I believe we need to establish a new order. From now on, you don't speak to me unless I ask you something. Understand?"

"Ummpphh."

"I didn't like ze tone of dat. Okay guys, let's vash out his mouth so he'll learn zum manners."

Two brutes lifted me deftly by the heels while steisskauph leaned back on his chair as if it were his throne. The punter would have joined in but he was on the bed with his shoe off rubbing his toes. I might have bruised them with a quick parry by my ribs. Maybe he broke something. The alumni might not have as good a season as they paid for, after all.

As they headed for the toilet I gave homage to Yogi Berra – deja vu all over again. If I could only black out this time maybe they would think I was dead and leave me alone. We reached the hallowed ground; they lifted me higher and slowly lowered me down. "Here's Johnny" I laughed to myself. With each passing moment, two thoughts circled my head, along with the toilet water as they added a couple of nice touches this time. Urine and flushing. Not that I could taste it as my mouth was taped shut, but you'd be surprised what you can smell under water. Revenge and I hate this fucking place.

Chapter 4:
Success At Last

Recovering at student health gave me time to pause. Where did I go wrong? Not only did I not succeed but also I wasn't invisible. I got caught and paid for it. Either I have to become more clever or pay for it even more dearly as I upped the ante.

The student nurse came in with another IV. I had always envisioned myself on the other end of one of those. Next time.

"I see you're finally awake. How are you feeling now? You know you nearly drowned in the lake. Lucky someone called 911 in time. How did you fall in? Your alcohol level was zero. Were you on drugs?"

Being a student maybe she didn't realize that she had to wait for an answer before asking the next questions and then another and another. "I don't remember anything. Maybe I stumbled, hit my head and fell in but I just don't know." If she was asking, then she doesn't know what happened. It also means steisskauph either is not a killer or he's just as inefficient as me. I guess that's why we go to school – to learn our trades better.

"Your friend Werner came by inquiring how you were but we couldn't let him in. I told him you were going to be all right. He had a strange look on his face. Are you sure he's your friend?"

"He's my roommate. Maybe he was hoping to get my bed. He likes it better but I got there first." I lied. It sounded lame but it's the best I could do with the dawn of consciousness having barely arrived.

"You know what's funny? He was just here a couple of days ago himself. He drank so hard on Friday night he passed out and was kept overnight. We sent him home the next morning. Don't you know he was back in an hour puking his guts out? Says the damn exterminators overdid his room and made him sicker than did his drinking. Took a day of airing out before he could go back to the room. Maybe that's what happened to you. Are you sensitive or allergic to bug spray?"

"Maybe so." So he was saved by alcohol! That's a switch. If he had gone back home that night rather than student health he would have been too drunk to notice the smell and probably would have woken up dead the next morning. Oh, that demon rum! "I'm feeling a whole bunch better. I'd like to go home."

"Can't go until the doctor says so."

She sounded hurt as if my wanting to go was a reflection on her and not the natural desire to be rid of all these annoying IV's and monitors. More interesting was the fact that the doctor had the final word. Yes, my decision to become one was probably right. No one questioned the doctor and his word was final.

As I was resting there, a man came in and inquired as to my identity. I confirmed it for him and he then presented me with an unusual looking piece of paper. As I started to read it, a deep foreboding came over me. There at the top read 'Plaintiff' and 'Defendant', just like the paper my father got years ago! I was being sued! I read on and it turns out one of the frosh football players, the punter no less, had broken his great toe while he was kicking me, was dropped from the team and lost his scholarship. He was being forced to leave school and he blamed me! He wanted more than $15,000.00 and would be seeing me in circuit court. At first, I didn't think this would do too much for my recovery, but after a little contemplation, it helped solidify my resolve to right the wrongs of society. That is, I'll get those little lawyer bastards if it's the last thing I do!

Chapter 5:
How Do the Homeless Stay Warm?

It was clear I couldn't go back to the dorm as long as steisskauph was there. Not if I valued my life. I had some relatives who lived in town but asking them for help would lead to too many questions. I could stay in the infirmary for another night but that would just delay the inevitable. I'd just have to sneak back during class hours, get what I wanted and find another place. With that resolved, I took renewed interest in my surroundings. I thought I might as well get familiar with the infirmary, as my future profession will involve working in such places. The walls were fairly stark, punctuated periodically by REAL medicine cabinets! Not the type we have in our bathrooms, which we only call medicine cabinets, but the nearest thing to medicine in them is underarm deodorant, which only keeps our friends from getting sick. No, these were real medicine cabinets, stocked full of real medicines. What they were for baffled me but I bet they were potent and could be put to good use.

There were several others beds in the infirmary but only the one next to me was occupied. He seemed like a nice guy and didn't look contagious from his back, so I felt safe in saying "Hi."

He turned toward me showing me his face for the first time. I then realized I might have been a bit hasty on ruling out contagious. His skin was an unusual shade of yellow and his face was covered in festering ulcers. I hoped that whatever he had couldn't leap the few feet between us because whatever he had, he had it good.

"Hi." He responded but grimaced in pain as he spoke. "The corners of my mouth are cracked and it hurts whenever I try to talk."

He looked in so much pain I hoped he was a law student. "What do you have?" I asked cutting to the chase in case there was still time for me to escape.

"I don't really know. I'm a vet student and they think it's something I got from some new monkeys we just imported from Africa. They've tried every antibiotic we have and so far it's only getting worse. They guess it's a virus or something. All I know is if I don't get better real soon I'm not gonna make it. These ulcers are all over my body. No one's coming near me without full gown, gloves, mask, the works. I'm surprised they even let you in here but I guess they're full everywhere else. Hope you don't catch it."

Pathetic, really pathetic, to see a grown man cry like that. But I couldn't help myself, as I saw my life slipping away. Then again, who's going to see it? A man who'll be dead before his next breath? Still, I had hoped for more self-control and another one of my famous plans. I'm not dead yet, and even if I'm doomed, I may still be able to take the law school with me. "Hey, I'm bummed to hear it man. Hope they can help you. Sorry if I can't stay longer but I gotta go. Bye."

I noticed on the shelves an environmental suit and some biological hazard bags that were full. They probably had his waste in them. I donned the suit and looked in the bags. They were full of pus soaked bandages and some test tubes of blood. Not knowing how I was going to use this stuff but knowing it was a start, I doubled bagged the bags, removed the suit and headed out. "Bye man, good luck."

"Bye."

The Devil Who Walked The Earth

I had the makings of a plan but not the details yet. It was now evening so when I went by the dorm, I could see steisskauph was back and I was out of luck for the night. There were a few protected areas where I could spend the night out and it was fairly mild, in the 60's, so I'd survive until morning. I walked down towards the "surekill" river, the name we affectionately called the river that flows through Philly because of the treacherous highway of the same name that runs along its banks. I found a nice secluded spot under some trees surrounded on three sides by some sizable boulders and settled in for the night.

I never noticed the Philly sky at night before. Mostly because I wasn't crazy enough to go out at night alone in this maniacal city and if I did go out I'd always keep my eyes averted to avoid giving the locals reason to ask "Are you looking at me?" and give them an excuse for a fight. So I noticed the night sky for the first time. It wasn't a pretty sight. The constant smog blotted out the stars and the moon had the same yellow glow as my doomed infirmary mate. I guess I wasn't missing anything, but you just don't know until you give it a try.

"Give what a try, you scum?" I must have been waxing poetic out loud as there was a bonefide bum standing menacingly over me repeating my words. "What are you doing in my spot? Get out! Get OUT! GET OUT!" His words became more shrill and hysterical with each syllable. (A good preview, I later reminisced, of my first wife's speech pattern.) Before I could respond, he grabbed one of my bags and started to furiously rip it apart. Fortunately, doubled bagged biological waste bags are formidable obstacles to the bare handed of the world and as he struggled with what he thought were my prized possessions, I was able to grab the other bags and escape with my life. Wow! A second death defying act in one day.

I glanced back once to see what the situation was and it turns out he was immersed in his life's work in getting that bag opened. He finally did and all the used dressings fell out over his head. He picked through each piece as it lay on the ground in minute detail. After several minutes, he found nothing he needed and threw it all in the river in disgust. He then lay down in my spot (oh my god, I'm starting to think like them!), apparently having completely forgotten about me. I was able to take a deep breath and look for another spot. I'd either have to defend it better or risk losing my goods to the next displaced vagrant.

A little further down the river I found another clump of rocks and trees hidden back up the ridge a bit, thus a little more secluded. It dawned on me this one didn't have the stale smell of urine around it so it probably wasn't already claimed. Just to be safe though, I hid the bags a short distance away in a shallow hollow, covered them with twigs and leaves and settled in for an undisturbed sleep for the rest of the night.

I woke with the sun and amazingly didn't feel tired. Both awakening alive after sleeping unprotected outside in the center of Philly and not being tired were inconceivable just the day before. This might be both literally and figuratively a new dawn for me. Maybe I should have been a cowboy.

I gathered the remaining bags and trekked back to the dorm. By the time I got there, steisskauph was gone. Amazingly, my key still worked and I let myself in. My stuff was still intact but there really wasn't enough to worry about, especially if my plan was to work. I took a few small items, money, wallet and such but left everything else untouched. After donning a pair of gloves and a mask I took from the infirmary I opened one of the remaining bags and withdrew two items. One was a pus saturated dressing, which I smeared all over his washcloth. The other was a tube of blood that I carefully opened and poured a few drops in his mouthwash. After everything was secured back in the bags, I took one last look to see if there was anything else I needed or should do. Seeing none, I opened the door, didn't look back and locked up. To make the bright red bags a little less conspicuous, I put them in my laundry bag and set out for the housing office.

"Hi there. I'm dissatisfied with my current sleeping arrangements and would like to know if you have anything available, a single preferably."

As it turned out, because it was towards the end of the school year, there were a number of vacancies due to dropouts and I was given a single. I arranged for a friend to get my stuff under the watchful eye of one of the campus cops and settled in for what would hopefully be a quiet finish to the semester.

Reading the paper a few weeks later, I wasn't surprised to read about a bum being found dead, covered with pustules which they thought was a staph infection but the autopsy was inconclusive. Steisskauph tubed it several days later and there was an unusually high fish die off that summer, all with strange lesions. I kept my biological waste bags well hidden and well preserved until I could learn more.

Chapter 6:
Am I Brave Enough to Make a New World?

Being a civil engineering student gave me access to the great minds of the world and the great materials of the lab. Together they would surely help me prevail in my struggle against the "evil ones" as I'd taken to calling lawyers.

I'd get almost daily confirmation of their perfidy in the headlines of the paper. Today's fodder: "Couple have fender bender, sue Disney for millions". The article went on to state that a feuding couple, engaged but in the middle of a dispute rammed their cars into each other in Disney World's parking lot, resulting in relatively minor damage. One sued the other for pain and suffering and included Disney as a codefendant because there was a pothole in the parking lot that had to be avoided in the pursuit, thereby making the injuries worse. A truly novel legal theory to be sure but the jury bought it, assigning one percent of the liability to Disney. The actual damages were less than $1000.00 but they awarded a million dollars for pain and suffering to the plaintiff. The defendant was declared a pauper and couldn't afford to pay the award. Therefore, under the theory of joint and several liability, Disney was responsible for it all, not just the one percent for which they were judged responsible. Thus, the fighting couple got a million dollars for a fight they caused and an innocent bystander, Disney, had to pay. They were last seen leaving for their honeymoon on a cruise ship in Miami.

Only a lawyer could have turned the world on its ear as he did in that case. They had to be eliminated. Maybe we should preserve a few and put them on display in a glass container in the main square of each city. Passersby could press a button which would send an electric shock through their body. Even though the excruciating pain would be only a small fraction of that caused by even the most benign lawyer during his career, it would be enough. I wonder if Aldous Huxley ever had blueprints drawn up for that device when he wrote Brave New World?

Chapter 7:
A Nice Day Fishing

After my sophomore year, I took some time off and went to the Florida Keys. I needed time away from it all. School was hard and thinking was harder. I'd been vacationing in Miami for many years as a youth but college interrupted that and I hadn't been back in some time. I chose the Keys as a little different and the path less traveled.

I liked the heat, although I kept to the shade. The trees were quite stunted in the semitropical sun. No towering oaks like one found in north Florida. Nowadays, there were more foreign exotic invasives than anything else. Still, it was warm and green and pleasant. The water was everywhere and refreshing but there was none of the crystal clarity of the Bahamas or Caribbean.

I flew into Miami, rented a car and drove down US 1, over the Card Sound Bridge. I had never taken this road before (note to self: wrong turn – expensive toll). It ran right through a state park. I stopped at a road monument which said this was the only area in the western hemisphere where there lived native crocodiles along with alligators. Also, these crocodiles were salt water tolerant. Great, swim in the ocean and watch the sharks and crocodiles fight over you for supper.

It was early afternoon. I figured since I was stopped here already and there was public camping, I might as well stay the night and do a little exploring tomorrow. After I set up the tent, I waded in the water up to my mid shins, not daring to venture out any further. I hung up my towel to dry, and then settled in for a good read.

The view looking out over the water was quite relaxing. Gentle waves lapping at my feet. The water so warm you couldn't even feel it. You'd only feel its absence by cooling from the breeze over my intermittently exposed feet as each wave ebbed, only to be warmed again with each new flow.

Nothing could upset me now. Wrong. A stranger walked up, breaking my solitude on the isolated stretch of fine white sand I had found. So different from the renourished beaches to the north.

"Well howdy stranger" said the stranger. "How's the water?"

Lifting my eyes from my book, I saw a tallish, ruddy complexioned fellow, about my age and clearly having just gotten into town judging by his pale white skin. A question quickly crossed my mind: Would the tide come in and drown him if I buried him up to his neck in the sand before his flesh blistered off from the sun? But would it be worth the effort to do the burying given his tall stature? "Hi, nice place isn't it?" I replied.

"Sure is. I'm surprised to find anyone else here. I took so many wrong turns I was sure even breadcrumbs wouldn't help me find my way back. But here we are at what's got to be God's own vacation spot." drawled the stranger.

"You're a long way from Texas, I see. Just passing through?" I said hopefully, so my solitude could be regained, using my best John Wayne lingo.

Looking rather taken aback, he states "Oklahoma. Panhandle. A good 20 miles from Texas. Only an easterner couldn't tell the difference".

I look at him a little harder. Is he kidding or is he really serious in the apparent umbrage he's taken over my misidentification of his origin? "So solly, fo' honorable mistake, I just come over from old country." It's the best Charlie Chan imitation I could remember from the old movies. "Still, that's a mighty long distance from here. How'd you have the great misfortune of stumbling into these here parts?"

"You talk funny for an easterner but I guess that's to be expected. Actually, I'm down getting acquainted with the area. Just entering Miami Law in September and wanted to get a lay of the land."

"Well, I hope you're getting a nice intro." A law student, eh? "Planning to do some swimming while you're here?" The wheels are always turning.

"Probably so. Have you been in yet?" So naive.

"Sure have. Water's great. See that little sand bar out there a few hundred yards? Nice swim, well worth your while if you can make it."

"That little distance? Can probably make it with one kick." False bravado is always fun to watch. Especially if you've just laid a trap for the unsuspecting. He obviously didn't see the sign stating "no swimming: heavy shark and crocodile infestation". Scribbled underneath: "identifiable parts of violators will be prosecuted", but I had to put my towel somewhere.

"Have a go at it then and stop lollygagging. Time's a wasting". I almost couldn't control my glee.

"Don't blink. You don't want to miss this". With that he bounded off into the water, ran at full tilt until the water reached his groin then leaped forward into a shallow dive and stroked out towards the bar.

The water never gets greater than ten feet deep in this area but there's a moderate current digging a trough between shore and the sand bar. It's this current in a relatively confined area that herds the bait fish together and makes great hunting for the predators nicely enumerated on the "no swimming" sign.

To my delight I almost immediately saw a set of beady little eyes quickly converge on the steadily shrinking figure of the stranger. The whipping of it tail was quite clear, at least ten feet behind. An instant later the tell tale fin of a bull shark aimed steadily at the departing figure. Any time now and the moment of truth would be at hand. The two sinister figures met at the meal to be almost simultaneously, their mouths opening and closing hard into his flesh. A mighty struggle briefly ensued bringing a timely end to another one of the devil's spawn.

I lifted my book back up and started reading after this pleasant interlude. Several minutes later I caught some movement over the top of the book. There, to my amazement, was the stranger struggling to his feet, several large gaping areas were visible, one in his thigh and the other over his left abdomen. The blood was spurting and his pallor, previously quite striking, now reminded me of a polar bear caught in a snow storm. Had to flip down my sun glasses to avoid being blinded by the glare off his body. He stood several paces from me and spoke long enough to say "They spit me out, professional courtesy. By the way, they asked me to give you these." The last words were muffled by the sand entering his mouth as he collapsed at my feet.

I took the papers and saw it was a subpoena, written on water proof paper from the sharks. It turns out they had been waiting all day for me to go for a swim and were fuming that the person they attacked was not only not me, but a lawyer. They were suing me for fraud and mental anguish. Also, they wanted punitive damages because the lawyer was rotten and they were afraid they'd get food poisoning. Sheesh, it's true what they say about sharks, they play rough and don't mess around, and man, are they quick.

Quite annoyed at this turn of events, I grumbled as I picked up my chair, removed my towel I had draped over the "no swimming" sign and moved several yards down the beach. The nerve of some people, blocking my perfect view. After half an hour or so later, the good news struck me. The flies were no longer bothering me. They had found that the stranger made happier hunting grounds. By the time the sun started to set, I had my answer to my original question. The sun had fully blistered the stranger's skin before the rising tide finally drew his carcass back into the ocean.

Chapter 8: Inspiration from the Chaplain

I joined a frat and they let me spend the summer after my freshman year in their house. They had just one rule: don't call the fraternity a frat (it was like calling a country a ..., well you get the idea).

The brothers were nice enough and none were jocks. In fact, they'd all probably have heart attacks if the gym requirement wasn't dropped several years before. They affectionately referred to themselves as rummies and not because they played a lot of cards (as in gin rummy) but more for the gin. They actually did play a lot of cards but they never were able to keep score through their drunken stupor. Hearts was their favorite but, ironically, they were pretty heartless about it. They would form alliances, which to the uninitiated wasn't immediately obvious. They would gang up on any newcomer, dumping point after point until he'd have 100 and they'd have under 10. It was merciless and a fair amount of money would change hands. Fortunately, I never played for money so I could still afford to eat. On the other hand, they'd only let me play if they couldn't find a pigeon and were desperate for a third or fourth.

That summer at Penn in the frat house was pretty interesting. I still have bruises from where they'd inflict their discipline on me for calling it a frat but most of the time they were too weak from ethanol poisoning to do me much harm. Every once in a while they'd forget which hand they held the cigarette in so rather than a clean punch, my arm would be more of an ashtray where they'd inadvertently snuff out their cigarette. It was okay, I got even in plenty of ways.

Penn had a great library. They excelled in engineering and in medicine, two areas that I needed to master in order to implement my plan. It was uncensored and unmonitored too. You could go anywhere and read anything without anyone blinking an eye. My two favorite books could have been subtitled "homemade bomb making made easy" and "everyday lethal chemicals". They were thick books offering a wide variety of recipes for the average shopper. I organized my notes painstakingly but the reading took so much time that the summer ended before I was ready for action. I had plenty of time and nowhere to go. I wanted to get it right.

In September, the frat house filled up. There were just two of us there in the summer but 15 when school started. Privacy was at a premium so I had to be cautious lest someone might discover my notes. In a 100 years old house, there was a plethora of hiding spots. A loose board in the floor under my desk would be perfect and I felt confident they'd be safe there. Right next to the biological waste I was saving.

Plunging back into academics left little time for extracurricular activities and the notes stayed where they were for quite a while. On the other hand, frat life blossomed, filling my life with rich new experiences of human depravity accented by drunken abandon. I didn't drink which afforded me a unique vantage point for observing abnormal human behavior. I was able to set up my own little Skinner's Box to see how others would react to various noxious stimuli, most of the time not of my doing at all.

One of the most eye opening events occurred outside the frat's back parking lot. We shared a common entrance with the school's chapel which was also the home of the school's chaplain. There was a clearly marked "no parking zone" at the entrance to the lot. It was a difficult entrance at best, being narrow and up a short but steep driveway. One day I was looking out of my room which overlooked the driveway. There was a car blocking the no parking zone making ingress and egress possible only by driving up on the curb between two parked cars, turning sharply, first left on the sidewalk and then right up the driveway. It was so tight that anyone attempting it would invariably scrap the side of the car on the concrete retaining wall at the end of the driveway. Well, there was the chaplain attempting to maneuver his station wagon through this maze, scraping and banging both sides of his car the whole way. He finally gets up to the top of the driveway, but then he stops, puts the car in reverse and accelerates madly down the hill, smashing his rear squarely into the middle of the illegally parked car. The impact knocks the other car halfway out of his spot. The chaplain calmly drives up the ramp again and deftly turns into his spot. The damage to the other car was fairly impressive but the station wagon looked largely unscathed. I'm sitting there contemplating what this whole thing means about human nature. I mean, here's the upholder of the faith which espouses turn the other cheek, exacting the lord's wrath on an obvious sinner but doesn't that make him a sinner too? Before I could make a judgment as to whether or not this is some sign to me that the lord's work must be done by individuals here on earth, up comes a University tow truck and insult is added to injury for the hapless offender as his car is towed to who knows where. If the chaplain really has juice, the car will probably be floating down the river and out to sea before the hour's up.

In addition to the personal meaning for me, I now have some dirt on the chaplain that may come in handy someday. J. Edgar Hoover proved you can't know too much about both your enemies and friends alike if you want to stay in the game.

School went on and no lightening struck the chapel or chaplain so I guess he's home free. I graduated with an engineering degree and got accepted to Penn Med.

Chapter 9:
Try Something New

Why do women always label men as inconsiderate, oafs and boars, or worse, whenever they enter the bathroom and find the toilet seat up? It's as if they regard this affront as the height of disrespect, a shot across the bow in the battle of the sexes. Is there a moral imperative that the seat must be lowered after use? Has the legislature passed a law requiring the seat to be returned to the lowered position after use? Is there an eleventh commandment that's too sensitive to be mentioned along with the other ten in polite company that the seat must be lowered? What's the concern? Are they afraid of falling in? Unless you're Ally McBeal, most women's derrieres are way too wide for them to be able to fall in, let alone worry about it. Haven't they looked at themselves in a mirror recently?

On the other hand, is there a law requiring men to raise the seat before they use it? What do we care if it gets a little wet? It doesn't matter if we use industrial strength bleach on the seat followed by more radiation than they had in Hiroshima, women are going to clean it off again before use regardless of the absence of any visible foreign material. If there is no law, why do men, in fact, frequently, albeit not always, raise the seat before use? If we were the moral midgets implied in the complaints that we don't lower it after use, why would we think about, let alone bother, raising the seat before use?

What's more, why isn't there the same moral imperative or just the simple courtesy for women to raise the seat after use? They know full well the next person to use the seat will most likely be a man, most likely one of their "loved ones". As women are generally regarded as the gentler and more sensitive sex, raising the seat would demonstrate the respect they say men lack. I, for one, feel that lowering the seat has two added bonuses. First, it hides the mess you made all over the bowl and rim with your lousy drunken aim. Second, it adds a little shock value to anyone who raises the lid and sees the dried up fetid remains of your lousy aim. Neither of which are your primary goals but they add some pretty decent secondary gain.

Perhaps this struggle over the position of the toilet lid is not a mere power struggle but one more deeply rooted in sanitation and sensibilities? Granted, the simple act of raising or lowering the seat takes so little time and energy that it seems ridiculous to waste a second's thought on the subject. On the other hand, this is one of the aspects of life that traditionally has only been discussed behind closed doors, bathroom doors that is, largely between parent and child and only in hushed tones. This might give rise to the child's fear of the subject and loathing to bring it up in public. Naturally, the toilet represents the more repulsive aspects of human existence and is not something one would joyfully expound upon to the world. Thus, the struggle for control of the toilet seat position can be seen to arise from distaste of the unsavory nature of the activities that occur in the bathroom. So therefore, it leads naturally from this discourse that the only logical answer to this conundrum is not one of a power struggle nor one of sanitary consideration, but that it's the parents fault for making this subject so taboo that we've all been ruined for life in solving this issue!

All I know is that anyone who touches anything at all in the bathroom, especially a public one, is going to get it, and get it good! I solved the issue by entering a public bathroom only if someone else has opened the door for me, then by grabbing a paper towel before touching anything else and using it as a barrier between me and everything else I touch and finally by flushing with my foot. That had it licked for a while but now I can't get it out of my mind that the bottom of my shoe is eternally contaminated by the germs of everyone's who has ever lived and if I wear my shoes in my own house I'm doomed. As an aside, I now use this as a weapon against my enemies by putting my feet on their furniture and now they've got it good. I haven't resolved the dilemma that they're the very people who contaminated the toilets in the first place. Thus I'm merely giving them back their own germs, so does that count?

"Oh look, someone's entered the bathroom", I thought to myself as I was watching the video monitor I placed in the men's room at Penn Law. He opened the stall door, and yes, starts to lift the seat. A true gentleman. As the seat passes the halfway mark, the thin, almost transparent, fishing line moves through the pulleys, pulls the pin from its holder, releasing the hundred pound block of concrete suspended from the ceiling. The 12 foot drop occurs quickly and quietly. The block hits him squarely on the top of his head. A sharp snap is audible even through the cheap sound pickup of the video camera. It's all over in a flash. The crumpled body would lay unattended until the next patron needed to use the facilities.

What was that noise? Damn, the camera from the women's room couldn't pick up any images due to all the smoke from the explosion. Oh, well, I'll be able to see that in slow motion when I replay the tapes. Two law students up, two down. Nip them in the bud I've always heard it said.

Analyzing this later in my room, it became apparent that this took way too much time and was far too expensive to repeat the million times it would be necessary to eliminate all the lawyers in the U.S. alone. And even though I'll cherish and take comfort from those "snuff tapes" for years to come, it just wouldn't do as the final solution. I'll have to try something new.

Chapter 10: How Does It Feel?

My third year at Penn Med finally saw me out in the wards, taking care of real patients. I was able to write orders and make diagnoses. Most of them wrong, mind you, as a third year medical student doesn't have a clue. If it weren't for the interns looking over our shoulder, nobody would make it out of a teaching hospital alive. As it is, there's a 20% increase in mortality at teaching hospitals during July and August of each year, the months the new interns start. Which should alert you that even having an intern monitor medical students doesn't bode well for the patients. I'm not sure, but I think the government actually wants it this way as a plausibly deniable means of paring down the Medicaid ranks thereby keeping taxes under control.

It took a while to figure things out but after a few months you finally understood what you need to do to get by. There's a certain mindless routine even in the medical profession that if you can just get down right, you'll be able to get by without being brought up before too many committees. The rest of what needs to be done can be accomplished by asking for consults.

Over the years I've been able to judge how good a doctor really is by the number of consults per patient that he orders. If the number of consults exceeds the number of fingers on your hands, then that's clearly a terrible doc, one who suffered a maturation arrest as a third year student and one you should avoid like the plague.

At the other end of the scale is the doc who orders no consults whatsoever. He thinks he's the world's best doc and needs no one to help him or tell him what to do. Since no one can be an expert at everything, this cowboy is just as dangerous to life and limb as the one with too many consults, the only difference is this one doesn't even know how dangerous he is.

I actually met a GP once who told me he was the best internist, best obstetrician, even the best plastic surgeon he knows and doesn't need anyone to help him. Fortunately there were rules in the hospital requiring residency training in the various subspecialties so that he wasn't let loose to prey on the patients in the hospital. The real unfortunate ones in his practice were those he saw exclusively in his office and never survived to make it to the hospital.

Finally, there are the good docs, those who order appropriate consults, directed at the organ or system in question, who listen to the recommendations of the consultants, but are able to handle most problems on their own. These are the docs you should look for and trust if you're ever sick. These are the ones who not only paid attention in training but understood what was going on. The other 90% of docs are just there to make money and build up their ego.

So, as a third year medical student, I was finally able to start to put everything together that I had learned up until then. I could not only see that patients were sick but start to understand why they were so. I could start to understand how fragile we are, and in the case of lawyers, start to understand how to make even the strongest and healthiest succumb to my ministrations.

So it came about that during the third month of my third year, while on the Internal Medicine rotation, that I finally met my first lawyer patient. True, he was an old, ex-lawyer, obviously down on his luck in more ways than one, not the least of which was having me for his doctor but also in having to seek help in a charity hospital. But he had caused the usual amount of pain and suffering during his career as a typical lawyer and now was finally going to serve a good purpose in life - educating me in the flip side of medical care: creating suffering and ending life. Hippocrates turned over in his grave whenever I walked up to the plate to see a patient.

After reviewing his chart, I knocked on his door and entered the room. "Mr. Deaver?" I asked, somewhat rhetorically, knowing full well that the person in bed 201 by the door better well be James Deaver. If not, he might soon be missing a perfectly good organ if he's not careful and his roommate will be wondering how multiple enemas could possibly cure his brain tumor.

"Yes." He responded.

Even at this stage in my career I learned to be careful that I was dealing with the right patient. I had just last week wasted an hour on a Mr. Smith, but it was James not Robert, his roommate, who I actually was looking for. From then on I confirmed the first name too. "What's your first name, Mr. Deaver?" Killing two birds with one stone, I can both confirm that I have the correct patient and start my mental status exam. This part was for orientation. Orientation was made up of three parts: person, place and time. In the most severely demented, orientation to name was the last to go but by that time they were usually no longer able to speak. He spoke.

"James."

"Mr. Deaver, I'm a student doctor and would like to ask you a few questions, if you don't mind."

"That's fine. It's sort of boring in here and I could use the company." That was as honest a reply as I had heard up to that point from any patient. Usually they would roll their eyes or complain about something. I had developed a dislike from the beginning for whiners and found that just about everyone adopted an entitlement attitude once in an institution.

This was especially pronounced with the poorer and most downtrodden members of society. Apparently their miserable existence was so bad that when someone tried to be nice to them and help them, they took advantage of them and began to demand excessive service because they were patients and we were obligated to take care of all their needs.

This attitude became pervasive with the rise in health insurance and blossomed with Medicare and Medicaid. They were called "entitlement programs" so recipients began to get the idea that they were entitled to their health care and it better be free. This attitude spread to all spheres of their stay in the hospital including expecting the doctor to turn on their TV even when the clicker was well within their reach. The same attitude has subsequently spread to almost everybody in all spheres of society so now everyone demands their rights to everything and no one ever feels responsible for satisfying any of their own personal needs. It's always up to someone else because they're entitled to it. And if they don't get it, they just hire lawyers to take it from those who they want to get it from. The breakdown of civil society can thus be traced back to the 1960's Democrats with their "Great Society" and multiple entitlement programs.

He continued, "It's October 3, 2 PM and I'm in University Hospital. Look, I'm touching each of my forefingers to my nose with my eyes closed, tapped my toes on the floor and smell coffee on your breath. 100, 93, 86, 79, 72 – should I go on?"

He suddenly turned surly; apparently he'd been through a few of these exams before and wanted to get on to the meat of his problem. "Are we having a bad day or have I said something to offend you?" I tried to take the punch out of his anger by directly addressing his obvious attitudinal problem.

"When you walked in I decided to give you the benefit of the doubt but you're an automaton like all the rest. Asking me my first name is so beneath my dignity as to show utter disrespect for me. If you were half a doctor, you'd be able to do your mental status exam while talking to me about important things. Instead you waste my time and never solve anything."

"Look who's wasting time. You could have held your diatribe and channeled your anger in a more sociably acceptable manner so as to get your point across and not antagonize your audience. You are either a sociopath or a lawyer. Actually, I repeat myself."

"You sniveling little bastard! How dare you talk to me that way! I'll have your license for this!" he spit out.

"Okay, we'll need a tie breaker question." I sneered back at him.

"Out! Get out, get out now! Medic! Nurse! Help, I'm being abused! Help!" he was nearly beside himself now. He frantically rang his call bell as he was shouting. His face became so red I was able to rule out anemia as a diagnosis.

He was the first in a long line of patients who threw me out. Even then I took it quite sanguinely. People are basically scum and their opinion of me meant nothing to me. I didn't leave, partly out of spite, partly because I was hoping he'd have a stroke or heart attack and partly because I needed to finish the interview for my school work. So I just sat there, listening to his tantrum becoming more shrill with each passing moment.

He became so incensed that he started to climb out of bed to physically attack me. Unfortunately for him, I was sitting just out of reach and he forgot he was scheduled for hip surgery and wasn't allowed to put any weight on his leg. Nevertheless, he did and immediately fell to the floor. I couldn't tell if he was writhing in pain or cursing the gods for making him fall short of his mark. He lay an arms length from me and started to crawl, howling with each movement. For every inch he moved forward I gently rolled the wheel chair I had taken up residence in a similar distance backwards. He kicked his legs furiously behind him in a horizontal effort to pounce on me. With each attempt the rate of blood dripping from his leg grew heavier and finally the femur protruded through his skin, got caught on the foot of the bed and after one final but futile thrust, proceeded to rip the flesh from his hip to his knee. In doing so, he lacerated his femoral artery and rapidly was surrounded with a sea of red. Moments later, his wailing and movements stopped and he appeared to be no more.

I bent over to his ear and whispered, "I never got to ask you, what type of lawyer were you? Malpractice, perchance?"

During this five minute titanic struggle no one ever came in to answer the bell. I calmly walked over to the wall and turned it off. As nonchalantly as a stroll by the lake, I took the chart and meandered down to the nursing station. No one seemed to take notice so I spoke up and asked "Does anyone know who was taking care of James Deaver, the patient in room 201 by the door?"

The nurses looked at each other, as if deciding whether or not I was worthy of their time or they had better things to do. I guess they decided in my favor and one answered, "I am. How can I help you, doctor?"

"I was wondering if you could help point him out to me and maybe get a fresh set of vital signs so I include them in my HandP."

Reluctantly she rose, as if a large section of a bridge was being lifted by a crane that appeared to be half the size for the job and you weren't sure which way it would turn out. But she finally overcame her inertia and was up by me. "This way, doctor."

I always thought being called doctor was a good thing. How could she make me feel so belittled merely by the way she said "doctor"? So I walked "this way". If anyone was watching from the rear I would be headed for trouble because I swayed my butt as if it weighed the ton that hers really did.

We reached the room and as she turned the corner, she stopped with a start. "Oh my god, what happened here? Mr. Deaver has fallen and he's bleeding real bad!" She bent over him, took a pulse, looked for breathing and finding none she stood up and did something that surprised me. She kicked him in the head, not hard enough to cause bruising but hard enough that you wouldn't want to have been on the receiving end. She said to herself, "So long sucker, hope you died a miserable death you bastard lawyer you." I made a slight noise and she turned with a start. "You still here? I thought I told you to call a code! What are you doing here?"

Obviously feeling guilty and worried that I saw what she did and might report her, I quickly said, "I didn't see anything and, by the way, I hate lawyers too."

That seemed to settle down her rapidly rising concern. She gave me a conspiratorial wink and said, "Let's sit for a spell and make sure no signs of life appear. We wouldn't want to call a code if it isn't necessary."

"No maam, a code shouldn't be called unless we're sure we need one." So we sat for a spell.

She periodically poked him with her toes, "How we doing Mr. Deaver? Feeling any better yet?" After a while she looked at her watch and said, "It's almost time for my coffee break. How about we go down and have a cup. We'll give him some time to see if there're any new developments by the time we come back?"

"Good thinking. I could go for a bite about now. I'm on tonight and I'll need a little something to keep me going." I reached down and gave him a little poke. I was surprised how quickly a body cools off to room temperature.

She closed the curtains and the door and we strolled down to the cafeteria together. On the way I had mixed feelings. I was glad that he died and was glad that the nurses recognized lawyer scum when they see it, but was disappointed that I didn't get a chance to inject the potassium chloride I had in the syringe in my jacket pocket. I needed to know how much it would have taken and now I have to wait for my next lawyer patient. I just wonder how it would feel, me injecting the poison and him receiving it. That's okay, I guess, I'll find out next time.

Chapter 11: Incomprehension

I get a call from The Boss. I dread these calls.

"Come down to the office." He commands. "I want you to interview someone for north county. Our numbers up there are terrible and we need some help."

"Okay, when?" Like I have nothing else to do. Every meeting means less time for real work meaning more work the next day. Thanks for asking me down.

"Today at noon."

Great. Half an hour for a 45 minute trip if I drop everything and run to the car. It really doesn't matter, they never start anything on time anyway.

The trip down I-95 is actually pretty easy this time of day. The only collision I see on this trip is going north so the rubbernecking is minimal on my side. If I have any luck it'll be cleared up by the time I head back.

I pass the megamall just before the office. It never ceases to amaze me that busloads of silver haired citizens come every day from the west coast just to save a few bucks at the outlet mall. With any brains at all, they could point and click and frequently name their price on the web from the comfort of their home. But this way they get to socialize and get out. The problem is, it only takes one semidemented senior citizen who has forgotten the social graces of bathing to make the trip one living hell. Plus the farting and burping for two hours each way make for some interesting experiences. Fortunately, most of the passengers are too old to hear, see or smell and those that can, can't remember if they're the ones who did it or not. Actually, almost all take great pleasure in being able to expel gas from any orifice so everyone is pretty happy regardless. Except the bus driver. There've been cases where replacement drivers had to be found for the trip back home because the original driver said he'd rather walk home then go through that again. Passersby have been known to faint if caught walking too close to the doors when they're first opened and ancient memories of Elizabeth, New Jersey course through the minds of those strong enough to be able to escape on their feet. You've never experienced nasty until you hear the comments of the passengers as they offload and have to step over and around the unfortunate who've succumbed to the initial assault when the doors open. "How dare you block my way! Get up! How rude!" Some decide those lying in the way deserve what they get and step on them as they make their way straight to the shopping. Not a moment to be lost by going around. For good measure, not a few canes come in good use as prods.

I finally get to the office and of course there's another meeting going on. The receptionist perfunctorily tells me to have a seat and wait. So I go to sit down in my usual spot but am so startled that I have to do a double take. There's a guy sitting there but I'm not sure what to make of him. He's about my age and build but that's the only thing that seems earthly. He's staring into space, presumable recalling fondly his home planet. His hair makes Einstein's look like he just came from a salon. I thought polka dot ties went out in the '30's but at least it matches his pants. But the most startling feature, and one I don't think I've ever seen before outside of the asylum, was his face. Not so much the bone and skin structure, although they were unusual but not extraordinary, but his beard. Not really a beard either except in patches. He was clean shaven over about two thirds of his face but the other third, broken up and scattered randomly through his face, had at least a week's growth on it. I refused to believe he shaved this way on purpose, yet it was equally implausible to believe he didn't as this was too bizarre an appearance to not know what you're doing. Yet how could he drive, let alone not walk into walls, if he couldn't see what he had done?

I would probably have stood there in rapt contemplation indefinitely if I wasn't rescued from my inaction by The Boss opening the conference door.

"Hey guys, why don't you and Hob get acquainted until we're ready for you?"

Hob must have been the object of my attention as he suddenly came out of his stare and looked at me.

"Are you Hob?" I said, brilliantly.

"Yes, Hob Roff".

"How're you?"

"Great."

"Great. It's a little noisy here. Let's go out for a little walk." I watched him rise from the chair. He didn't seem to stagger so apparently didn't have a tremor and didn't walk into a wall so apparently he could see. We shook hands firmly and accurately, grabbing hold of each other on the first try, so hand eye coordination seemed intact so that didn't account for his shaving anomaly. The only thing left was psychosis so I was prepared for anything when we went out the front door.

After a bit of small talk we got down to the job requirements.

"Have you ever worked in skilled nursing homes?" I inquired.

"I've only had a few patients in them and rarely saw them. Just let the physical therapists handle the program." Hob didn't sound quite normal when he spoke but I couldn't quite put my finger on the pathology yet.

"Well, you've got to understand that we can't be run by PT, we've got to run the show. We're a managed care organization which means we do the managing. This tends to piss off just about everyone we come in contact with, from PT, social services, administration, families, to the patients themselves. The only people we don't piss off are the HMO's, unless, of course, we don't do a good job by expediting the patient's care and arranging timely discharges. Do you have really thick skin?"

"I think so."

Good, several words strung together in a seemingly meaningful way. With a little more training he might even be taught two or three syllable words. Better be careful not to get my hopes up prematurely.

"Great. Let's go back in, I think they're ready". A lie that amazingly enough turned out to be true. We walked to the back with The Boss, a large man who I'd dread to have to walk behind when he became 80. I could see myself lying face down, being trampled by the seasoned citizens I was thinking about earlier if he was ever to let one go from a touchas that large. We made it down the hall uneventfully but I did confirm that I could still hold my breath for 30 seconds if I really had to. You never know when this sort of survival training might come in handy. Actually, I did know. Every day. Walking past open doors to patient's rooms at the nursing homes was an endurance test in itself.

We sat down, went through a few pleasantries and made some general conversation about the job. I really didn't put much effort into this as it was inconceivable he would be hired. We thanked him and asked him to wait outside.

Once alone, I pointed out the obvious. "He hasn't seemed to have mastered the art of shaving at the tender age of 48, and his mother dresses him real funny. His command of the language is underwhelming and he's very, very strange."

"I agree." The Boss said. "Let see the next one."

The next one was also middle aged but a female. We invited her in, reviewed her resume and asked her about herself. I thought my hearing had gone as I could barely distinguish her voice from the sound of my own breathing. I politely asked her to speak a little louder but to no avail. Once again into the breech I thought to myself. "A little louder please". Nothing. "I'm sorry but I can't hear you, you're going to have to speak up. You're not going to be able to get your point across if no one can hear what you're saying."

"I am trying my best and I don't appreciate your comments. I don't have to be abused this way!"

Fails the thick skin test right there as the situation didn't even call for an answer, let alone a confrontation. Also fails the commander of men test too. You can't lead with a whisper.

"Thank you very much for coming, we'll let you know". The Boss comes through again.

She leaves and we're left with a dilemma. Dr. Jekyll or Mr. Hyde.

"We'll have to go with Hob." Says The Boss.

"Hob? Oh no. Can't we interview anyone else?"

"There is no one else and we need someone right now."

"The warm body theory?"

"That's right, we need a warm body to fill the slot."

"Okay, but I don't think it's going to work out."

Chapter 12: Incompetence

Hob and I agreed to meet at the hospital's doctor's lounge to start our first day on rounds together. I'm to train him for a week and then give him his own set of nursing homes. It appears he got there long enough before me to have already eaten and then gone to that place he visits when left alone. He's the proverbial person who stands out in a crowd. Not for his ebullient personality but because everyone else gives him a lot of room. He's sitting in the far corner at a table, alone, a quiet oasis in an otherwise boisterous room full of doctorly camaraderie. Wisps of conversations float throughout the room like a dollar bill being puffed continually out of reach on a breezy day. The winners in the previous day's market always sound louder than the losers. Who needs a place to rent, leaving voluntarily, or involuntarily, from their partners. Whose kids are on the honor roll, how much it costs to keep them there. Some mixed feelings on their kids' brilliance because it means an extra year in practice to pay for an Ivy League school rather than the state's schools. All these conversations swirl around Hob but none seem to penetrate. He remains an oblivioma.

"Hi Hob, how're you today?" I ask.

"Fine." Hob replies.

He seems unsure of himself as if he was rudely awakened in the middle of his daydream.

"Ready to get started?" I add as I sit down for a roll and juice.

"Sure."

I have gotten over the shock of Hob's physical appearance but others in the room obviously are quite surprised. Furtive glances are cast as surreptitiously as possible, but they are hard to mask as the duration of stare exceeds that usually considered socially acceptable. And with good cause as Hob must have dolled himself special for this special day. I can't tell whether or not mousse was involved, (I doubt it because that would involve a skill I doubt he could possess and a style beyond his grasp), but if his hair was lacquered, it would cut a swath that would have taken out half the doctors in the hospital as he walked down the hall. It is beyond Einstein and possibly even beyond Einstein's comprehension how somebody could call himself a professional and have hair this unruly.

Once you got past the hair, you're then assaulted with the bizarro beard. I could imagine him telling the barber "A little here, a little there. Oh, just close your eyes and make it random!"

Having been a doctor for 20 years, no matter what I saw, it couldn't upset my stomach and interfere with a good meal. What am I talking about? This is hospital food! The show Hob's putting on actually improved the taste of the food.

Not a few of my friends ignore me. The few more stouthearted ones call me aside and ask if everything was all right. "No time to talk, big promotion, gotta run, see ya."

Hob says he parked his car a distance away. I want to drive anyway so we hop in mine and start off. The first home was actually just across the street so I don't even bother with my seatbelt. Hob almost panics.

"Stop! I can't figure out how to buckle my belt."

"We're only going through the parking lot. Don't worry."

"No! Help me put my belt on!"

"Okay, okay, don't bust a gasket." I put the car in park, look at Hob and ask, "You need help with the belt?"

"Yes."

"Do you see the belt?"

"No."

"Didn't you say you use a seatbelt when you drive by yourself?"

"Yes, but it's always on the left and I don't see one there."

Oy! "Look, it's over there on your right, do you see it now?"

"Yes, now I do, but it's on the wrong side."

"The wrong side?" I ask incredulously. "You don't know it's on the other side when you sit in the passenger seat?"

"I never sit in the passenger seat so I never have to use it over here. I just thought they'd both be in the same place. Why aren't they?"

"They aren't because they aren't. Tell me, can't you figure it out yourself?"

"No, I have a hard time figuring new things out since my accident. Now I can't find the thing that buckles me in."

That might start to explain a few things. " Do you see the strap?"

"Yes, but I don't see the end, the part that buckles in."

Lord help me. "Grab hold of the part you see, slide your hands down towards the floor and when you can't slide any further, you'll find the buckle. Grab hold of it and pull up towards you."

Hob does as he is told and is rewarded with sight of the buckle. "Now what?"

...8,9,10. "Okay, take the buckle and snap it into the opening over here on your left, see it?" Click. "That's it, good. You're no longer a virgin. Ready to go?"

"Okay."

We slip out of park, coast 100 feet and slide into the spot labeled "Doctors Only". I look forward to watching Hob try to get out of the belt. I am prepared to blow off the rest of the day, if necessary, to watch. I used to hate to watch grown men cry until Hob and the unlatch caper. He struggled mightily with it for quite a few minutes with cries for help interspersed with his sobs of agony As it turns out, my fun was cut short after only a few cryptic hints on how to unlatch the belt when a nurse comes by on her way to work and takes pity on Hob, reaches over and lets him out.

"So tell me Hob, when you buy a car, how many credit hours do you receive in Seatbelt Etiquette and Repair 101?"

"I can't help it, I have trouble with seatbelts."

No shit.

We finally enter the nursing home. Once again my breath holding practice is put to good use. It's interesting putting the smells together with the bodies. God was kind in removing our senses when he blessed us with our smells. I now get a sense as to why so many Jews are doctors. We are the chosen ones, in this case chosen to receive the largest noses so we can suffer the smells even more acutely than our less well endowed brethren. Please God, once in a while, choose someone else.

I explain to Hob the basic concept of efficient management of the patient's stay in the skilled nursing facility, abbreviated SNF and pronounced "sniff". This involves a delicate balance of knowing when the patients can leave and when they must stay. I pride myself in saying that no patient leaves one moment before they're time. But not one moment later, either! There's a battleground between those two moments though.

We see a patient. Hob doesn't seem to have a clue as to what to say as I ask him to interview the patient. I'm hoping that I don't have to teach him medicine too. I decide to start off on something easy.

"Let me show you how to do the discharge summary. It's real easy. Here's a card that lists what we need to dictate in the order needed. Let's go through a dry run and then you can dictate it."

"Okay".

Hob, don't fail me now!

Hob takes the card and picks up the phone. I reach over and press the button to hang it up. "No, this is a dry run, you don't need the phone."

"Oh."

Oy. "Let me go through this with you once. First you need to dial the number."

Hob picks up the phone.

"PUT IT DOWN! You pick it up one more time and I'll break your fingers."

Hob puts down the phone.

"Thanks." I say. This is great. "Next you enter your doctor code, work type and patient's social security number. It's easiest to do this on hook so you can use one hand to dial and one to keep your place as you're looking up the numbers. Then you'll hear a little beep and you can start dictating. First the center number, then the patient's name. Next the date and place of admission, then the date and place discharged to. Next, the admitting diagnoses, the discharge diagnoses which are almost always the same so I just say 'the same' and finally the meds and any follow up orders. It's real easy and once you get the rhythm of it, it takes only about a minute to do. Ready?" I say, hoping beyond hope.

"Okay." He says as he reaches for the phone.

Click. My swift fingers reply. "Dry run, remember? You don't even have a chart in front of you. What were you going to say?"

"You're right. Sorry."

Hob is becoming infuriating yet pitiful. Stay calm. Act, and we all know it's only an act, professionally. "Okay, try it, make believe you've already called in and are ready to dictate."

"This is Dr. Roff dictating a ..."

"No. Stop. Where on the card or in what I said does it say you need to say your name? It doesn't. Your code is your name and it's wasteful, confusing and redundant to say it again. Now start again and follow the card."

"This is Dr. Roff ..."

"What are you doing? Weren't you here a second ago or was it your evil twin who was here when I told you you don't need to say your name?"

"Sorry."

"Try again, no name. Start with the phrase 'center number'. Go."

"Center number ... what is a center number?"

"It's a number given to each of the primary care doctor's offices. It's a six digit number. Just make one up. No, use 123456. Okay?"

"This is ..."

"No! Center number."

"Center number 123456. This is Dr. ..."

"Nooooo!!!! Okay, stop. Let me write it down and all you have to do is read it."

"Okay."

I wrote down in fairly precise detail a script that should take him through a dictation. So help me God if he screws this up. "Okay, read this."

"Center number 123456, patient John Doe, admitted to south Florida nursing home on January 17, 2000, discharged to ..."

He read on with only a small amount of ad libbing but basically was about right. "Okay, let's try the real thing. Here's a chart, look it over, get familiar with the components that you'll need to do a good dictation and let 'er rip." I realize that my optimism is most likely totally unwarranted despite that pep talk, but hey, we've been at this for 15 minutes already, maybe he'll pull it off.

The first thing Hob does is pick up the phone.

Click. I reach over and do my thing. "Remember, leave it on the hook when you're inputting the initial codes."

"Okay." Says Hob.

Why am I getting the impression when he says "okay" it really means something different on the planet from where he comes, like "stress test" or "bite me"? "Try again, phone on the hook." As I say these words I see my hand shoot out and catch his hand with his fingers wrapped around the handle but just before it actually lifts off the cradle. "Let go of the phone and step away from the handle!" Shocked from his reverie, he actually lets go. "Good, now press this button over here that says 'speaker'. Excellent! Now you hear the dial tone?" Hob shakes his head. "Good. Enter in the phone number ..." Hob's now humming along like a well oiled zombie. The phones rings and the dictating service answers. "... now enter the doctor code and work type, good, now the social security number. Okay. NOW, pick up the phone and dictate like it's written."

"This is Dr. Hob ..."

Click. Hanging up was the only conscious act I could remember that I did for the next few minutes. I close my eyes. The Keys, boating, flying – wonderful, beautiful thoughts traverse my mind. I open one eye to see if I was dreaming or if my nightmares had become reality. Eeeeeekkkk! He's still there. Oh well, it's only my sanity at stake, nothing important. "Hob, do you notice you can't hear anything on the phone anymore? Do you know why? Well let me tell you why. I hung up. Do you know why I hung up? No? It's because you failed to read the script as written. You did so in practice (albeit with a lot of practice) but you struck out at the plate. You don't need to say your name. It's redundant and in this case it's confusing as you're dictating with my number and saying your name. Don't do it. Okay."

"Okay."

Did I hear him say 'I'll be dancing on your grave before long!'? Nah.

The Devil Who Walked The Earth

We went through three more Clicks! before he came close enough for government work. Anyway, we moved on.

After finishing at the first home and we drove off to the next. I'm not much of a conversationalist under the best of circumstances but with Hob's stellar wit, let's just say the radio is heaven sent.

After driving to several homes, Hob says something. I am so startled I almost drive off the road. "Do I really have this job?" He looks at me imploringly. It may be the first time his stare is directed towards a terrestrial object.

"Yes." I respond, wishing it isn't so.

He thinks about my answer for a minute, then says, "Do I really have this job?"

This takes me aback a bit. What is he getting at? Is there something I don't know or is it just his insecurity? "Why yes, you do. I already told you so. They're not interviewing anyone else and they've put you on the payroll. That's as hired as you can get. Don't worry."

"I've just got to be sure that I really have it, do I?"

"I've already answered that question and I won't answer it again."

"So I do have it?"

I've developed an icy stare I usually reserve for nurses and ancillary personnel when they hesitate to jump to when I tell them to do so. I'm told it's withering. I'm not even sure I could stand up to it. Hob now suffers a full, unadulterated blast of it. There are no innocent bystanders to absorb or deflect any of the full brunt away from my intended victim.

All Hob can muster is a few 'I'm sorry's' which relieves me of having to launch a verbal assault at close quarters which could turn really nasty.

After an appropriate cooling off period, I turn to Hob and ask him why he keeps asking.

Hob replies, "Well, I've been on so many interviews and haven't been able to get an offer that I just want to make sure I really have this job."

"What were the problems or excuses for no offers?" I am interested in seeing what others have told him.

"Well, some said I was too old, others said they didn't need anyone..." (How could he go on a job interview and then be told there were no openings? That's chutzpah!) "... others said I had too many malpractice suits, and there were other reasons but I can't remember them all."

TOO MANY MALPRACTICE SUITS! We sort of missed that in our 'we need a warm body' deliberations. I cringe thinking about having to delve into this subject further and decide to hold off for another day.

"Anyway, I'm glad I got this job because if I didn't I wouldn't have been able to take it anymore and was going to kill myself."

There were few words that could make me sweat. However, contemplating firing him all day and then being presented with this was enough to make me do so. Rapid fire thoughts reviewing the scenarios played through my mind for the next few minutes. Top amongst them were not so much Hob's suicide but perhaps his wanting to take those responsible for his predicament with him. One read about it often enough in the paper to make that concern a real one. I feel it best to let this issue lie for the time being and give Hob another chance.

Chapter 13: Enough

The problem is that his "one more chance" dragged out his one week training period to four. Something had to be done. He was draining me physically and spiritually. I'm even suffering from guilt by association. We walked into one nursing home and the social worker, THE SOCIAL WORKER!, the one person patients could rely on for help and compassion, pulled me aside and asked how long the 'clown doctor' was going to be with me. Similar comments abounded. I stopped making excuses and told them not much longer.

Hob embarrassed me at virtually every turn and at every level. Socially he had no redeeming value, medically he was terrible. I would have to whisper in his ear what to ask the patient. I remember one time we walked in together to see one patient and introduced ourselves. I asked the patient a few preliminary questions and asked Hob if he could take it from here. He said he could so I walked out. I turned around and there was Hob following me out. I asked him what he was doing and he said he thought we had finished. "Only if the only thing you need to know about him is his name." I responded. "Get back in there and talk to and examine him."

"Okay."

"Okay." I replied. Translation: may a thousand little devils flay your skin with pitchforks.

We got through the day by my doing all the work. The next day Hob met me at the usual place so we could drive together to make rounds. Only today I had to leave early and didn't want to have to bring him back to his car, so I asked him to follow me. "Do you remember how to get there?"

"Oh course." Replied Hob.

"Ha!" is all I could think to myself. So we set off, Hob following like a man with his shadow. Until the first turn. Now the first turn is a little tricky. There was a bend in the road. Some people might even have called it a corner but it really wasn't. Negotiating this maneuver seemed to have stumped Hob. I continued to watch him shrink in my rear view mirror as he remained stationary at the so called corner for the longest time as I continued to drive. He got smaller and smaller until he disappeared altogether as the road continued on. I'm not sure how or why he finally moved. Maybe it was the cars honking behind him, maybe it was some divine inspiration. Whatever it was, I know that he did indeed move as he wasn't there when I came back to that very corner at the end of the day. However, he never showed up for work. He never called, beeped, paged, sent smoke signals nor used psychic telepathy to contact me either.

He did show up for work the next day as if nothing happened. So to indulge my curiosity, I asked him, "Hob, what happened yesterday?"

"What do you mean?" replied Hob.

... 7, 8, 9, 10. "I mean, why didn't you show up at the nursing home?"

"You drove around the corner and I lost sight of you." Hob said obliviously.

"Well, that brings up two questions. Why didn't you turn at the corner too and why, after you finally did turn at the corner, as I assume you must have as you're now here and not still there, didn't you drive to the nursing home?" I asked, looking for a place to sit anticipating I'd fall down from the shock of the answer as if I wasn't fundamentally already in shock.

"There were other cars coming and after I did turn, you were gone and I couldn't find you." Responded Hob, still not aware of the significance of what he was saying.

"Surely you're familiar with the rules governing the right of way? That is to say cars turning right at an intersection have the right of way over cars turning left into oncoming lanes of traffic. They did teach you that in moron school didn't they? And you have heard of the telephone and you do know the office number, why didn't you call me or have me beeped?" I realized I was losing all semblance of civility and with that last remark had crossed over the line of no return.

"I didn't realize the office could beep you." Hob was now looking a little pale, perhaps realizing the situation was deteriorating.

"We've been making rounds for four weeks. I get beeped every few minutes. Who do you think was beeping me? You think the patients somehow have figured out my number and the office remains clueless, relying on the kindness of the patients to find me for them? Regardless of how I get beeped, couldn't you have gone to a kindly nurse, helpful social worker, benign administrator, even one of our patients and thrown yourself at their mercy and begged for them to beep me? Couldn't you have done something to find me? Maybe you should have turned yourself in at the police station and told them you were lost. Anything except doing nothing. But no, you did nothing except drive around in a meaningless manner for what I assume was several hours looking for me until you finally gave up and went home. And now you're back this morning as if nothing happened. Well, something did happen. You won! You get the twit of the year award. And the committee is meeting even as we speak to retire the award as they are hard pressed to think of anyone that could top this, and they've seen some doozies!"

I took a breath. "Go home. Don't come back. Call The Boss and tell him I can't use you and see if he has anything else for you to do."

After all I've said, Hob didn't look surprised or hurt until I said I couldn't use him. He has now replaced the picture in the dictionary as the definition of an oblivioma – a lump of a person who's totally oblivious to his surroundings.

I was so relieved to get rid of Hob, I actually wasn't thoroughly unhappy about going to work that day. By the end of the day the joy of that relief had worn off but it was nice while it lasted. At least I still can anticipate the good news when I check for Hob in the obits every day. So far no joy. It also leaves open the possibility that he'll come back and sue for not hiring him. To do that though, my lawyers tell me he'll have to prove that I maliciously caused his motor cycle accident several years ago. It seems unlikely but it can't be ruled out entirely, with our legal system and all. They're just trying to be optimistic for me because they're the defendant's bar, after all. I know that they're secretly rooting for the plaintiff's bar to come through with something though. It's just they're nature and they can't help it. It's also why I don't differentiate between the two when I do my master planning.

Chapter 14: Things to DO

Pilot

Sky.
Fly!
Why?
Superfly!!!

Life's not all work. Sometimes I actually think there is a God. Someone separate from the all pervasive evil that rules our daily lives. Some benign being that actually doesn't care whether or not we suffer so we have a fighting chance to grab a few moments of respite, even fun, even, dare I say it, joy.

In the undoubtedly futile effort to extend this sense of well being beyond the natural borders of the weekend, I've bought a boat and a plane and learned to fly. I figured that reflecting on these pleasantries during the week would give me strength to survive to the weekend. Of course this foolish notion caused me to be severely punished for my insolence by the Evil One. Amongst the many adversities he's thrown at me for this attempt at respite from his evil rule during the week, he's created these bottomless holes in both the sky and sea and has charged me with trying to fill them with all the money I make and all the money I can borrow. The really diabolical part is that he has granted me a long life and the ability to work endless hours. Thus I'm neither ever relieved of the burden nor free of debt. But then the benign being temporarily rules and I get to use the boat and fly the plane for a brief while and all is right in the world. I can see now where Karl Marx figured it out. Religion is the opiate of the masses. It was free (it was all that they could afford anyway) and it gave them hope that someday the benign one would triumph over the evil one. Ha! Don't count on it.

Anyway, I figured a little fun is better than none so I took the bait of the Evil One and attempted to have fun. First I took up flying. If you believe Sigmund Freud's premise that thrills are just death defying acts that we do in an effort to give us a (false) sense of security that we (as opposed to all that came before us and those that will follow) can beat death, then you can understand why people fly.

Here you are in a paper thin metal skin with an engine half the size of your car engine and notoriously less reliable, traveling thousands of feet above the ground and completely unconcerned that a penny dropped from the height of the Empire State Building will turn red hot and bore entirely through anyone unlucky enough to be struck by it. But it doesn't matter as we'll live forever and the Evil One is taking the weekend off. Of course the Benign One will only take notice when he reads the obit column on Monday to get a chuckle as he sees who was so foolish as to think that he cared.

I finally got up the courage to fly. Well, not so much to fly as to tell my wife I wanted to fly. She took it very well, far better than I expected. Maybe it was the way I presented it. It was in outline form actually. Cash assets on the left, insurance policies and pension plan assets on the right. The right was far more impressive than the left and she was favorably impressed. In fact, she was downright enthusiastic.

I was really honored by the dance that she did whenever I left for my lessons. She said it was a Midwest tradition indicating good luck for the men going out to hunt. I was a little surprised that there wasn't an equally festive dance for when we returned from the hunt but she said there just wasn't. I could see the disappointment in her eyes in this realization. I suggested she do the same dance when I came home as she did when I left but she said it just wouldn't be right. She never could bring herself to do it on my return. I once went to the library to see what dances were available from any culture for the womenfolk to celebrate the menfolk's return but I couldn't find one! There were plenty for the leaving part, just none for the return. It was an oversight I vowed to correct someday.

Learning to fly was actually great fun. And it really wasn't very hard. The hardest part was finding the airport when you're up in the air and wanted to go home. You'd look out on miles of sameness and had to try to pick out where you were. Another hard part was trying to figure out where the imaginary lines of controlled airspace were drawn when you didn't even know where you were. I solved this problem in the beginning by just circling the airport. My instructor tried to insist on flying somewhere else but I wasn't going to be fooled into leaving and never finding home again. He said he did it all the time but I just thought he was too young for that to be true and he wanted to hijack the plane on my credit card. No siree Bob, I was staying right there and wouldn't lower my gun until I was safely in my car and he was no longer in sight. He tried to tell me firearms were illegal on planes but I was ready for him. I looked it up and that only applied to commercial flights. Anyway, possession was nine tenths of the law and, Lord knows, I was possessed.

I learned a few maneuvers and must have been really good. He usually couldn't wait to get back down so he could tell all his fellow instructors what I did that day. I was proud but wouldn't allow him to short change himself. I insisted that I fly all the hours mandated by the FAA for all the regular students and not allow him to make a special exception for me to cut the required hours in half. And the FAA was so nice to me. They'd have an agent there at the gate to greet me personally every single time I flew. It seemed they took a special interest in me. They'd follow my every step with their radar and then show me the pretty tracks my plane left. They even went so far as to point out all those elusive boundaries they'd call "controlled airspace" and showed me how I was in it most of the time. It gave me a sense of well being that they were always watching out for me and even keeping all those other planes away from me when they got too close. I've never met such nice civil servants before. And so polite. Kept calling me sir and asking me if I understood what they were saying. They wouldn't move on to the next subject until I said I did. But of course I didn't. They were always talking in such technical terms. Who knows whether anyone could understand them? But I didn't want to hold them up from tutoring others in the finer points of flying so I just said I did and they'd move on to the next subject. They even wanted to make sure I knew all my rights as a citizen and asked me several times about that. That part must have been tricky because they always read it off a little card they carried around with them. Nice fellows but it must have been a stressful job for them because I never saw the same one twice. When I asked what happened to the one from last week, it turned out they usually were transferred to exotic places like Fairbanks and Diego Garcia. Some, I was told, volunteered for combat missions but I knew they were pulling my leg when they said they needed it for some rest and relaxation. I liked kidders and I wished them well.

I finally got to take my check out ride. To honor the event I presented my examiner with the following poem.

CONCURRENCY

Today's the checkout ride
My most important day,
The plane is so cramped
Hope the instructor's not gay

Preflight's a breeze
Radio check and advisory,
We taxi to the runway
Which way is thirty-three?

Turn into the wind
Run up is smooth,
Rocks blow behind
Into the 1-5-2

Short field takeoff
I can do it,
Into the dirt
Soft field is it

Into the air
Quick and easy,
Don't look down
Makes me queasy

S-turns, stalls
Instruments too,
We're flying into
The wild blue

Take me down
Pleads the instructor,
No problem, mon
No reason for fluster

Pull the throttle
Set the flaps,
Make the call
Just get me back

Soft field, short field
It doesn't matter,
Give me time
I'll get better

There's the runway
Now in sight,
A few more feet
Such a fright

Glenn Allen

A gentle landing
The wheels touch down,
Oh what a feeling
We're on the ground

A little bounce
It's okay,
We'll get back down
And home today

A little gas
To settle back,
Oops too much
We're on the grass

Into the air
A third time now,
Look, we just
Missed that cow

A sheepish grin
As we walked away,
We made it back
A good landing today

And ponder this
If you would my friend,
We get to use
The plane again

How you did it
I can't plainly see,
But you got your license
And concurrency

He must have had a bad day because he was a little grouchy and the poem didn't have the desired effect on his spirits.

"Are you sure you want to do this? It's probably a waste of your money. From what I hear, you're bad news." said the examiner.

At first I didn't know how to take him. But then I figured out his gruff exterior just hid a teddy bear, gave him a big laugh and said, "Let's go!"

I certainly had him pegged. He went from a big, bad, mean guy to a scared little boy who let out a laugh that I heard once before but couldn't quite place it. I finally figured out it was the laugh Police commander Dreyfus made as they were carrying him out in a straight jacket, away from Inspector Clouseau, at the end of the Pink Panther movie. I took that as a good sign. A man with a good sense of humor.

I wasn't sure whether or not I'd need the gun. He looked a lot older and more experienced than my instructors and probably wouldn't be as afraid to fly as the instructors were. But who could really tell in advance and I decided to bring it along just in case. It would be especially handy if the examiner tried to pull the same crap as the instructor and tried to trick me to leave sight of the airport. He actually did try once to trick me but just briefly and halfheartedly and it didn't take much to get him to abandon such a silly effort. The check ride actually was pretty brief, which once again I took as a good sign. The examiner said he saw all he needed to see and we were back on the ground in no time. In fact, he was so helpful he begged me to let him land the plane. I figured he hadn't flown in a while and was a little rusty and needed the practice so I said what the hell and let him do it even though I was paying for the time. It's hard to deny a grown man's wish when he's crying like that. Also, I'd be there to help him if he looked a little tentative. He did okay though, even with that bad shaking he had developed soon after takeoff.

Once we got down, I said if I didn't pass I was going to ask for him again and I'd let him land the plane again since I saw how much he liked it. I mean, I've seen people kiss the ground before but never the wheels, wings and propeller. I bet that next time he'll wait until it stops spinning though but I'm sure with plastic surgery his nose and lips will be even better than they were before. Frankly, the nose job was long overdue anyway.

He said he'll pass me but made me promise that I'd call him everytime I go up in the future. I said that would be a little inconvenient and I really wouldn't want to take him on every trip anyway. The disappointment was palpable. I guess that crushed him because he said if I didn't let him know when I was flying, he'll never fly again. I considered that such a shame but I also considered that with the fear he showed when we were flying, maybe this decision should have been made a long time ago. I wished him well and asked him to say hello to all the FAA gents I've met. It seemed he was planning on a long trip to all of the places they said they were going to. If they're that popular, maybe I should go too.

I had quite a bounce in my step as I left Lantana airport for the last time. I waived goodbye to my instructor who looked jubilate after hearing I passed the test. I also waived to that nice but quiet new foreign exchange student my instructor had just started with. Mohammed Atta I think was his name. Doesn't look like he'll amount to much and I doubt I'll be seeing him again.

Chapter 15: The Bitter End

Flying wasn't my only interest. As I mentioned earlier, I greatly enjoyed boating. I think it was my one true love. So I took (almost) all of my hard earned money and bought a boat. Actually, that's not true. I bought dozens of boats. Not necessarily all at the same time but at one point I did own four simultaneously. A sailboat, a run about, a cabin cruiser and a dingy. You might not consider a dingy a boat in its own right but I suggest you find a way to get from the anchorage to the shore in a nonboat. It can be done but you either have to be prepared to get a little wet or know where the rocks are.

People have said to me "Do you really need so many boats?" My response has changed over the years from a sort of apologetic "Yes" to my current lament, "I don't have enough boats." In fact, I once added up the proper number of boats one should have (all at once, mind you) and have come up with a conservative figure of 14. I mean, what's a well dressed man to do if he doesn't have the right boat for the occasion? I say that's a conservative number because the more you own the more the cost becomes prohibitive in dockage fees alone. But the real problem is that it's just not right if you can't dock the boat behind your house and of course you need a decent selection for each of your vacation houses. So as you can see, I've tried to keep it reasonable.

Of course, what's the use of owning a boat if you don't use it? On the other hand, I've found over the years that no matter how much the boat costs, it's still a pittance compared with the cost of actually running it. So what's a dedicated boater to do?

Find a friend. Actually, anybody will do. If you do find a friend (a rich one preferably), he can go out with you over and over and share the costs. If he's not much of a friend, you can resolve the sometimes awkward problem of not asking him out again by simply pushing him overboard and let the fish take care of him. You need to put a little forethought into that maneuver before you, that is, he, takes the plunge. You must first pooh pooh the notion that boating may be dangerous and therefore the wearing of a life preserver is silly and redundant. Heck, you're on a boat for god's sake. Second, you need to be able to read a chart and insure that you're not going to be doing the pushing onto a sandbar or in the intracoastal waterway. There might be others around to see the deed and you wouldn't want him simply swimming or walking home. Not only would that still leave the awkward issue of asking him out again, but might also raise other somewhat thorny questions that are more annoying than the one you were trying to avoid in the first place.

I personally have had to resort to the one way trip method only a handful of times unless you insist on counting each member of a family individually rather than lumping them as one.

Talk of this option always reminds me of one of my favorite lawyer jokes: What do you call 400 lawyers chained together at the bottom of the sea? Answer: A good start.

That then reminds me of another of my favorite lawyer jokes (but so true): Why do laboratory researchers prefer lawyers over rats? Answer: 1. There are more lawyers than rats. 2. They don't become as attached to the lawyers as they do the rats. 3. There are no animal rights groups for lawyers. 4. There are just some things that rats won't do.

Of course, since you can't really know the outcome of the voyage before you get back, the only way to insure that he'll pay his portion is to collect up front. That way you won't be inhibited to choose the one way trip choice based solely on economic factors. Do make sure you erase any one way trippers from your phone book so you won't make the mistake of calling him up and asking him to go out again. Just in case the investigators are still on the case.

Thus having at least one friend is the solution in the long run for reining in the operating costs of boating. Remember to please refrain from using the word pigeon unless you're skeet shooting off the back of the boat. (Note: skeet shooting is frequently a good profit center for the boat owner if the prizes aren't too expensive, or better yet, you use blanks to remove any chance of your friend hitting the target.)

So, as it was, I found such a friend. Blarney was his name. A good hearted soul but more of a landlubber than an able bodied seaman. In fact, in certain ways he reminded me of my old friend Hob. I bet Hob would have loved the trip out.

Blarney loved the sea and would have spent his whole life on it if he could. He literally would have done so if he ever went out alone as he couldn't tell east if he was watching the sun rise. He couldn't run the engines or steer the boat if he had John Paul Jones standing there telling him what to do. And most of all, he couldn't anchor.

Lords knows he tried. Over and over. Not only doing the same thing wrong but branching out in the most clever ways, coming up with previously unheard of ways to do it wrong. Old salts shook their heads in disbelief when his escapades were recounted. Some were even impressed that after 5000 years of boating, new ways to screw up were still being discovered. Not necessarily by chance mind you. No, Blarney left very little to chance. He would study the manual for anchoring cover to cover each time we went out. He would spend hours out front practicing for the moment when he heard the words "Drop anchor!"

And still he'd get it wrong. Miserably wrong. From winding the line the wrong way on the winch, thus letting out more line rather than drawing it in when we were getting ready to leave to forgetting to release the various shackles holding the anchor on the boat when trying to drop the anchor, Blarney got it wrong. My voice would become hoarse by the end of the day trying to shout instructions down from the bridge. I would have been better off drifting for all the good the instructions did.

My favorite miscue, which only happened once, proving that given the proper incentive even Blarney could learn, happened one day when we were out moderately deep. I've instructed Blarney to let out a length of line that was equal to the standard seven times the depth. Blarney never remembered to ask the depth so I always had to remind him how much. He'd then proceed to let out a length that was related to the depth only in that they were both numbers able to be expressed by mathematical characters. This one day I decided to see how much Blarney had learned over the past three years and didn't ask him how much line he was letting out. I knew it was way too much but just wanted to see what he'd do. So much line was going out of the boat that we were actually riding higher in the water. I still wasn't going to say anything. Then it happened. It wasn't so much anything happening but rather nothing was happening. That is to say, the main attraction at the moment was watching the line go out and at that moment there was no line going out. In fact, there was no line. Blarney had allowed all the line to go out. The line abandoned ship. I repeat this fact now as I had to repeat it then. I was dumbfounded. There was no more line to let out. The line had reached the bitter end moments before I did.

I called to Blarney "I think that's enough. Why don't you cleat it off now?"

Blarney looked for the line but couldn't find it. He turned towards me and held up his hands and shrugged. I saw my opening and took it. I put the boat in reverse, slammed the throttle to full open and watched as Blarney did a perfect reverse 360 in the layout position over the pulpit and into the water. Having accomplished my purpose, I slowed the boat down and had an epiphany! What a great maneuver for a mass, one way ride, deck clearing. Blarney didn't fit into that category (yet), he always paid his way.

"Hey, Blarney, while you're down there do you think you can grab hold of the anchor line for me? It's only 50 feet down and I'd really appreciate it. If you think it might take a while, I can go back and get you some help." God, I love these loud speakers. Makes you feel like you're really communicating.

Blarney was actually obliging me as I spoke as he kept dipping below the water and always came back up more excited each time, like he had spotted the line and was trying to tell me he'd get it next time. I couldn't hear what he was saying. Maybe I should get me one of those hand held waterproof loud speakers for the next time I needed to hear what the guests had on their mind. I was really impressed with how much water he was able to spray with one mouthful though. Thought I'd commission a fountain for my garden when we get back and call it the "Blarney".

Finally, it looked like Blarney had given up on looking anymore, at least he didn't seem to have as much enthusiasm as he did a few minutes earlier. He just sort of floated on the surface always looking down but apparently just couldn't spot the line. We all felt it was time to give up on the search. I worked the boat over to him and had the ladies help me pluck him out of the water and onto the swim platform. He seemed a little heavier than I remembered him, but that might have been the wet clothes and drinking too much. As we hauled him out, we got the surprise of our lives – there was the anchor line wrapped around his legs. No wonder he wasn't kicking so much, it was as tight as a noose.

What luck! I unwrapped the line, inspecting it carefully to make sure it wasn't nicked on something like his fingernails or the small pocketknife he clutched in his hand. But no! It was okay. The others finished bringing Blarney on board and I went forward and finished anchoring the boat. Our day wasn't ruined after all.

Blarney eventually woke up but barely remembered a thing which would have been a bit of a problem if I had to charge him for damaged line. But since the line was okay it saved me a little hassle. Just in case, I resolved to raise the rates next time to allow for a damage deposit/contingency fund. I also used some of it to buy Blarney a new book: "Anchoring for Imbeciles". I hope he likes it, it's dedicated to him.

The episode must have done something to Blarney's inventive spirit because after that episode, he never came up with any more clever ways to foul up the anchoring. He would always do it the same way from then on. He'd stand up front, staring into space and drooling while I took care of all the line work. He wasn't much of a conversationalist anymore either but on the bright side he never again complained about the rapidly escalating costs of going boating with me.

I bought and still have the "Blarney" fountain in my front yard to remind me of the good old days.

Chapter 16: First Things First

Life as a hospitalist can be intense. Sometimes you have to create your own intensity.

It was pointed out to me once by a very good friend that arguing with lesser people makes one's self less. We were standing in a buffet line during a break in a CPR refresher course when an EMT asked me a question regarding a subtle medical point. I was able to give him a reasonably succinct answer which should have settled the issue. Instead, he started arguing a blatantly ridiculous line of reasoning and I, like a fool, tried to set him straight. A thankfully brief time later my friend tapped me on the shoulder and whispered in my ear: "He's an EMT, he doesn't know anything, why are you even talking to him, let alone arguing?"

That hit me like a lightening bolt! Indeed, why was I even talking to him? He was so inferior that it was a total waste of breath to deal with him in other than a master/servant relationship. Well, that eye opener stayed with me forever. It didn't stop me from trying to help people see the light but it did stop me from caring whether or not they did and cut my heretofore virtually epic discussions with the hoi poloi very short.

Except for a few circumstances.

One of my favorite "educational" digressions regarded the universal but mindless repetition of the phrase "God bless you" when someone sneezed. For one who found religion antithetical to rational existence, I could neither bring myself to utter such a sentiment nor understand how billions of people could do so so reflexively and not think twice of it. And why just with sneezing? Why not burping or farting or eating or anything else that we all do? Why sneezing alone? And why invoke God in such an activity? Was sneezing evil or potentially injurious to our health? What was it about sneezing?

I finally found out in college. It came up in a philosophy course. We were discussing the origins and progressions of philosophy throughout the middle ages to modern times. Karl Marx' statement that "religion was the opiate of the masses" came up. He felt that the ruling classes fostered religion upon the masses to keep them from rebelling. The masses lived like peasants, which, of course, they were. They worked, ate and slept in dirt. They then saw the lord of the manor ride by in his fine clothes upon his white steed and disappear beyond his castle walls. There were a thousand peasants for each nobleman. They could easily overwhelm all of the nobility in short order if they had a mind to. So how could the ruling class keep their foot on the necks of their serfs without fear? Religion! Religion promised the oppressed that they would be rewarded in the next life for the sacrifices they made in the current one. It didn't matter to the noblemen whether or not there was afterlife so long as they got theirs in the current one. So all the promises of religion, empty or not, were a small price to pay to keep their privileges intact in the here and now by subduing discontentment and rebellion.

The above is just a prelude to the answer to the original question, but it points out the mindset that is necessary to answer the question. That is, medieval and magical thinking is necessary to be religious. In the medieval ages, it was believed (and apparently many still do today) that if you let down your constant vigilance, little devils would leap into your body through your mouth if you opened your mouth and closed your eyes simultaneously. This is the very set of circumstances that occur when you sneeze. Therefore, in order to exorcise your body of this evil, everyone would say "God bless you" forcing the buggers out into the open, having to await the next sneeze for another try to take over the eternal soul of some other poor peasant. With all these devils lying in wait for us, it's a wonder any of us ever survived. On the other hand, maybe they have succeeded on a select few whom we can easily recognize as lawyers! It's an intriguing thought even if one doesn't believe in religion. I mean, what better way is there to explain the existence of an entire class of beings that make Hitler appear moderate?

Anyway, as diametrically opposed to religion as I am, I take every opportunity to point out the absurdity of religion, magical thinking and the foibles of humans whenever I can in a way that even a simpleton couldn't misunderstand.

An example of a typical interchange goes like this:

Me: sneeze, sneeze, sneeze, sneeze ... (up to my record of 16 times in a row – I've got terrible allergies and yes, I know I should see a doctor. Ha, ha.)

Shmuck (stupid hideous miserable un clean klunk): God bless you, etc. (Up to four or five times typically, although some stay with me the full length of the paroxysm.)

Me: So you believe in magic and devils?

Shmuck: No, why did you say that?

And I launch into the above explanation. We all have a good laugh and they never say "God bless you" to me again. It doesn't stop them from saying it to the remotest of strangers they meet everywhere else and every time they sneeze, but at least I don't have to listen to that drivel again. Have either one of us learned anything or is there even the remotest of benefits to be derived from this? Not really, but I do get to feel superior for a while even while smiling at them through a half sneer and they're distracted from the drudgery of their lives for a few moments. Almost like a religious experience in that way for them. They still dread Friday the 13th, won't walk under any ladder, avoid stepping on a crack and are horrified if they break a mirror. So basically, they continue on in their almost dreamlike state of existence, unquestioning and unthinking. They almost deserve the cruel fate they are dealt in dealing with lawyers.

Sometimes my nightmares find me alone in the forest and I start to sneeze. There's absolutely no one there to hear me. Who's going to bless me so I won't go to hell? I wake up in a sweat, look around and see filing cabinets filled with summons and court papers and realize that I am already there.

Another one of the ways that the little people annoy me is the typical nurse's brain dead way of calling people by their last name first followed by their first name as if in their professional life all convention is thrown out the window and the rules of the world are reversed.

Beep: "Call Nurse Jones re new admission at Del-Boca rehab." So I dial the number to Del-Boca rehab and they answer "Hello, Del-Boca rehab." I say Nurse Jones please. They connect me and Nurse Jones says: "Doctor, this is Nurse Jones at Del-Boca rehab and I'm calling to have you confirm the orders on Smith John."

By the fourth time I'm reminded that this is Del-Boca rehab I'm getting a little annoyed. The nurse says it like I should be surprised I'm speaking to someone at Del-Boca rehab, as if I dialed a series of random digits and just happened to hit their number by luck at precisely the time they needed me. What great luck! Suffice it to say that's another one of my peeves but I usually let it go for the bigger game, unless I have an inordinate amount of free time and really want to torture the nurse with two peeves at once. That usually causes them to either hang up, report me to the administrator or run screaming from the phone trying to pull off their head. When that happens I get to do it all over again with the next nurse who picks up the phone the previous one dropped but, as I said, I've got to have nothing else to do to play that one out to the end. Too big a dose of sarcasm even makes me feel bored after a while. So I usually let the smaller issue drop and go right for the meat: last names first.

"Smith John? That's a strange name, I've never heard a name like that before. I can't tell, is that a boy or girl? What nationality is that?"

Nurse Jones: "It's a boy. His name is John, John Smith."

"John John Smith? I have two patients?"

"No, one patient. His name is Smith, John." Replies the nurse.

"I understand, one patient with the strange name Smith John and another called John John Smith."

"No doctor, you have one patient. His first name is John and his last name is Smith."

"Oh, why didn't you say so in the first place? I thought his first name was Smith and his last name was John. But that's only because that's what you said. I mean, you don't go around introducing yourself as Jones nurse, you called yourself nurse Jones. That is, you said your first name first. Which, interestingly enough, is how the first name is defined, that is, the first name spoken is called the first name. At least that's how we do it in America. Isn't it how you do it in your native country, the Philippines isn't it?"

"No, I'm American and you know it so stop that."

"Alright, so tell me about this patient Jones nurse ..." Click. Damn, now I've got to call back. The hell with it, if they want me they'll just have to call me back. Anyway, I enjoy my daily talks with the administrator. In the meantime I've got to make calls to three more rehabs, so I'll have plenty more opportunities to help them put first things first there too.

Chapter 17: Detective Freed

Detective Jim Freed is a 20 year veteran but is still perplexed as to whether or not there was any link in the string of homicides in which he's now been called upon to be the lead investigator.

New York is a big place with more than it's share of death, although the Mayor had just given an upbeat news conference touting the great strides the city had made in becoming more livable, not the least important of which was a 26.3% drop in murders since he took office. Coupled with the good economic news, the reduction in crime stats virtually reassures his reelection next year.

Nevertheless, the series of recent murders in midtown had been noticed as unusual even by New York standards. Five people in two weeks in just one section of town. These weren't street people, druggies or bums. Each was killed in his office with a single shot through the heart. None had a rap sheet, none were in the news, none had been noticed as anything other than reasonably decent people by the people in the surrounding offices.

Jim is reviewing the files around the kitchen table, as is his custom before leaving home to go to work, when there is a knock at the door. His wife gets up and lets in the man dressed in the uniform of the city police. Jim, still engrossed in the files doesn't even look up when the policeman, walks up to the table where Jim is sitting and speaks.

"Jim Freed?"

Sensing that the deep voice didn't resonate as he'd expect his wife's to, Jim finally looks up and is not a slight bit surprised to see a uniformed officer in his house. "Yes officer, may I help you?"

"Are you Jim Freed?" the uniform asks again in an officious manner.

As his style clearly did not indicate a social visit, Jim begins to sense there is a serious problem. Another murder? However he didn't recognize this officer and a subordinate wouldn't have sounded that way. "Yes, I'm Jim Freed."

"Detective Freed, I'm with the process server division and I have some papers here for you. Please sign that you've received them."

Detective Freed was on the serving end of this scenario many times since he was a rookie but up to now never felt firsthand the emotions one goes through on the receiving end. He takes the papers, signs the receipt and gives the now somewhat moist pen to the policeman. The officer thanks Jim, turns, and with a nod to Mrs. Freed, lets himself out. As the door clicks shut, Jim, though a little shaken, regains his sense of presence and opens the envelope.

Detective Freed, having been on the streets for over two decades considers himself a battle proven veteran who's seen it all. He prides himself that he could keep his composure even when viewing the most grizzly murder scenes including a few dismemberment cases he'd been involved with over the years. Then how come there is blood starting to percolate from the painful spot on his right forefinger where the paper had sliced him while he was opening the envelope?

He licks his finger with a little disbelief that is a stepping stone for the much greater disbelief that overcomes him as he starts to read the contents of the letter. A sense of dread begins to overcome him even before he reads the first word as he has to unfold the papers, not the usual trifold typical of common letter paper but an extra fold was necessary to accommodate the 8 ½" x 14" paper used by the legal profession. "This is not good" he begins to repeat to himself as he reads the caption:

In Re: the First District Superior Court of the City of New York
Plaintiff: Jenny Freed
VS
Respondent: Jim Freed
Man and Wife
Plaintiff hereby petitions the court for dissolution of marriage due to irreconcilable differences.

The rest becomes a blur. Here he is, sitting across the table from his wife of 22 years and she has him served with divorce papers and hadn't even said a word about it to him. How could this be? If true, would this be worse than the fate of the five most recent victims he is working on? Probably so, as only the living could feel pain and he is most definitely feeling pain. A long look at his wife seemed to last an eternity as silence settles over the room.

"For once he's not engrossed in his papers and is paying some attention to me." thinks Jenny. It's a little late and definitely for the wrong reason, but the attention is welcomed nonetheless, perhaps for the last time.

"Do you want to let me in on what's going on?" Jim said, finally breaking the spell of unreality that settled over him.

"I want a divorce". Jenny said more boldly than perhaps anything she had said in the 22 years of marriage. Jim towered over Jenny, and being somewhat meek to start with, she rarely spoke her mind. All decisions of any import were always left by default to Jim and though she resented never being asked her opinion, she always acquiesced. She had felt trapped by a sense of economic slavery in an unequal marriage. That is, until she became better acquainted with a sweet little man who she'd known in passing for years from shopping in the local grocery store. She heard he lost his wife and he learned how unhappy she was and offered to help, as his job, it turned out, was divorce attorney. Having finally found a way out, the affair was just what the doctor ordered. She could now have a new life. And Jim could rot in his.

"That's it? No discussion? No 'let's work this out?' No nothing?" Jim's breathing is slow and deliberate, as it always becomes when he wills himself to remain calm in a crisis.

"No. No discussion. No nothing. I'll be gone by the time you get back from work. My lawyer will be in touch. Get one yourself. Let's make this as painless as possible. No kids makes this easier but after 22 years it's still not easy. But it's too hard to stay together, so, as I said, that's it." Jenny isn't emotional. She had years of suppressed emotion training by living with Jim to prepare for this and uses it as an exit strategy to fall back on. She is more than ready to leave and, in fact, is more than half packed.

Jim continues to look at her but she is already fading from his mind. "I'll think about it".

"Fine. But you'll have to let my lawyer know. The address is at the bottom of the papers. It's been nice but I have had enough. I wish you well." At which point Jenny gets up, turns her back and disappears into the bedroom.

Jim continues to stare at the space where Jenny was but is no more.

Chapter 18: All in a Day's Work

"**Detective** Freed, you take the lead in the downtown murders. We've found five dead in one office last night and we're still counting. Sort of a fine "hi, how are ya?" to the clean up crew that discovered them early this morning. There are so many offices and they're all locked that they've still not even checked each one yet." Lt. Krumpk stated. He'd been known as Krupke after the officer in West Side Story since he joined the force 20 years ago, although he was now senior enough that no one called him that to his face anymore except for the chief and one captain. This was attributable not only to respect for seniority and but also a fear of being exiled to the night shift in Bedford-Stuyvesant like that rookie in 1985 discovered was his fate after having the temerity to sing the whole song at a benefit skit one night. Rank has its privileges and getting away with outright revenge was one of them. "You get on over there now and mop this whole thing up."

Detective Jim Freed wasn't feeling in a real good, investigative, police mood today, having just had the rug pulled out from under him at home this morning. Nonetheless, duty called and he tried to put the late unpleasantness out of his mind, at least for now. He turned to his two subordinates, laid the situation out to them and almost made it out the door when he was stopped by a man in a suit and a visitor's pass hanging from his pocket.

"Detective James Freed?" asked the suit.

Uh oh, thought Jim, it's always bad news when someone calls you by your full name in such a formal way. "Yes." He responded while reading the badge: Robert Sutch, process server. Now what? he thought, he can't be divorced twice, can he?

"I hereby serve you with these papers. Read them and act accordingly. Good day officer." With that Mr. Sutch turned and left.

The name Robert Sutch was emblazoned in Officer Freed's memory. "Woe be to him if he even double parks in my presence." He thought to himself. And with that the day's first hint of a smile crossed Jim's lips. Jim opened the papers and found that his wife's attorney/lover works fast. He now was restrained from going within 500 feet of his wife or their house. That was a bit upsetting but what really got his attention was the address of the law office. The damn gigolo had listed Jim's house as his office address. Jim's pillow hadn't even cooled from his night's sleep when his wife's lawyer had already moved in.

"Whoa there big boy, lose your balance?" asked Officer Stimkowski as he grabbed and steadied Jim as his knees buckled just a bit while reading the notice.

"No, no, I'm fine, just a small misstep. I'm okay. Thanks for the catch though. We'll put you at shortstop at the next department picnic." Jim could not help but feel a little shaken but it was embarrassing to admit it, even to himself. "Shaken, stirred and rotisseried is what that puke will get." Jim's anger surprised him. Letting one's anger get the best of one's self only led to review boards and letters in one's personnel file. But everyman can only be pushed so hard until the pushing starts going the other way. This might be his line in the sand.

"Okay boys, let's go play in our new sandbox." The three of them piled into an unmarked car and took off for the downtown offices. It was in an area that had seen better days but was still quite respectable. Upon arriving, they were met by the usual contingent of uniformed police and allowed through after showing their ID's. They ducked under the yellow crime scene tape and took the elevator upstairs to the 41st floor. They were greeted by more uniforms and a plaque on the wall: Dudley, Chism and Houd, Attorneys-at-Law. This immediately had the same effect on Freed as it had on everyone who had ever heard of the firm for the past 20 years, ever since Johnny Carson first announced that his law firm was Dewey, Cheatum and Howe on national TV. At first the firm ignored the jokes, then they did what any self respecting attorney would do, threatened Johnny and NBC with a law suit. Failing that, they decided it wasn't worthwhile to spend the money to change their letterhead, thus fulfilling all the requirements necessary to be an upstanding member of the bar: self-absorption, ignorance, frugality to a fault and with no sense of humor whatsoever.

"Who's in charge here?" demanded Detective Freed in his least amused voice.

"I am." Responded Sergeant Billingsly, a rather large fullback type, which was precisely what he was in college but wasn't good enough to make the pros.

"I'm Detective Freed and I'll be leading the investigation. Tell me what you've got so far."

"Well, it seems that this law firm occupied the entire 41st through 44th floors and we've not started searching 43 and 44. It seems every door is locked and there are no keys to be found. We're having to pick every lock rather than have a $10,000.00 bill to fix the locks and windows if we were to break them down, so things are kind of slow here. We sure could use more help." Officer Billinsgly briefed Detective Freed on several other problems and went through a few more details.

"How many dead so far?" queried Freed.

"Five on the 41st floor and we just found three more on the 42nd."

"Okay, you've almost finished the 42nd, I'll take my two men to the 44th while you start on the 43rd. Let me know when you're done. Okay boys, let's go upstairs." With that they got back on the elevator which was conveniently being held by an officer who stuck his foot in front of the doors. This resulted in an annoying intermittent clatter during his conversation with Billingsly as the door kept crashing down on his foot and then jarring open every few seconds. Freed pondered which would break first, the door or his officer's foot. He didn't have time to wait around and find out. Maybe they'll have time at their next stakeout. Get up an office pool and maybe make some money. Money sure was going to be in short supply for the foreseeable future if what he knew about law suits was true.

From the elevator speaker a dulcet female tone announced "44th floor" and they exited briskly as the door opened. They were greeted by only one uniform guarding the vestibule to a distinctly more upscale version of the offices seen downstairs. "This is clearly the senior partners' floor." announced Freed as if this wasn't readily apparent to his two underlings. "Okay, Braver, you take the left hallway, Wang, you take the right one and I'll take the middle one." The middle one wasn't so much a hallway as a large and remarkably well appointed reception area. The door was locked of course. The name distinctively gold leafed onto the window read: James B. Brown III, Managing Partner. In smaller letters but unmistakable was: Appointment Necessary. "Well, here's my appointment card." said Freed as he took out his service revolver and used the butt to smash out the window. He had enough of lawyers for the day and wasn't going to let an officious little jerk impede a murder investigation. He reached inside, unlatched the door and proceeded in. The receptionist's desk was neat and tidy, except for the receptionist who managed to sully the near part of her desk, chair and carpet with a burgundy colored stain. "Tsk, tsk, there'll be a little smaller paycheck for the next 30 years to pay to replace the items you so carelessly damaged Ms. Jones or whatever your name was." Thought Detective Freed. He was past caring about lawyers and their henchman at this time. The thought was creeping into his mind that maybe some sane person was actually doing some good deed, but he knew he would have to keep such thoughts to himself, at least for now.

Detective Freed was temporarily stymied at the next door. This one was solid oak and clearly required a bit more heft than the handle of a service revolver. Fortunately, the Firm had provided a suitably sturdy coffee table that looked like it could do the job. It held up just long enough that the third impulse against the door shattered both the door and the table simultaneously in a sort of miniature demonstration of mutually assured destruction that was the buzzword of the cold war. But this war was decidedly warmer than that.

Once inside, Jim found what he expected, a body slumped back in the chair, half in half out. The awkward position that only a corpse could assume for any length of time. However, upon closer inspection, he could see that Mr. Brown, Managing Partner, was still breathing. There was a knife protruding from his chest and the blood stain emanating outward around it was prodigious but somehow he managed to hang on, if just barely. Maybe the perpetrator should have used a wooden stake to do in the head vampire. Jim leaned in closer to take his pulse when Brown opened his eyes and whispered faintly, "Doctor, doctor."

Jim said of course he'll get a doctor and stood up. He was about to go out for help but them stopped and looked around. He saw the mementos of a life's work. Newspaper headlines of people, usually famous people, Brown had successfully sued; Mafia chieftains, all smiles after their acquittals; and corporations brought to their knees. He recognized a few of the people as ones he himself or officers in his precinct had arrested. A lot of good police work went down the drain due to an arcane point of law dredged up by these lawyer snakes. He felt helpless time and time again but there was nothing he could do, because, after all, the prosecutors were lawyers too and they clearly stuck together to defend "the law" rather than fight for justice.

Jim walked to the demolished door, saw no one nearby and returned to lawyer Brown. Still breathing and his eyes were still open. His right arm moved as if he was trying to reach out to Jim. "Doctor did this, doctor …" Brown slowly lowered his arm down but his eyes remained fixed on Jim. All Jim could think of was that James B. Brown III was setting the groundwork for the mother of all malpractice suits and it was all he could take. Jim grabbed hold of the knife and pushed it in two more inches, up to the hilt. Another large wave of blood exuded from James B. Brown III's chest until no more came and his breathing ceased. Jim didn't dwell on why the knife still had two inches left and why Brown was still alive. He just felt good about doing the right thing and feeling good about himself for the first time in a long time. "All in a day's work, Mr. Brown".

Watching on the hidden camera over the mantle place of the fake fireplace, I thought, "Detective Freed", whose name was clearly legible from his police ID hanging from his left breast pocket with a little panning in of the lenses, "you're mine!" I felt pleased in completing another day's job done well.

Chapter 19:
Already Doomed

"Hey, Jim! You got a message about the lawyer massacre, some kook who says he saw it all but won't leave his name. Will only speak to you. Said something about good hunting, Jim Bowie. Says will call back in a while and you're to leave a number where you can be reached. They come out of the woodwork on all these bizarre cases."

"Thanks Tom, I'll be in my office for a while. It doesn't hurt to check out every lead, no matter how farfetched." Jim hoped that Tom didn't see the sweat start to bead on his brow or the stagger in his step as he momentarily thought he'd die from the jolt he received from the sudden surge of adrenaline that inevitably accompanies extreme fear. Did this joker really know about him and the knife or was this just a random crank call that somehow hit a nerve? Jim steadied himself, walked into his office, missing only that one beat and sank into his chair, wondering and afraid of what lay on the other side of the next phone call.

After a short while, Jim was able to push his concerns aside and fell back into the comfortable rhythm of typing up a police report, even one as unusual and bloody as this one. Thirty five people dead, almost half of them lawyers, and all but one dead on arrival, but no one else will ever know that. Forensics was still working on gathering evidence and probably would be for two or three more days, there was just so much death to be investigated.

After half a dozen routine calls, it caught Jim by surprise when the caller said, "Hello, Detective Freed, or should I say the new Jack the Ripper?"

Jim froze, could barely speak and croaked out a hoarse, "Who is this?"

"Don't worry for now who this is, what we really need to determine is who you are? We need to know if what you did today was just an isolated act of heroism or if you are a dedicated marathoner for the cause." said the electronically altered voice on the other end.

"I don't know what you're talking about, what are you saying, who is this, what do you want?"

"Now, now Detective Freed, no reason to get upset but I certainly hate repetitiousness, except when performing the good deed you did today. And don't worry about covering your tracks, you know this phone conversation isn't recorded by your office and you know I couldn't legally record it so you have nothing to worry about. How about we set up a little meeting? I have some home videos to show you and we have a little partnership deal we need to make. How about tonight after work? Go to the phone booth on 3rd avenue outside the station house and wait for my call, let's say five-ish? See you then." Click. I love these electronic voice changers, they make me so invisible. I walked away from the phone booth on 3rd avenue, went into the deli and ordered nice hot pastrami, my favorite and waited. It was 4:15 and I could make this a leisurely snack while I waited. I slipped the exam gloves into my pocket that I had used to avoid leaving fingerprints on the phone. They come in handy for so many different jobs.

Jim sat back in his chair. What should he do? If he confessed his actions, maybe said he slipped and pushed the knife in by mistake, he might get off with probation or nothing but he'd always be suspect and would probably have to resign anyway. Then what would he do? Night watchman? Don't think so. That was assuming that the phone call was a bluff and there was no videotape. How could there be anyway? But how could there be a witness when there was no witness to be seen. Jim was careful of that, but was he careful enough? What if he went to the meeting to see what it was about? Nothing would be lost, no commitment made, all his options still open and he'd have more information in order to make a better decision. If there really was a tape and a witness, he was doomed. Or was he? What did the caller call him - a hero? Did that mean that the whole thing was a setup? That a surveillance camera was set up to catch him or whoever entered that room? By the police? No, they weren't capable of such forethought or deviousness and their inability to keep a secret was legendary. So someone else, light years ahead of the police must have set this up. But why? They obviously could have finished the job themselves, why leave the biggest fish alive? Did he know I would be there? That would have taken a good bit of intelligence work and even more luck if I was the target. If I wasn't the target then it's just my luck. But isn't it just my luck? I got to kill a big shot lawyer who's been a thorn in the department's side for decades and if I'm really a hero in this guys eyes, does it mean I get to kill more of the bastards, maybe even my soon to be ex's boyfriend? There might be an up side to this whole thing and it can't hurt to find out. I'm already doomed anyway.

Chapter 20:
Tea in the House of Evil

Jim was prompt, arriving at the phone booth two minutes early. I was watching from the bar across the street. He appeared to be alone. I was hidden behind some plants so he wouldn't be able to see me if he tried to see if he was being followed. After waiting two minutes, I dialed the number from a cell phone I had lifted from a stranger on the subway and he promptly picked up the phone. I set the tape recorder to play so no one could hear what I said. The message was short and repeated twice. Another location of another public phone. He looked around, saw nothing suspicious and headed off to the next location. The other phone was only three blocks away but it gave me the opportunity to see what, if any, surveillance he'd set up at this site and cleared out with him. As it was, I spotted no one and was satisfied he was on his own. I finished my coke, walked out and went into the Chinese restaurant next door.

A few minutes later I called the second number, and told him to go to the Chinese restaurant where I was. He was to ask to be seated at a table in the back. I told the waiter I was going out for a smoke and would be right back. I crossed the street, pretended to do a little window shopping and got lost in the crowd. I spotted him a few minutes later. I wiped off any fingerprints from the cell phone and threw it in a garbage can. After waiting a few more minutes, I went inside to join him.

I told the waiter I spotted a friend and was going to join him. Walking back casually towards his table, I could see Detective Freed gauging me as a serious personal threat and cataloging me as a policeman might do for his report. "Jim", I said warmly, extending my hand as an old friend might do, "so how are you tonight? Wife okay?" Not just thrust the knife but twist it as it sinks in.

Jim was a little surprised at first but quickly caught on and played the game well. "Just fine, and yours?"

"Good. Let's say we order first and talk later?"

"Okay, waiter – I'll have some wonton soup and a spring roll."

"Sounds good, I'm not too hungry tonight, I'll have the same. Oh, and waiter, please bring some tea. Thanks."

Jim must have thought how can this guy be so polite and jovial when he's clearly a cold blooded killer, extortionist and who knows what other evil lurks in his breast.

The waiter left after a shallow nod of the head and I got down to business. "Jim, and I hope you don't mind me calling you Jim as I feel I know you well. Hell, I probably know you better than your soon to be ex-wife does as I know your real, innermost thoughts. I know how you'd be when left to your own devices. I know you're able to act on your impulses and damn the law. I know how you really feel about lawyers. That you'd like to kill them if you could and in fact did when the opportunity arose. You're the type of person I'm looking for. Someone with brains, courage and motivation to do the right thing. And I don't even have to convince you what the right thing is, you're already doing it. So I have a proposition for you. Are you interested in hearing me further?"

Jim knew what I was talking about although he still couldn't quite figure out how I knew what I seemed so sure about knowing. "Assuming I have a clue what you're talking about, what is it that you want?"

"Of course you have a clue, and just to make sure that you have no doubt about it, I'm going to show you a print of a most poignant scene that happened today and still have a whole videotape stored away somewhere real secure that the print is taken from. Also, just to set some ground rules, I'm not alone and I'm not foolish enough to not realize you might want to recover any incriminating information I might have on you to make sure that it can't be used against you, perhaps by doing me some harm. Let me assure you, I'm not that foolish. There are several copies of the tape, all of which will be released if I'm not heard from within two hours of this meeting and every 24 hours from now on, at least until we can trust you. If some harm was to befall me, we wouldn't think of reciprocating in kind against you. No, we would just release the tape and see how you fare in prison. I understand that if they're able to keep you in solitary, some cops have lived for up to five years before the inmates find a way to get you. On the other hand, the odds of you getting enthusiastic counsel is pretty close to nil seeing your crime was lawyer killing. I do believe, given the above scenario, regardless of any post event remorse, your best course lies with teaming up with us. By the way, here's the print I promised you."

Jim took the picture and studied it hard. It was a little grainy coming off an ink jet printer but it was clear enough. Jim's face was unmistakable looking up and around having just finished off the job with his fingers encircling the knife. Where was the camera hidden was Jim's main thought. He now had to make a decision, throw in with this group or throw himself on the mercy of the court, turn state's evidence and round them up.

Seeing him lost in thought, I felt it was best to remind Jim that his choice was freedom with me or life long wondering if this was his last day from revenge from my group. But more importantly, throwing his lot in with me would give his otherwise desolate life some meaning. He could finally do some good, eliminate the lawyers who were the enablers of the criminals he hated so much.

"I want to see the whole film."

"Done, eat up and we'll see it together. I can't get enough of great art like that."

It didn't take long to finish our meal. I carefully wiped my fingerprints off all the utensils, chair, glass and everything else I touched. I even asked Jim to pay to prevent him exchanging the check or any money I used to pay the bill with his and then fingerprinting it. These precautions didn't escape Jim's notice but he didn't seem inclined to force the issue right now. In fact, he even started to admire the efforts made to protect myself. He was starting to gain a little confidence I might even be able to protect him.

As we got up, I pondered the thoughts that must be going through Jim's head. Perhaps he was clever enough to see the irony of our situation as we had Tea in the House of Evil.

Chapter 21: Are Nurses Worse Than Lawyers?

I've long contemplated, after all the lawyers are gone, what will I do for sport? Oh, there are numerous targets such as endangered animals, various other professions like bankers, and in-laws. However, with only a brief review of all the options needed, the answer was quite obvious: nurses. Decades of torture at their hands deserved some redress. And the torture wasn't just self perceived, virtually every patient I ever spoke to had a litany of complaints about the nursing care they received, so in a way, as with lawyers, a selective thinning of the herd was in society's best interest.

I used to think it was clever to tape the call button down so the nurse would someday have to enter the room to at least turn it off before the smell of a rotting carcass wafted down the halls after the patient had been ringing the bell for several days. That was before I came to the realization that the majority of nurses became immune to the sound of the bell by their third day on the job. Therefore they never responded to the bell to turn it off, no matter how insistently it rang. That effort failed also for lack of tape to tape the bell down because it soon became known in nursing circles what I was doing and they systematically hid the tape from me.

Throwing bedpans into the hallway to get attention, especially metal ones that were full, also worked for a while but that not only required patients who could lift the bed pan, let alone move their bowels to fill it, but also required the patient to be given a bedpan in the first place, which interestingly enough, was a somewhat rare event. It was rare for several reasons. For one, the nurse had to respond to the patient's bell, but as noted above, that was fairly unlikely. Also, the patient actually had to hit the pan, which given their feeble state and poor eyesight, was a 50/50 proposition at best. If the patient did successfully navigate the above bureaucratic maze, the nurse would have to help the patient off and clean them. If the nurses didn't do it on a timely basis, only then might the pan end up in the hallway (if the patient was strong enough to do so). All this added up to more work for the nurse, so as to maximize break time, they just seemed to decide, either as a group or through some nurse telepathy, to do away with bedpans and let the patients go in their bed. Thus, all the work would fall on the aides' shoulders to change the linens and clean the patients. The nurses could then concentrate on more productive matters like chilling their stethoscopes, complaining there's no soap as an excuse to not wash their hands and dulling the tips of their large bore needles.

None of the above was as bad as what they did to me though. There always were the snippy little things like calling me at 2 am to verify orders of patients who were admitted the day before, or worse yet, saying they beeped me by mistake and were sorry they woke me. There was a remedy for that though. I would call the night nurse around noon (their midnight) and tell them how much I appreciated their care of my patients. They rarely tried a repeat performance and were somewhat shocked I was able to get their unlisted home number. It was easy, you only needed one well placed ally per facility.

They did a number of other annoying little things, which individually weren't so bad, but collectively sealed their fate.

Some of my favorites include the time the nurse called me and stated the patient fell and hurt their hip. Should they get an x-ray of the hip or of some other place? My response was we should probably not disturb the hip in case it was injured but x-raying some other place, the nurse's choice, seemed like a good idea.

Another nurse called me to ask if the patient should be allowed to go to the bathroom. I thought about it for a while and responded that I don't think it would be a good idea to allow this so I said no. They responded that the patient had to go bad and she might burst if she didn't go soon. I told them to write an order in the chart explicitly stating it was against doctor's orders for the patient to burst.

The foreign language speaking nurses had their own set of problems relating to being unable to master most of the simplest concepts of our language let alone our idioms. When asked when the patient arrived at the facility, the Creole speaking nurse replied "the 8th of 30th".

I asked "what was the name of the 30th month of the year"?

She responded that the patient came in last month.

"Oh, you mean August?"

"Yes, the 8th of 30th."

"Let me get this straight, you're telling me she came in last month, August, which you think is the 30th month of the year?"

"Yes, August."

"Okay, just so I know, what is the name of the 29th month of the year?"

"Doctor, there are only 12 months in the year. Why are you saying these things?"

"I'm saying them because it's hard to understand you. Your English is bad."

"What do you mean my English is bad?" She moves the mouthpiece away and asks the other nurses in the background "Do you think my English is bad? The doctor says he doesn't understand me when I say the 8th of 30th. Do you understand me?"

"Not really." I hear in the background.

"What do you mean by that?" she now starts to sound indignant.

"Look," I say, "let's just get on with the orders." I yell into the speaker.

She hands the phone to another nurse grumbling the whole time "my English is good. It's the 8th of 30th."

I think I have the wrong number.

So I wonder, as I'm listening to the drivel from both the previous nurse and the current drone, are they doing this on purpose or are they congenitally stupid. I do concede that if I went to a foreign country and I spoke their language as badly as these nurses coming to my country speak English, that there would be a legitimate cause for action to have me drawn and quartered and my parts slathered in honey and left for the ants to pick my bones clean.

But I didn't go to a foreign country, these nurses did. I'll never know if they're smart or dumb. I'll never be able to get that far because they don't speak the language and there's no communicating with them. Having said that, if their actions are all that I have to go by, then they are indeed worse than worthless as they can't do what I ask them to do and they're just taking up the space another nurse who was competent and could speak the language could be taking.

Are they as bad as lawyers? We'll see.

Chapter 22: Don't Piss Me Off

Daffy (short for Daphne), the HMO case manager calls me up, more frazzled and frustrated than usual. "We have another problem at Avenue Manor. They've blocked two more discharges last night for the most ridiculous reasons. That makes four this week alone. I don't know what to do."

"What was the reason for the delays this time?" I sighed. The same call, another day.

"They said the equipment didn't arrive from the supply company yet." Daffy replied.

"Why not, this time?" The burden of leadership is heavy.

"They said it wasn't ordered on time to get here."

"But aren't they the ones responsible to do the ordering?" I asked, becoming slightly more interested.

"YESSSS." Daffy hissed.

"So let's see: they know a patient's to be discharged several days in the future. They know they're responsible to order the equipment and have it ready by the time of discharge. They then don't order on a timely basis and when the equipment doesn't arrive they cancel the discharge because the equipment's not there. Their real reason for doing so? So they can bill for another day or two and make more money."

"Correct." Daffy replies brightly.

"Anything else they do I need to know about?" Already starting to gird my loins for battle.

"Well yes, a whole bunch of things. They refuse to set reasonable goals in physical therapy, refuse to write sensible discharge summaries, set the patient and family against us and are generally belligerent and antagonistic." Daffy lamented.

"So what do you want me to do?" a glint of glee entering my eyes.

"The only thing we can do is send our patients elsewhere." She answered with some trepidation.

"Okay let me talk with Farty and see what he has to say." Farty of course wasn't his real name but that's what everyone who's ever stood behind him for more than a moment called him. He practiced some exotic eastern religion which apparently worshipped the bean. Its messiah, who was said to have descended from the beanstalk first made famous by Jack, was greatly anticipated and whose return was supposed to be hastened by bean eating. I only met Farty in person once, even though he's been my employee for some time now. But since I've assigned him to another county, we do enjoy our regular phone conversations. I just wished he'd stop asking to be reassigned to a place closer to home, but since I worked near his home too, I felt it prudent to achieve some geographical separation. "Hi, how are things?" I always just said 'Hi' and he always knew who it was. I did this for two reasons: even I thought it was rude to call him Farty to his face, it had been so long since I called him anything else, I couldn't remember his real name. The other reason, I'm getting so old I can barely remember my own name and "Hi" was such a benign enough generic greeting, it was hard to get myself in trouble by using it.

"Just fine, what's up?" he replied pleasantly as always. Farty was well admired for his niceness, just always from a distance or in passing. Here was one doc not prone to many curbside consults. "Phhthththhhh" was audible as a deep vibration in the background. Good, old reliable Farty.

"Just been discussing the situation at Avenue Manor and wanted to get your input. Daffy feels we should pull out and I wanted to know what you thought."

"Actually, as much as I try not to make waves, I have to agree. It's the only place where I get angry calls and that's from everyone conceivable, including distant cousins of patients. One time I got a call on my cell phone but lost the signal and hit *69 and it turns out it was from a cemetery with only one watchman and he denied making the call. That was weird. It appears that the ringleader is the administrator. He's real haughty and nasty and refuses to listen to my concerns. He's an arrogant pig, immature and incompetent. In any case, any place else would be better." Farty was on a roll.

"Listen, I want you to tell me what you really think, don't sugar coat it. That's okay, never mind, I can read between the lines and will take it from here." I now had to find another place to send our patients and then get the HMO's to agree to do so.

Piece of cake. Nursing homes were beating down our doors to send them patients. I once had an administrator tell me that he lost money on every patient we send him. This was while he was asking me why my census was so low. I remember a skit they did once on Saturday Night Live. One actor was playing a banker and the other a reporter interviewing him. The banker said the name of his bank was The Change Bank of New York and the reporter asked the banker what the bank did. The reply was that they made change. For instance if you wanted change for a dollar and wanted four quarters they could do that, they were the Change Bank. Or five dimes and ten nickels, they could do that. He went on to give several more examples of how to break a dollar bill, each time ending with "We can do that, we're the Change Bank". Finally the reporter asked how they made any money doing that. The banker answered: volume. So every time I here someone complain about the reimbursements from the HMO's, I think of that skit and laugh, sometimes out loud which either really confuses or consternates the administrator, as I think of the hypocrisy of complaining of losing money with each admission and then asking for more. Li'l Abner had 'kickums' that would bend over and beg to be kicked in the butt. I would have loved to do that literally to half the administrators I met. Actually, to all of them, but I wouldn't want to soil my shoe on the other half. Finding a willing nursing home wouldn't be a challenge.

On the other hand, convincing an HMO to change its referral patterns based on my whim could sometimes be like tying a rope to the Rock of Gibraltar and trying to tow it up to England. Never one to back out of a challenge, I thought this might be a good change from the rather boring and pedestrian sport of nurse baiting I engage in when things are slow.

So I ask around to find if there are any alternatives, get some other opinions and zero in on my tethered goat, Manner of Death Care. I ask for the administrator and after the usual pleasantries which consisted of confirming who he was and introducing myself, I got down to business. "So how's business?"

"Well, we are always looking to fill the house and we have a few beds empty." Replied the innocent administrator, not realizing that the hole he had just dug for himself merely by talking to me was rapidly becoming a bottomless pit.

"Would you like another 20 or so patients as an average daily census increase?" Come a little closer said the spider to the fly.

"Twenty you say. That's quite a few patients but I'm sure we could handle it and would love to give it a try." Snap!!! As the bear trap closed tight around his leg.

"Good. I would like to start using your facility for my patients, but (Aha! I thought I heard him say), you need to be willing to work with us in our requirements for our patients. Specifically, we need a case manager who realizes no one stays in the nursing home forever, in fact they only stay for a week on average and therefore discharge planning must be started and finished almost before the patients have a chance to settle in. And, they must be made to feel that this is appropriate and good for them. We also need a physical therapy department who's realistic in their goals and realizes that there's therapy available even after the patients leave the nursing home. If we can work together, then things will be great, if not, here today, gone tomorrow." That wasn't a veiled threat, that was an open one.

"Agreed. When do we start?" God, he was eager. Probably drowning in red ink. I could have asked for and probably received a room for my relatives to stay in when they visit. That would teach them (the relatives, that is).

"Soon. I need to inform the people I need to inform. Don't panic, it will take a few weeks." I hung up and called Daffy. "Okay, I got you another place. Now we'll both have to write letters of request and wait."

"Okay." Replied Daffy.

A few days later I got a call from the head case manager of the HMO, a lady I liken to a Viking warrior but without the grace. "So I hear you want to bump off another nursing home." Even I, known as 'the devil who walks the earth', am a little intimidated when on the phone with her. I've vowed not to speak her name openly for fear it would open the gates of hell and unleash its demons on mankind.

"Yeah, but I've got another place lined up, everyone's on board and it'll be good for your company." Speaking quickly allowed me to back out like the cowardly lion when he faced the wizard.

"Okay, we'll give it a shot." Click.

"Bye." I said to the dead line. Let the games begin. And they did. Within two weeks, almost all of our patients at Avenue Manor were gone. There were a few stragglers Farty had to see but they were dwindling rapidly. Unfortunately, he had to suffer through a series of verbal assaults from the administrator on down to the janitor. The administrator called the HMO and demanded a hearing. He said he was never warned that there was a problem and it was unfair to do this to him. Never once was he apologetic but remained true to form, haughty and arrogant as ever. After a month of this tact, he realized he was in trouble. He made the double error of taking Farty into his office and closing the door. He virtually got down on his knees, begging for patients, breaking down in tears. Raw meat for Farty. He had never before experienced the power that the bottom line has on people. Seeing a grown man prostrate himself made his stomach turn. It just makes me hungry. After a few minutes of groveling, the administrator drew silent, developed a strange, almost green hue to his face and fell over unconscious. Farty, taking this as the end of their discussion, decided to leave the office, but being the kind sole that he was, closed the door after him to preserve whatever remaining dignity the administrator had. He was discovered by his secretary just in the nick of time and after several weeks in intensive care, the administrator made a miraculous recovery. His family was told he was probably minutes from death from asphyxiation but the doctors couldn't officially say from what. Everyone knew not to bring Farty in for questioning.

So there was a tranquil interlude for several weeks due to Farty's inadvertent intervention. But eventually the administrator was back on the job, more determined than ever to fight and win this battle, as if he were fighting for his job. Which, of course, he knew he was. The administrator was back on the phone with the Viking, demanding his hearing. It was granted. A victory! Do you know how to spell pyrrhic?

He and his regional manager were to meet with her and an HMO medical director the next day.

I got a call from the medical director after the meeting stating that they told the administrator that the choice of facilities was solely up to me. He also told me that during the meeting the administrator 'bellowed' at the Viking demanding that the patients be allowed to return to his facility. They came close to blows. Oh goody, more fodder. So I get the call.

"We'd like to set up a meeting at your convenience to discuss this situation. When can you come up to meet us?" asked the administrator in a most condescending manner.

'Never' was my first thought but I finally settled on "Never. But we can talk on the phone when I have time. Call me back at 3 pm." God, that felt good. I'm in charge and I set the time and manner. This only works when you hold all the cards. Don't try this at home with your parents, kids. You'll get mighty hungry not be able to sit down for dinner until the skin on your butt heals.

So at three o'clock I get the call. "Hi doctor. We're on a conference call with the regional and district managers and Dr. Isaac" says the administrator. (So that's his name, but his first name still eludes me. Or is that his first name? I can never tell with some people.) "We'd like to talk to you about the situation here at Avenue Manor. We have a real nice facility here and would like you to send your patients here. We are fully licensed …"

"Look, I know the situation at your facility". I said, cutting him off. I just didn't have time for this nonsense. "Let me tell you how it is. For the past year you have been ignoring our pleas for cooperation. You've been thwarting our discharge plans with self-fulfilling actions that prevent a safe discharge on a timely basis. You've been turning the patients and families against us causing us untold and undeserved grief. Your case manager and physical therapist are more of a hindrance than a help. Your nurses are all agency nurses, they are totally clueless and their names are not pronounceable in English, a language, by the way, they apparently have never heard of. We've been complaining about this for a year and you tell me you know nothing of this. You might want to ask yourself why."

The regional manager, Spruce, speaks up, "I can see you're dissatisfied but we'd like a chance to set it straight. Send us your patients and you'll see the changes I put in."

"Look, I'm not going to change my mind on this just because you ask. Your actions have drowned out your words. On the other hand, you'll be getting patients from time to time and if what you say you've done is true, we'll know it and can readdress this issue in the future. I've got to go now, but Spruce, tell you what, give me a call right back in private. In private, you understand?"

"Yes". A more dejected man with a glimmer of false hope I've never seen.

A minute later, Spruce calls back. "Hi, Spruce. Picture this: the universe has just disintegrated and Hell has frozen over." I waited a moment for effect and continued. "That's when you'll see our next patient." Another pause. "As long as your administrator remains at your facility".

Spruce gathers his thoughts and responds "Can you give me a little clue as to why you feel that way?" as if specifics can ever undo a feeling once your mind's made up.

"Let's start with that little performance this morning (with the Viking). Do you think you're going to get anywhere like that?"

"No, you're right that wasn't good." Spruce admits.

"Now take my docs. I've had two in there for the past year and they refuse to go back. They tell me that your administrator is juvenile, arrogant and incompetent. Look at it this way, I have my two docs and the HMO case manager complaining to your administrator and other staff daily and it is only getting worse. Yet your administrator says he's heard nothing. That means he's either lying, ignoring the complaints he's heard, ignoring the complainers or has intimidated his staff so they won't come to him with the complaints. Regardless, it's clear he's incompetent and it's clear he doesn't have the necessary temperament for the job. Just remind yourself of his performance today and that he remains arrogant and unrepentant up to this moment. I'm not telling you to make any personnel changes, I'm just saying we can't work with the people that are there at this time. If you're willing to work with us, we need the following changes: a new administrator, head nurse, head of physical therapy, case manager and medical director."

"Thanks very much for your insight. I'll be thinking about what to do." Said Spruce, a broken man.

"Okay, bye." As I hung up, I noticed a half dozen department heads of the nursing home from which I was calling surrounding me. You might say it was indiscreet to hold this conversation in the middle of a nursing station, but short of bragging, this was the best way to let others be put on notice. "Hi guys, what did you think? Was I clear or do you think he didn't understand what I was saying?"

"Oh, it was clear. How did you put it? Oh yes, 'Hell will freeze over' before you send another patient until he fires his administrator and half his staff. Even we got the message, or should I say firing squad, and we only heard half the conversation?" I always liked Bob, the head of physical therapy, he was quick and smart and knew how to play ball.

"Good, I just wanted him to remember in the future to DON'T PISS ME OFF! Good day gents, it's back to work for me." They lingered briefly, the show was over but they were a little shell-shocked. 'Let me see' I said to myself as I took out my logbook. Oh yes, that's administrator number three. Ironically, the facility where I was would log administrator number four next week but she didn't know it yet. I called her Betty Boop because she was an airhead but that wasn't really unkind to the original Betty Boop because she at least had some redeeming qualities.

I called back Farty. "Well, what did you think?"

"Awesome boss. My chin is still dropped to my chest. By the way, when do I get my next raise?"

"When I've paid for my condo. You know the best part of my screwing people over like this is the cigarette afterwards. By the way, are you familiar with the concept of tithing?"

"Ooops, look at the time. Gotta go, see ya."

Chapter 23:
A Public Service Announcement: "Warning: Failure to wash your hands after shaking hands and then rubbing your eyes may lead to blindness."

(*Editorial* response: Stop all your hand wringing over hand washing)

Shaking hands hasn't always been my bete noir. I remember fondly the early days of my professional career when I volunteered at the Florida State Hand Shaking Clinic. Those were exciting times where much of the early medical investigations into the hazards of hand shaking were first undertaken.

It was there that I first learned about the necessity of proper hand washing techniques. There was an epidemic, especially among the young people, of hand shaking related illnesses. The clinic tried their best to try to educate the population about the dire need to maintain good and safe hand shaking techniques but not many people were listening.

As the epidemic worsened, the Conservatives wanted everyone to stop shaking hands altogether except under the watchful gaze of a responsible family member. That wasn't a popular or practical solution. The Liberals advocated giving out free gloves to try to break the endless cycle of hand shaking followed by recurrent infections, frequently requiring intramuscular shots to cure increasingly resistant infections. This worked for a while but people soon became blasé about using gloves every time they shook hands, even with strangers. We were taught that every time you shook hands with someone you were shaking hands with everybody the other person had ever shaken hands with. Pretty soon, people were letting down their guard and started shaking hands with gloves that they had previously used to shake hands with other people. They became too lazy to come to the clinic to exchange used gloves for new ones. They soon forgot how bad things were before they used gloves to shake hands. Many even neglected to use gloves at all when they shook hands. The epidemic grew out of control anew.

I resigned from the Florida State Hand Shaking Clinic in disgust and despair. I grew cool to strangers. I wasn't about to fall prey to the hand shaking epidemic. I vowed to find someone with clean hands and only shake her's. I began to believe that a monogamous hand shaking relationship was the only way to be able to enjoy hand shaking again without the artificiality of wearing a glove. But alas, finding someone who was clean and pure enough to enter this relationship was proving to be quite difficult. Where could I find such a person? Certainly not at public rest rooms, although that would afford me the opportunity to observe one's hand washing techniques first hand, but that would limit me to unisex sinks and the number of those dwindled as the hand shaking epidemic flourished.

I withdrew into myself, staying mostly at home, consoling myself by shaking my own hands in the privacy and safety of my own home. That worked for a while but my hands soon became too chafed from the frequent hand shaking habit I was developing. My hands became fatigued and limp with over use. I found I couldn't even shake my own hands without fear. What was I to do?

The answer came to me one day. Fall back on my core values! Do that which I had set out to do from the beginning, the thing that had sustained me time and time again. The ideas that gave me strength and purpose. Something to live for. I was renewed again and could set out into the world with greater vigor. I could hold my head high as I was able to rise above the indiscriminate hand shaking that was destroying the nation.

I called Sandy and Bulldog. "I'm ready! Let's go forth again and do good and leave the carnal pleasures of hand shaking to those lesser beings who needed something to hold onto more firm than a lofty ideal. Let the real work of man begin again."

"Uh, what do you have in mind?" Bulldog drooled out the words along with saliva from the side of his mouth as I had called him at two AM.

"The usual." I responded with glee. "Let's go forth and kill all the lawyers and stop our hand wringing about what we can't have and can't do."

"That's great but how exactly do you plan to do this?" snzzzzz.

"Let's go to the court house in the morning and greet all the lawyers we can find. We'll go up to them, tell them we really appreciate their work and say 'shake'. With any luck they won't wash their hands all day and we might be able to kill them with kindness by quitting time."

"Um, sounds good. Let's just hope their germs don't overwhelm us. G'nite." Click.

Hmmm. Good point. Maybe we'll just wear gloves. Okay, that's a plan.

Chapter 24:
I Have a Job to Do

As part of my full time pursuit of eliminating the scourge of lawyers, I have taken work as a hospitalist. This is a relatively new concept whereby a physician, usually an Internist, has decided to limit his practice to working in a hospital or skilled nursing facility. It pays the bills, hones my skills for my real job and not infrequently allows me to further my main goals at the same time. That is to say, lawyers and their evil brood are not infrequently my patients.

As a hospitalist, I have no patients of my own. I merely see the patients of many other primary care doctors who've either chosen to have me see their patients or are forbidden by the HMO's from seeing their patients while hospitalized because we handle the situation much better. What do I mean by better? Simply put, we get the patients out of the hospital faster. Much faster. Tens of millions of dollars a year faster per hospitalist. And what do we get in return? Long, almost unbelievably long hours, low pay, the undying enmity of the patient, his family and the entire staff of every institution we set foot in. So why do we do it? We need a job, relish confrontation and covet the power to tell others what to do.

This reminds me of the most apropos definition of a physician I have seen to date. It was contained in a Dilbert cartoon strip. Dogbert has set himself up as a career counselor. Standing in front of him was a short, stocky, bald headed, no necked character dressed in a tee shirt with stripes making him look like an escaped death row inmate.

Dogbert was reviewing the aptitude test results the character had just taken and said, "It says here that you like to remove vital organs from helpless people. That means you're best suited to be either a doctor or mass murderer. What do you think of people?"

The character replies "They're worthless insects I crush beneath my feet".

At which point Dogbert says, "We'll need a tie breaker question."

Except for a few liars and a few docs I don't really know enough to have them tell me the truth, the above interchange describes how almost all doctors, regardless of their field, feel after a few years in practice and a malpractice suit or two. By the same token, the same holds true for just about everyone I've ever known in any field. The only difference is that doctors can do something about it, legally, and get away with it.

Let me give you an example. A lawyer comes in with a stroke and can no longer eat without a feeding tube. He's confined to bed, paralyzed on one side, can't talk or interact in any way but he is conscious. Traditionally, the typical physician would take the family aside and tell them that a feeding tube is necessary and that the patient will have to be placed on a ventilator. He'll be confined to bed, tied down if necessary and sedated so he'll be drowsy but still conscious.

What a perfect way to torture someone, stick all sorts of tubes and needles in him, limit his freedom to blinking his eyes and giving him a life sentence. You wouldn't have to actually kill him, he'd die on his own as his only means of escape.

So you see, doctors have been torturing patients legally for decades. They don't have to actually kill the patient as he does it himself. But not for months and not before he suffers from the ignominy of having strangers clean him up every day, once a day, whether he needs it or not. Not before he develops horrible bed sores causing untold pain and suffering; blood clots embolizing to the lungs causing a drowning sensation of shortness of breath if he lives through it with the attendant panic that goes along with it; various bladder and bowel infections (nothing like a good case of diarrhea to cut down on those annoying visitors) and, if he's lucky, a pneumonia to finally do him in. Yep, nothing like the caring attitude of the family doctor to steer his patient's family in the right direction in these life and death situations.

The only problem was that this approach was nondiscriminating. Both the good and the bad among us were subjected to the same degradation. What the medical profession needed was some good old pessimism that they could impart to the loved one's family.

"The situation is hopeless. We could either keep your parent alive artificially but the pain and suffering would be unbearable and he'd die just the same in short order, if he was lucky. If not, he would linger in unspeakable horror and bankrupt the family to boot. No, what I would recommend is hospice and let him go in peace and dignity."

Now that's what I'd call a great doctor. Unfortunately, not all families can be educated that way and they stick to the old, outmoded, so-called "Western" idea that life at all costs is better in every case than the alternative.

So they'd reply "I understand what you're saying but I feel obligated to give my parent every chance I can to keep him/her alive. I believe when god wants him, he'll come and get him."

To which I typically reply, in as sympathetic tone as I can "god has not only come for your parent but he's outside furiously beating on the door to let him in but you've barricaded it and put in earplugs."

"Maybe so, but I just as soon want to wait until he breaths his last before I stop what we're doing."

"Okay, that's your right, I'll do what I can to make him comfortable." "Oh nurse," I think to myself, "please hand me that curare we keep for special occasions, I feel merciful tonight." Of course, that's only if the patient is not a lawyer. In that case I keep them as uncomfortable as humanly possible to tolerate and every visit I whisper in his ear "so lawyer, how does it feel on the other side of the suit? Not as much fun getting it as you had dishing it out, is it? Something to look forward to, my new issue of toxicology came today. I'll have a little something new for you when I return. Now remember, don't die on me, I haven't finished with you yet." I'm always surprised how a seemingly immobile person can grimace like that. All I know is that it gives me great satisfaction, knowing I have a job to do and I do it well.

Chapter 25: A Good Plan

After I dropped Jim off a few blocks from his house, I drove back to see Bulldog and Sandy. On the way, I called in to Debbie, the communications officer who had responsibility for monitoring the various wiretaps we had illegally placed. "Anything I should know about on Detective Freed?"

"Unless he's using a code even the Navajos couldn't break, he's playing this straight as an arrow." Debbie replied. Debbie had a great job, just sitting around all day, not far from the fridge and her never ending pile of sweets. One look at her and Sandy's wife would have had a heart attack on the spot. She had to go the Tall and Stout shop just to buy something to sit on. I knew we'd be needing a replacement sooner than later because her poor body just couldn't hold out much longer. Gravity was sure to win.

"That's great. Let me know if I need to know anything. He just got home."

"I know he's home. Don't you think I'm paying attention to the monitors?"

"Okay, thanks, bye." Debbie could be gruff, especially if she wasn't eating or someone was interrupting her eating. She must be a little hypoglycemic. Maybe I should send her another care package and be a little more diligent in my search for her replacement.

I pulled up to the motel room again and again didn't have to knock as the door opened in front of me. "Don't you guys do anything but watch the door?" I asked jokingly.

"We anticipate your arrival so bad it almost hurts." said Sandy. I almost believed him.

"Okay, let's get down to business. Jim's acceptable, right?" I looked at the other two nodding their heads in the affirmative. "Good. We'll get back to him later. Let's give him a couple of days to settle in and see what he comes up with. In the meantime, our latest operation seems to have gone without a hitch. It certainly made a statement but not everyone understands what the statement is. Since we're not in this for the notoriety, there's no reason to clue anybody in by telling them. The more off guard we can keep them, the easier it'll be for us. So, did you bring what I asked you to?"

Sandy and Bulldog both held up the last page of their respective city's phone book as did I. Each one contained a full page ad of a personal liability firm, exhorting the citizens of their cities to sue their fellow man if they felt wronged even in some vague manner. I knew that they wouldn't have any trouble finding them as virtually every phonebook in the country now was monopolized by these types of ads.

"As you can see, the scourge of the earth has taken to the advertising media as never before. You can't watch daytime TV without every other ad being by a lawyer telling of rights we never knew we had being trampled by virtually everyone alive and we were due money for it. I know eliminating a few of the worst offenders won't make them all go away but it'd surely make them think twice about frivolous lawsuits and trying to legislate new laws from the bench. I think we should proceed with these three targets for starters. In the meantime, the planning for the June graduations will continue and be fine tuned. The method we used in the Brown case seems to work just fine. Any questions?" I really loved these guys and the work we were doing gave us a great opportunity to be together. The work was almost just a bonus.

Bulldog asked "Who should we do first?"

"Your choice." I replied.

"Okay, unless Sandy objects, let's do mine first. I knew this was coming. I've already cased the joint and have the particulars worked out. If it fits in everyone's plans we could do it Friday and be home for the weekend."

"No problems here, I just wish we could be productive every day rather than just once a week." Sandy lamented.

"I know, but you've got to remember, these jobs are just to set the tone. There are too many lawyers and too little time if we continue this on a retail level. You know that the US has 5% of the world's population and 90% of the lawyers, topping a million currently. In order to accomplish our purpose we have to switch to wholesale and that's where the law school graduations are relevant. We've picked a day with the most number of graduations, 10, by the way, because once we do them, there won't be any mass gatherings for a while. The ABA meeting will probably be our next best shot and we'll already have that rigged so we won't have to worry about the increased security after June. Let's hope they are the same defiant bunch of assholes as ever and they don't cancel or move their convention. Okay, Bulldog, pass out the plans."

Bulldog did so and started to review them with us. Jones, Witherspoon and Dinkens, a prestigious and well established law firm with offices in downtown Jacksonville. They owned their own two story building so we didn't need to worry about elevators and guards on the ground floor of some of the taller office buildings overlooking the St. John's River as it meandered through the heart of the city. There were 22 lawyers employed at Jones et al and 54 paralegals, secretaries and other ancillary personnel. Bulldog called three different times to make appointments with the three principles and found a day that they'd all be in the office. The air conditioners were located in a relatively isolated area and our service truck would not appear suspicious parked there. We had ample supplies of halothane to put everybody to sleep so we could enter the building without concern. The halothane would only put them to sleep, it was unlikely to kill them so we still had to go room by room to finish them off. Knives were our preferred method because we were a hands on group. We did have guns with silencers for reticent victims and for newcomers into the building which were always kept at the ready. I estimated it should take fifteen minutes to finish up.

"There's one thing I haven't told you that makes this all the more sweet." Bulldog added. "My sister, with whom I'm engaged in a really nasty inheritance lawsuit, has an appointment there at three, so I'm hoping that fits in with your return flight plans."

"Always glad to accommodate whenever we can." chimed in Sandy. "That's one more lawyer too. One of us will do her if you don't think you're up to it."

"You'd have to fight me off if you even think of ruining my pleasure. She ceased being a sister in anything but name decades ago. She's mine." Bulldog's red face and clenched fists left no doubt of the depth of his feelings.

"She's all yours Bulldog, but we're there to support you in any way possible." I said to help slowly ease him down. I've seen Bulldog get this way in only two situations, discussing his sister or discussing lawyers and we were doing both now. This was a good plan and we all agreed to meet Friday to carry it out.

Chapter 26:
One Good Turn Deserves Another

Officer Jim Freed received the papers calling for his divorce arbitration on March 3rd. He was to appear in Judge Walters' chamber for the settlement conference with his lawyer. His wife had already demanded temporary alimony which, amazingly enough, was denied as she had already withdrawn their entire life's savings on the day she left and was living with her lawyer. Even the judge saw the irony and injustice in that. That was analogous to the Mendez brothers shooting their parents and then throwing themselves on the mercy of the court because they were orphans.

Jim wasn't looking forward to this proceeding as he didn't really want to see his wife again nor her lawyer, the low life scumbag who instigated this whole affair. He was concerned that he'd lose control and use the weapon that had heretofore been holstered for his entire 20 year career, except for cleaning and target practice.

Jim had been only peripherally involved with our operation and usually only in a minor advisory capacity. Nonetheless, he knew he was up to his neck in capital offenses and a slew of other charges carrying a long stretch of mandatory prison time for what he knew and what he did. He hadn't asked anything from us but as his thoughts began to ramble, he came upon the idea that maybe it was time to ask us to help him for once.

Jim picked up the special cell phone we gave him if he ever had to communicate with us. He touched the speed dial button number one (there was only one number programmed in speed dial) and listened as the phone rang.

Sandy picked it up on the first ring and said "Hi, Jim. What's up?"

Jim was used to the prompt and cheery voice at the other end. Sandy, always fearing the worst, put up the bravest front and sublimated his feeling from dread to cheer as a sort of self help antidepressant psychotherapy that he had read about in Reader's Digest. It seemed to be working, at least it had Jim fooled. "I have a favor to ask of the group that would be quite meaningful for me."

"Shoot." Replied Sandy, using his favorite policeman jibe.

"I was wondering if you'd kill my wife and her lawyer for me?" Jim always wondered whether or not the 128 digit encoded scrambler on the phone really was as decipher proof as we assured him. Maybe yes and maybe no he pondered, but he was still a free man so even if it wasn't foolproof, at least no one was concerned enough about them to try to break the code. "I was impressed with the way you did in that scumbag lawyer and his receptionist the other day. The department hasn't come up with the first clue and a few of the guys who knew him are actually giving the perps a few kudos for selection of target and nastiness of departure. They'd nail you to the wall if they caught you but wouldn't be overly harsh in the capture."

"I'll discuss it with the others, and since it involves a lawyer, if it doesn't interfere with our overall plans, we might be able to fit it in. I know I'll vote for it."

"You know I'm involved in a divorce and it has to look like an accident. I'd be the prime suspect any other way."

"You know we like you too much to let anything bad happen to you. Our middle name is 'Accidents-R-Us. Don't worry, we'll take care of you. By the way, we had nothing to do with the incident you're alluding to, but wish we had been. We'll be in touch soon. Bye."

Sandy sounded reassuring and optimistic and Jim felt a little better. He knew that the denial was merely proforma to allow for deniability if the issue came up later. He hoped that if he'd be able to extricate himself from at least this one complication to his already overly complicated life that he'd be able to live a reasonably comfortable life in retirement from his savings and pension. He'd still have to somehow extricate himself from us. But he knew that might take some time and doing. He wanted to be able to save for his old age even though it was looking less and less like he'd make it that far due to his association with us. Worse yet, he feared his old age might become expense free, down to the striped clothing the state would be providing for him if things didn't go just perfectly. For now he was at our mercy.

Sandy hung up, turned to me and asked what I thought. I had been listening on the speaker we have hooked up so no one has to repeat the conversation for the others.

"I've got the plans almost entirely worked out, we have a month to kill, in this case literally, before we have to go to Chicago and it would keep us sharp. Let's work on it but keep Jim out of the picture so his reaction will be genuine surprise and he won't be able to slip up and give away details that he doesn't know." I looked forward to a little side job and the opportunity to bind Detective freed eternally to our cause. Especially since he was alert and astute enough to put two and two together about our recent caper even though the MO was entirely different than anything else we had done up to that point.

What did we know? His soon to be ex wife was shacked up with her lover/lawyer. They had absconded with all his money and were demanding more. The lawyer had a small but reasonably busy practice in a small office building, several miles from the court house and several miles from her old home. They lived a few blocks from the office. They had two cars, she had a 1998 Volvo S70 and he had a 1990 Nissan Sentra.

That was a rundown on their obvious assets. What did we need to know? What were his usual office hours, did he go out to lunch, where and for how long? Did he take the same route to work every day? Did they go out to eat or stay home?

What about her? Did she work, where, what were her hours? Did she go to club meetings, volunteer, stay at home?

These were just a few of the details we needed to know, they could almost be placed in checklist form for future jobs, the blanks filled in and the job take care of itself. No, every job is unique even if seemingly similar in facts. This wasn't going to be a particularly tough assignment though and didn't call for the ritualized killing the last one demanded.

"Sandy, since you said we'd try to help, you need to live up to your word. Take Bulldog and go on our usual fact finding tour of the targets and let me know how you think we should do this. Car accident, carbon monoxide poisoning, murder suicide, even robbery/murder. Whatever you think might be best. I'd like to get this out of the way sooner than later so we can position ourselves in Chicago and concentrate on the ABA."

"Be right on it." Sandy said with his usual alacrity. "Come on Bulldog, we've got a little reconnoitering to do."

"Coming dear." called back Bulldog. He got up from the couch he was lying on, put on his shoes and ambled after Sandy.

Bulldog probably needed less rest and more exercise but it's hard to teach an old dog new tricks and Bulldog was more stubborn than most. On the other hand, he's not let us down and makes up for his somewhat excessive bulk by his sheer, well, bulldogedness.

I went back to my planning. Doing in a whole bunch of people in a public building was going to be somewhat tricky, but I think I found the way. We need a little bit of learned skills though before we'd be able to get it right. I pulled the classified out of the paper, made a few calls and had three job interviews lined up for tomorrow, one for each of us. If luck stayed with us and we were hired, our work would be all but done.

After a couple of hours of further planning and details, I called it a day and went out for supper. I knew Sandy and Bulldog wouldn't be back for two or three days. They would do an all night surveillance just to make sure the ex and her lawyer weren't into kinky, all night type stuff. I closed up shop and headed on out. As I walked to the car, I wondered if we could use Detective Freed with us in Chicago. An extra man might come in handy and he owed us more now. As we all knew, one good turn deserves another.

Chapter 27:
They Died With Their Boots On

Sandy and Bulldog showed up three days later. They smelled a little gamey and looked the part. It was both a tribute to their dedication and a bow to reality that they didn't really buy into this personal hygiene craze that started in Versailles three hundred years ago. I was used to it, knew after they checked in with me that they'd take care of this nonessential detail, so I merely cranked up the A/C a few degrees to get the air circulating and waited for them to gather their thoughts.

Bulldog spoke first, "Boy are they dull. Dull, dull, dull. If they didn't actually move from time to time, I'd have thought they were already dead, or at least wished they were. If they have any sense at all, they'll die of boredom before we can get to them. Boy, are they dull."

Bulldog enjoyed a little spice in life and could never figure out the home body/couch potato thing. We all need a little rest to recharge the batteries. Bulldog would say they don't need any batteries, they're not going anywhere or doing anything. That was alright with me, just made easier, sitting duck, targets.

"So not your idea of a wild partying couple, eh?" I offered. "What's the scoop, Sandy? Are we going to be able to make this look real?"

Sandy studied his notes for a few more moments and said, "Yeah, we can do it easy enough. Here's what I recommend, I've written it down for you. I can barely keep warm in this place. I'm going home, have a bite to eat, lie down and maybe have a bath. See ya."

"Me too." said Bulldog who trooped out after Sandy.

"Reverse the order." I stage whispered after them but I doubt they remembered the order to reverse anyway. It was cold in here, I had to crank up the A/C a little more than usual. They were starting to smell like nursing home inmates. That alone gave me a chill.

I read over Sandy's plan and thought it was reasonable and doable and spared Detective Freed of any obvious involvement.

I beeped them a message a minute later: "Be sure to be back by 8 AM, we have job interviews at 9 AM".

Eight AM sharp they showed up back at the office smelling fresh as daisies.

"I liked your plan Sandy, we'll implement it this week. It's only Tuesday, let's shoot for Friday, give Detective Freed's coworkers a little something especially pungent to enjoy when the bodies are discovered, probably Monday or Tuesday. In the meantime, here are the job interviews we need to go on." I said, handing them typed out directions and contact people. "Sandy, you apply for the fire sprinkler installation job. Bulldog, you go for the gasoline delivery job. I'll work on building maintenance. Probably a week or two will give us enough experience and know how, if we ask the right questions and pay attention to the details, that we'll need for the ABA job. Any questions?"

"Who's the third person going to be?" asked Sandy.

"I've got her picked out. We'll meet back here Friday at 3 PM. We'll go over the details and then get to work by 4:30 PM. I'll have it all set up for you then. Good luck on your job interviews."

We all headed out to our cars, drove off to offer ourselves up as employees at our soon to be new jobs and relaxed for a while, the planning was done for now.

Friday arrived in no time, time flies by when you're having fun. None of us could get all the grime and grease off us despite 20 minutes of intensive washing with industrial strength cleaners. The only spots that were dirt free were those areas where the skin actually started to come off from rubbing too vigorously. We decided a little dirt never hurt anyone.

"So here's the deal. Jim will be here with a prostitute he just arrested. She thinks she'll get off if she does a little favor for Detective Freed's friends. Well give her the heroin shot here so she'll be docile the rest of the night. Once he delivers her here, Freed is done and he'll go home."

"When's he due here?" asked Sandy.

"Any minute now. Let's grab a quick snack now or we can go out to eat together later if you like." We always had some food to nosh on, usually our individual favorites. Almost as if a ritual before battle, we'd take in our favorite pleasure in case it was our last. Frozen grits and bacon bits for Bulldog, heated in the microwave, almost made them edible for those so inclined. I just couldn't imagine anyone being so desperate or depraved as to be so inclined. Sandy was partial to 20 year old scotch but his wife made him stop some time ago so he settled for Godiva chocolate. I always had a batch of rainbow cookies on hand. These were a marzipan delight little known to most of the world except a civilized few from a particular religious sect. We preferred it that way.

Jim drove up a short while later, had a really skuzzy, down trodden, 'you expect me to pay for that?' looking whore. Clearly no one will miss her except some might note that the streets seem a little cleaner for some reason but no one would be able to put their finger on exactly why.

She entered to room somewhat gingerly. She certainly wasn't afraid of getting raped. Hell, that was her job. Neither was she afraid of being beaten, that was almost expected by this time in her career since no pimp would have her in his stable. They had reputations to uphold, you know. No, she was concerned that she wouldn't get her fix. We looked too clean cut to have a stash on us. She was wrong about her assessment of us being too clean cut but she was right she wasn't going to get her fix. She was already high and we didn't need to waste expensive heroin on her. Instead we gave her 5 mg of Xanax IV and she was just as happy in her sleep as heroin would have made her. Since they don't make Xanax for IV use, we merely crushed the tablets, dissolved them in ethanol and injected it in her veins. If she wasn't to have died that night anyway, she surely would have died of endocarditis from the bacteria on our hands in short order in addition to being stroked out from the undissolved debris from the tablets sooner than that.

It was getting dark when we loaded her into the trunk. We used a steamer trunk to hide her. We drove over to 11528 6th Ave. This was a three story apartment building with eight apartments on each floor. There was an outer door that wasn't locked leading to a small lobby with an elevator ascending to the upper levels straight ahead and two hallways leading in opposite directions. There was a Harry O'Connor listed as living in apt 3B. Beside his name was penciled in Jenny Freed. We rode the elevator up along with our steamer trunk and our bag of goods. Getting off on the third floor, we went to the right and knocked on the door for 3B. Harry looked through the peephole, saw me dressed as a pizza delivery boy and said, "That was quick, I just called a few minutes ago."

"Mr. O'Connor, you order pizza every night. We just have it ready for you now so you don't have to wait." I said.

Harry thought about that for a second, opened the door and was immediately maced. Sandy rushed in, found Jenny paralyzed by fear and indecision, sitting inches from the phone, yet not moving.

Sandy maced her anyway. He then picked up the phone, called the pizza place, apologized and cancelled the order. They said thanks but they'd have to bill his credit card anyway but would give him a store credit which he readily accepted and expressed his thanks for their understanding.

Bulldog, having emptied the trunk, carried the lightened load downstairs into the car and waited there for us.

Harry and Jenny were both writhing on the floor, temporarily incapacitated. We worked fast. We carried Harry into the bedroom, tied his arms and legs to the four corners of the bed. We then laid the whore on top of him. Bulldog shot her three times in the back and chest from the bedroom doorway. He then saw where she lay on Harry, reached across and shot Harry three times, once in the head, once in the chest and the third on up between the legs of the whore into his genitals. We then carried Jenny into the bedroom, put the gun in her hands, aimed it towards her heart and squeezed. We let her drop to the floor, picked up our bags and left. The noise was loud but the rooms were well insulated, not many people were home on a Friday night and the ones who were minded their own business. No one so much as looked out their peephole, let alone opened their door or called the police. They would have seen two men with full facial hair and large hats if they did.

We made a clean getaway and, as predicted, it wasn't until Monday afternoon that O'Connor's secretary finally called to tell the police that her employer hadn't shown up for work. They made a courtesy visit to his home but the smell from under the door made it clear it wouldn't end that way.

The newspaper echoed the coroner's inquest: "Triple murder/homicide in lover's triangle". Reminiscent of the early porno movies, the two lovers were naked except for their shoes. I love to be quirky.

Chapter 28: Another Fine Mess

Jim became numb as he watched the video. He saw himself enter the room, immediately seeing the still live lawyer, but stopping to check out the room before attending the victim. He remembered the feeling of recognition as he realized who the victim was. He remembered his disgust as he saw his defeats glorified upon the walls of the stricken lawyer. He relived the utter dejection he felt as his wife of twenty years sat there as the divorce papers were served. He also remembered the sense of peace and calm as he watched himself finish off the partially completed job. Could a lifetime of events really be compressed into this 24 hour day? And it's not even over yet. Jim sat there after the tape was done. It came down to now or never. Yes or no? Jim looked around, saw nothing in the room to sway him one way or another. It had to come from him. Jim contemplated the situation. I hate lawyers. This guy's giving me an opportunity to act on this hate which has been festering for so long. I've got to go for it. There's nothing left for me in my old life, maybe there will be something good for me in my new one.

"Okay, I'm in. No reservations, no regrets. I'm with you. Only insofar as lawyers and other criminals go. No self enrichment, no criminal activity beyond the above goals." Jim said.

"Of course, our objectives are lawyers and the criminals they protect. Not the good, productive people of our country. Welcome aboard."

"What do we do now?" Jim said almost enthusiastically. He seemed to have thrown in with us hook, line and sinker.

"I think the first thing we do is help you out of your current legal difficulties so you won't have any distractions. You go to work, work on 'our case' but find no useful leads and let it end up in the cold case file in six or so months. Stay on it until it does just to make sure. Also get involved in public corruption cases so we'll know who the most important targets are and, with any networking you can do, we'll be able to target more effectively in other cities and states so it won't look like all the spate of deaths are localized to here. We'll also read the papers and find targets unrelated to any that you're working on so there won't be a trail back to you."

"What are you going to do to solve my legal difficulties without it looking suspicious?" Jim asked with a little worried tone now that the reality of future planning was hitting home.

"Don't you worry, we already have solved your problem. While you were out investigating and taking some action on your own, we arranged a murder-suicide at your house. Try to act surprised and upset when you go home. Yes, keep that expression, that's perfect."

Jim looked like he was about to puke, the knowledge that his wife and her lawyer husband were dead in his home was another blow in a day when he thought he'd taken so many blows he was numb to any more, but he wasn't. In fact, he actually did throw up. I wasn't worried, the hotel would clean it up. They were used to little messes like this and always kept a ready janitorial staff at hand. You had to when you rented by the hour and couldn't keep the next guest waiting. Nevertheless, Jim rapidly regained his composure, realized he was in with no getting out and hurried exited the front door with me. We went in opposite directions and I told him to expect a call in a couple of days. We had a lot of work to do and couldn't waste much time. Right after the funeral we'll get down to business. I had a few associates Jim would have to meet. Bulldog and Sandy were good men. We were about to get a lot of work done.

Chapter 29: A Few Good Men

I read about the tragic events at Detective Freed's home two days ago. Jim did a great acting job and the coroner confirmed the murder-suicide from carbon monoxide poisoning in the garage. The stun gun left no marks so there was nothing else to find to dispute the coroner's impression. The funeral was today. A large contingent of his station house showed up and Jim was given a few days off. He agreed to take off today but said he'd be back tomorrow.

I gave him a call when I knew he was back home. "Hey Jim, I'm real sorry about your wife. How about meeting me for a drink to help you forget?" I played it coy just in case there was anyone doing some wiretapping that we didn't count on.

"Sure."

"Great, meet me at Clancy's. I'll be waiting for you."

There was a Clancy's just down the block but I was waiting around the corner in my car and we drove off for a different type of rendezvous. Sandy and Bulldog had gotten in the night before. They wanted to meet Detective Freed to size him up and see whether or not he could be trusted in a pinch. He'd done well so far but nothing could substitute for personal contact in evaluating a person's character.

We drove up to the motel where they were staying. They had picked a first floor unit in the back where comings and goings could occur with a minimum of casual observations by passersby. We drove right up to the door, hopped out and before even knocking, the door opened and we walked in.

I introduced Jim to the others. Bulldog got his name as much for his physical appearance as for the tenaciousness of his style. He was thick, not fat, especially around his thorax and neck, built like a linebacker and just as quick. Sandy had a more pear like shape, tending towards the paunchy despite his never ending diets du jour which his wife concocted up for him. He would have starved to death if he ate just what she allowed so he was always sneaking some in and then denying it to her. She couldn't figure it out so she just fed him less. And, of course, the less she fed him the more he cheated. The only thing left for her to do was to lock him in a room and feed him nothing until he finally either ate the door and escaped or did in fact lose weight. Sandy always carried a lock pick with him just in case she ever did carry out her threat.

Together, they sized up Jim. His physical appearance was average in many ways which actually was good so he wouldn't necessarily be easily recognized in a crowd. He'd just blend in, do what he had to do, and be on his way. Jim was above average in intelligence. That was obvious in the way he sized up his new partners. He had to make sure they wouldn't be the weakest link in the chain holding him up.

Everyone was pleased at first glance and the meeting was therefore short and sweet. The instructions for getting in contact with each other were established and committed to memory. The goals of the organization were clearly laid out and several immediate actions were planned. Jim wasn't yet entrusted with the scope and size of the group but it was made clear that the less he knew regarding each member and the less they knew about him, the better for all involved.

We didn't want a psycho or sociopath in our group, they were just bad news and couldn't differentiate a cause from a lark. No, we, like the Marines, wanted a few good men and Detective Freed was definitely one.

Chapter 30: Hope for the Best, Plan for the Worst

Training is important, whether it's to be a doctor or the right hand of god. What we were doing could be interpreted differently by different people based on which side of the fence they were standing. For instance, if you were a lawyer, you probably wouldn't consider us on the side of god. If you were just about anyone else who'd ever suffered from the miscarriage of justice practiced by lawyers, you'd probably think otherwise.

In any case, we definitely needed to practice, so we obtained specimens needed to help us fine tune our skills. Therefore, every month or so, the three of us would make an appointment at a solo lawyer's office on Fridays at the end of the day, under a fictitious name of course. We'd show up at staggered times so the first one there could scope out the location and make sure it would be suitable and safe for our plan.

We had all seen enough police shows to realize that it would be difficult to not leave some clue. We consulted with Detective Freed on a number of occasions about how to avoid such slipups. It became clear that we needed to not shed a hair if we hoped to stay in business long. So we came up with a plan to minimize our risk. We would buy clothes with the most common type of cloth so as to eliminate almost no suspects when the threads were analyzed. Our clothes would cover as much of our body as they could to prevent shedding of our skin. We obviously wouldn't smoke, spit or drink while we were there. We would shampoo and then mousse our hair so virtually none would fall out while we were there. And finally, we would cover all of our exposed skin and several inches into the covered areas with the same plastic spray used by doctors who wanted to eliminate exposure to diseases when examining patients. The plastic would form an impermeable barrier to liquids for several hours and would prevent shedding of any of our skin during that time. We thus could enter an office, be there for hours and leave no identifiable trace that we were ever there.

One of our training sessions took place on a sunny spring afternoon. Bulldog shows up first about 3:30 PM, half an hour before our appointment. He introduces himself to the receptionist/secretary/paralegal as this is a one person office and there was only one employee. As is typical of such offices, the receptionist is harried, gruff and less than pleasant. But we knew that from our screening phone calls. We chose offices with annoying personnel to make it all the more pleasant for us later on.

Bulldog walks up to the desk, sees the name plate of the receptionist, C. Rhabi, and introduces himself. "Hi, I'm here to see Mr. Piker. I have an appointment for 4 PM."

A few moments later, Ms. Rhabi condescends to acknowledge Bulldog's presence by halfway looking up over her reading glasses and says "And you are?" as if there were hundreds of clients filling up her office, she couldn't possibly keep them all straight and it would be just fine with her if most of them left so she'd be able to catch up on her work some day. In fact, as Bulldog glimpsed the calendar upside down, just a fraction of a second before Ms. Rhabi moved her right arm over the relevant sections in a practiced move that she must have perfected to taunt all the previous visitors, he could see he was the only appointment penciled in for the entire afternoon. Penciled in, he mused, rather than in pen, most likely because so few actually kept their appointment or stayed long enough after the sign in process for Piker to actually see anyone, and almost certainly not twice.

"Well, Ms. C. Rhabi, and I assume all your friend (using the singular perhaps inappropriately for the grammatical context but not the social context, as Bulldog assumed everyone had a friend but doubted she had two), affectionately calls you 'crabby', it appears that there's only one scheduled so I don't suspect it would take a great leap of faith on your part to surmise I might be that one, would it?" I love that Bulldog, imitation (of me) is the highest form of flattery.

"If I were to suggest a name and it wasn't you, then I would be guilty of violating a confidence and subject myself and these offices to lawsuit. We just won't allow that to happen. Now, I repeat, and for the last time, mind you, who are you?"

God, I'm going to enjoy today's outing, mused Bulldog. "Why, hush my mouth, I do feel put right in the place where I belong. Where are my manners?" Bulldog's southern gentility shining through, although it did sound just a touch affected coming from a big man like him. "Allowing me to introduce myself," switching to a Boris Badanoff accent, "I am Jubilation T. Cornpone, colonel, Confederate Airforce, at your service maam." Looking at her glassed over eyes and blank expression, Bulldog was sure the literary references were totally wasted on her. As he is fond of saying, woe to anyone who over estimates the intelligence of the average citizen.

"Alright, Mr. Cornball, have a seat and Mr. Piker will see you at 4 PM if the rest of your party is on time."

Bulldog sat down, his skin crinkling a little under the plastic layer recently applied. He pulled out his cell phone, pressed a few buttons to speed dial me and said, "Come on down, the water's fine." He clicked off, replaced the phone in his pocket, looked right at crabby, as he'll always remember her from now on, and smiled the smile of one who knew something you didn't.

Bulldog didn't have to wait long as we were parked in the lot across the street. Sandy opened the door, gesturing for me to enter with a long sweeping wave of his arm, evoking images of a gentleman from days of yore. Accepting his offer, I went in, nodded to Bulldog and announced to Ms. C. Rhabi, as her desktop nameplate proclaimed, that we were all here and were looking forward to meeting with Mr. Piker.

After the obligatory several second delay between my speaking and her acknowledgement, she condescended to look up her characteristic half way and says "And who are you?"

I couldn't suppress the same grin Bulldog was wearing, I knew this was going to be fun. "Why I'm Jubilation J. Cornpone, along with my brothers T. and S. we've come to seek the counsel and advice of the learned Mr. Piker and would be much obliged if we could see him right away." We had chosen a southern motif for this outing and were having a good time with it.

A loud voice interrupted our pleasant conversation, "Mrs. Rhabi, please send in the Cornpone party."

She glanced at her watch, 4 PM was noted and a scowl briefly appearing across her face as if she was disappointed that we weren't made to wait longer. I wondered how long a wait would be enough to satisfy the insatiable. "You may go in to see Mr. Piker now." Dismissing us with a wave of her hand in the general direction of the inner sanctum. She hadn't noticed it before, but saw S. carrying a moderate sized mirror with him. "Curious" she thought to herself but soon went back to her self absorbed reading of what appeared to be a popular magazine, "People" or "US" by the looks of it. With any luck, she may have a footnote in it, but more likely "Newsweek" or "Time" will chronicle her 15 minutes of posthumous fame. She didn't take any notice of the briefcase I was carrying.

Mr. Piker was a wormy, slimy looking fellow, mid 40's, balding, graying and greasy. And that was just a description of his chest hairs, those that were still visible poking out from under his gold chains. His scalp hair looked like Einstein's would have looked after being plugged into 220 volts, but without the panache. Piker came around his desk and extended his hand to us. I was sure glad I was insulated in my plastic suit of armor. Otherwise, there wouldn't have been enough bleach to disinfect me if I soaked in it for a week after touching him.

I extended my hand and exchanged the usual pleasantries. Piker motioned to the chairs arranged in a semicircle around the far side of the desk for us to all sit. Sandy closed the door behind him and took the seat closest to it to act as the quick reaction force in case of emergency.

Neither Piker nor Crabby noticed the lack of incoming phone calls. It was late in the day, they rarely got calls anyway and those were mostly solicitations. Sandy had cut the phone lines earlier, as is his habit. We just didn't want to be disturbed. Our business here wouldn't allow it.

Getting down to business, Piker opened with, "So, how can I help you gentlemen?"

I responded, "We have a little something we've been working on that we want to show you. Let me start by putting this mirror on your desk, if you'd be so kind."

"Why, of course. Let's see what we have." A bemused smile coming over Piker's face. 'Could this be a patent case or are these just salesmen wasting my time on toupees or makeovers?' he thought. He had fallen for that last week and maybe word spreads quickly about suckers and he wasn't about to let someone snooker him again.

On cue, Bulldog stood up, brought the mirror over to the desk, clearing aside a series of old paper coffee cups and crumbled note papers with apparent scribbles on them. He couldn't see anything on the desk that a self respecting cleaning service would allow to stay there. He set the mirror up on its stand and saw Piker admiring himself in it almost immediately. He adjusted his chains "just so" but it wasn't clear to anyone else in the room what "just so" did for him.

Bulldog stood over to one side of the desk, allowing Piker to continue his preening. It also served as a good staging point in case I needed help. Sandy shifted in his seat to allow quick access to the door to neutralize Crabby in case she was alerted to a problem by too much noise. One hand in his pocket, finger on the trigger, the other positioned near the door.

I came to the other side of the desk, placing the briefcase just to the side of the mirror. I opened it with the top towards the mirror so Piker could just see inside if he leaned over towards it. Thus he took his eyes off the mirror and away from Bulldog.

"I wonder what they're going to do with that roll of duct tape in there, and what are those shiny metal things under the tape?" thought Piker as he peered at the contents.

Bulldog took advantage of this momentary distraction, pulled out the club from his specially tailored jacket with an elongated pocket and bopped Piker one on the back of his head so quickly it was over in an instant. I caught Piker before he fell and propped him back in his chair.

Sandy cracked the door; Crabby was reading her trash magazine, having heard nothing, blissfully ignorant of the events taking place behind her. He maintained a vigil through the crack, just in case.

I removed the all purpose, god's gift to mankind, duct tape, and started to wrap Piker up. First I tied his hands to the arms of his wooden executive chair. The cheap construction didn't call for any padding and the arm rest were narrow enough to allow for a quick and easy taping. Next, I taped his mouth shut, then his torso and finally his legs. I used a liberal amount of tape (one of the few times 'liberal' wasn't considered a dirty word) on all because the amount of stress on them would soon test its mettle. Bulldog then brought over a second arm chair and placed it side by side with Piker's. We were now ready for Crabby. I motioned to Sandy. He opened the door wider and said to Crabby, "Oh, maam,

Mr. Piker asked me to ask you to come in with your pad, if you don't mind."

'Don't mind! Don't mind!!!' steamed Crabby. 'Why, that bastard is going to make me stay late on a Friday and he never pays overtime. I ought to resign right now and let him lose the only paying client of the day, that's what I ought to do.' She was working herself into a near frenzy as she reached for her coffee ring stained pad and stood up. Ice coursed in her veins as she looked at Sandy and said "Step aside."

Sandy smiled his big southern style du jour smile and said "Surely maam, much obliged."

Crabby swept past him, turned the corner and stepped into the room. Just as she entered, despite being partially obscured by the mirror, she could see Piker taped to his chair. Then the lights went out.

Sandy put his club back in his pocket and picked Crabby off the floor. She was bleeding on both sides of her head. Over the occiput where Sandy hit her causing a three inch laceration and on the forehead where there was a four inch laceration from hitting the side of a chair on the way down. I noted these things out of habit and also added them up in my mind. Emergency office visit after hours, $250.00, seven inches of lacerations to sew up, complex, plastic, at $150.00 per inch and two follow up visits with suture removal, $100.00 each for a total of $1500.00. Hey Crabby, you may not agree with me now, but I'm about to do you a favor. I'm so expensive, even I couldn't afford me and you certainly wouldn't be able to on the chincy salary that cheapskate pays you. If you couldn't afford to fix these things that just happened to you, you'd be forced to go through the rest of your life known as scarface, and you wouldn't want that, would you? Your heirs will be grateful at least leaving them an extra $1500.00 you didn't spend on yourself. Not only that, you never could stick to your diet, I thought as I struggled to lug her considerable mass over to the other chair. Sandy and Bulldog were enjoying watching my sweat start to bubble under the plastic film. "Come on guys, let's not blow this just to satisfy your own amusement at my expense. The real fun is about to start and you don't need me for hors d'oeuvres."

Chastened, they came over to help, Bulldog easily lifting her almost by himself. "My, you are buff, big boy. What are you doing after the show?" I cooed.

Bulldog, being all man, blushed at even the thought of a homosexual encounter. Not that I was anything but kidding, but he was almost apoplectic at some of the news stories, especially about the priests that were in the news recently. Bulldog was a regular Catholic churchgoer and the series of revelations about pedophilia were shaking him to the core. He said nothing though and deftly placed Crabby upright in the chair. Sandy made quick work of taping her and we were ready.

We didn't want to waste time in nonconstructive ways so I waved an ammonia ampoule under their noses, resulting in the expected quick start and a return to a painful consciousness.

They could see themselves in the mirror, each bound and gagged. There was obvious fear in their eyes, the unknown being a strong inducer of such an emotion.

"I can see you're upset and you must be confused at what's happening." starting my usual speech to the victims. "Ms. Rhabi probably is an ingénue at this game but I suspect, you, Mr. Piker, have taken quite some pride in inducing this fear and loathing in people when you've had the upper hand, knew the answers before the questions were asked, knew the outcome almost as soon as the situation was starting to unfold. You, who know the law as only lawyers do, who can manipulate it in ways of your choosing for whoever pays you more. You, of no moral compass, who's needle twists towards money as more useful needles turn towards the north. Yes, I suspect you've felt the feeling I'm now feeling as I hold all the power over you, as surely as I've felt the feeling you must be feeling now when the shoe was on the other foot. Well, I hope you like it. Actually, no, I hope you hate it, hate it as much I did and do when I have to deal with the immoral scoundrels who call themselves lawyers. Who only feel a sense of moral outrage at the injustice of not being paid in full, regardless of the outcome of their client's case, regardless of whether or not you've tried hard to win. You, whose ilk worships only money and don't care whose lives you ruin as long as you get yours. Well, the shoe is on the other foot and my revenge shan't be bankruptcy, despair and ruin, which lasts a lifetime, but the painful and merciful end of your retched life a lot quicker than you merciless and pitiless demons would ever consider for your victims."

I turned around and whispered to Sandy and Bulldog, "How was that? Did I sound sinister enough? Do they seem to understand what is now in store for them? Was it too longwinded?"

"I don't want to sound too critical, but I think the melodrama was a bit too much. How about a more matter of fact approach and being a little more succinct?" offered Bulldog.

"Sandy?"

"I agree, less bull, and that's not a pun Bulldog, and more physical pain. Try poking them while you're talking to try to make the point more salient. And again, no pun intended."

Sandy's idea was good but it might distract them from the words and I thought the words would magnify their pain. On the other hand, why waste a lot of time on talk, they're not going to be able to write a critical review later anyway. "Okay, you guys are right. Less bull, more to the point. Okay, who's first?"

"If we want to make the lawyer suffer more, let's do his aide first. He'll have a little more graphic idea of what's in store for him." opined Bulldog, clearly the better philosopher of the two.

"Okay, she goes first." I turned back to the two, now clearly terrified, 'test specimens' as we called them in our planning session. "I have bad news and worse news. Which would you like to hear first?"

Piker was now twisting at his bonds, hoping to wiggle out of one more predicament, but this time he couldn't subvert justice by his twisted logic. The laws of nature were not subject to lies as he had always found the laws of man to be easily subverted in the past. No, the glue on and the tensile strength of the fabric would be as totally unconcerned with his pleadings, if he could speak and wasn't bound, as I was in watching his efforts.

"The bad news", I continued "is I have your lab test results back and you only have one day to live." I waited for a reaction but they were largely ignoring me, which was alright as I was largely speaking for my own amusement at this point. "The worse news is that I've been trying to reach you since yesterday." Sandy and Bulldog both gave a snicker. They had heard this a number of times as it was one of my favorite doctor black humor jokes. But being the faithful group that they were, accorded me the respect of a snicker that friendship mandates.

Unperturbed with their snickers, I continued, "Do you know what a sperm and a lawyer have in common?" They both shook their heads no. "They both have only a one in a million chance of becoming a human."

Neither Bulldog nor Sandy had heard that one and were now uncontrollably laughing.

On the other hand, Crabby was crying inconsolably. At the same time she didn't take her eyes off of me. She knew her fate was in my hands and she was hoping against hope that she'd be able to get out of here in one piece. I was watching her too as I reached into the briefcase and pulled out a long, shinny, clearly newly sharpened knife. Her eyes visibly dilated, a sign of excessive adrenaline discharge, just the response I was trying to evoke. Even though the whole ritual would be over in short order, I wanted to make the most of the time we had together. It's hard to compress a lifetime of payback in a few short minutes but I wanted to do the best I could to do so.

"Now, now, don't worry Ms. Rhabi, I'll be quick and merciful. Yes, there will be some pain, that's inevitable, in fact that's actually the point. But it won't last long and then you'll be free, as opposed to the many people whose lives you've ruined by aligning yourself with the so called legal profession."

In soto vocce Bulldog said "Loooong winnnnded."

Glancing back a little sheepishly, I whispered back "Okay, okay, I get the point. I'm moving on. Better yet, here, you take the knife and you do it."

Sandy adjusted the mirror so Crabby could see herself squarely in the mirror.

Bulldog gleefully took possession of the knife. Walking over and behind Crabby he says "You know, you remind me not a little of my sister. So here." He reached across the front of her neck with the knife and quickly and deftly sliced transversely across from left to right, firmly and deeply, cutting her skin, trachea and esophagus to the cervical vertebra.

Crabby watched the mirror in horror as she saw the knife come across her neck. The searing pain was unbearable. Her last conscious thought was this couldn't be happening to her as she saw the blood squirt from the carotid artery. She never saw the second carotid give forth its life sustaining supply of nutrients as her world went black and she was gone.

Piker, for his part, redoubled his efforts to break free but duct tape didn't get its well deserved reputation for tenacity by judicial decree. It held tight, seeming to even beckon Piker to get off the stick and try harder.

Sandy repositioned the mirror again so now Piker could see his reflection head on. He couldn't believe what he was seeing. A man usually so in control was now staring at a wild man reverting to primeval instincts. He tried to thrash about, to regain control and have a fighting chance of escape but his efforts remained futile. If he could just get the tape off his mouth he knew he could talk his way out. He'd done it a thousand times before, he could do it again. For god's sake, his life depended on it.

I walked over to the open briefcase once again. This time I lifted out not a shiny, razor sharp instrument but a dull, ragged, pitted, derelict of a knife, barely worthy of its name. I had found it in a junk yard several weeks ago and knew right away what a lofty position it would hold in my world. For here was not just the instrument to be used to dispatch a lawyer, it was to be able to inflict a fitting retribution to the lawyer. It would be slow and oh so painful. Just what the doctor ordered.

I had always wondered how the samari had the guts (pun intended) to disembowel themselves. It seemed like an impossible task to take your own life in such a painful manner. If you were going to do yourself in it seemed better to take the least painful way out. I always wanted to see it done and now was a perfect opportunity.

By now, Piker was beside himself, tears rolled from his eyes, now wide with terror. He tried thrashing about but because he was well tapped in, was only able to manage a moderate rocking of the chair. He panic grew greater as I approached him with the knife. Actually I only assumed it was a knife by the overall shape as it was so rusty and encrusted with debris that no metallic structure was visible.

I leaned over and whispered in his ear, "I know this is going to hurt you a whole lot more than it hurts me. My only regret is that it isn't going to hurt you as much as all the pain you've caused."

I told Piker, "Now watch in the mirror as I attempt to sever your neck with this knife. He became practically apocalyptic. I took the knife and tried to cut his neck but it just left a nasty abrasion. I tried a sawing action which started to shred the skin. Piker rolled his eyes up into his head. He clearly wasn't following instructions so I took the sharp knife and cut off his eyelids so he couldn't close his eyes. This caused him to faint. Sandy then stepped in with his favorite device, a ball peen hammer, and started smashing Piker's toes until he woke up. That actually worked after the two small toes on each foot were flattened. Little bits of flesh shot off the tips of the toes and blood oozed onto the rug.

Once Piker woke I started the sawing again, not getting anywhere fast. The knife actually became duller, if that was possible, because large shards of flesh were getting caught on the barbs of the knife. I had to stop after almost every stroke to remove them to allow the knife to take another bite rather than just glide over the now fairly copiously bleeding raw skin of his neck. A few more strokes and he fainted again. This time it took four toes including the right great toe being almost pulverized by Sandy for Piker to wake up. He was now glassy eyed and moaning but conscious. A few more strokes and the trachea was entered. The mixture of blood and mucous was started to be blown out through the small opening like a kid's soapy solution through a loop. We all stopped and watched for a moment to see if this was of lasting interest but after a moment's reflection we decided it wasn't and proceeded on.

Piker kept fainting and we ran out of toes. Sandy opened Piker's pant, cut off his testicles and placed them on the desk. He hit one with the hammer but the blow was slightly off center and the testicle went flying off into the corner, bounced a few times, ricocheted off the wall and finally rolled to rest under a chair. He took the other one, placed it on the floor under a legal text he found in the bookcase. He climbed up on the desk and jumped full force onto the book. This time the testicle was trapped and stayed where Sandy put it. He reached down, lifted the book and found a silver dollar sized testicle pancake. Pleased with his work, Sandy took the pancake and placed in on Piker's head like a yarmulke.

My arm was getting tired as using a dull knife is tough work. Bulldog stepped in to finish off the job. He made rapid work of the soft tissues. He got more than a little soaked from the carotids bursting and finally gave up sawing at the vertebrae. The knife got stuck and he just couldn't get a good enough grip on the handle from the blood and mucous spray to dislodge it. So we decided to leave it there. Sandy and I had enough for the day so we started to get our things together.

"Okay, we're done. We've had a good evening but it's after 5:00. I'm hungry and I want to go home." I said, hoping to bring an end to the festivities and get out before any unexpected guest shows up although we knew there would be no cleaning girl or worried friend looking for either of our victims for a long time to come. Most likely the bill collectors would be the first to be concerned that these two were missing.

We picked up our equipment, walked with a light hearted step out of the room and headed on out. Sandy took one last glimpse back, admiring his final touch and pulled the outer door shut behind him. We left the appointment book to give the police a lead. They'd spend many a wasted day trying to track down the Cornpone family and probably be pissed when they found out they were mythical. That wouldn't motivate them to work harder, it would just make them pissed.

We had peeled off our "work" clothes with all the blood splattered over them, stuffed them in a carry all and placed them in the trunk with the rest of our gear. We got in the car, it started without hesitation and we drove off. After dropping the guys off at their cars, I drove off to my home for a little RandR. While by myself, I was able to reflect on the earlier proceedings. We had accomplished a few goals. First and foremost, we eliminated another lawyer and his willing accomplice. Second, we had gained experience in planning and executing a job. Third, we continued to become deeper and deeper involved in our work developing an unshakeable camaraderie that would be necessary to protect ourselves as the going got tough. We had to be able to trust each other implicitly and had to make sure that no one would become squeamish or have second thoughts. It was clear that all our goals were accomplished and we were ready to move forward. Taking an hour or more per lawyer would mean it would take us longer than our combined lifetimes to even start to make a dent in the number of lawyers out there. We also couldn't hope to kill them all even with mass murder techniques. No, our means had to make the lawyers want to quit the profession voluntarily if they hoped to live. Today's effort was just a bit of fun leading to the more serious work ahead.

I drove up to the garage, put the car away and sat down with a nice TV dinner to relax for the night. Tomorrow, I'd start work on the next step in our plan, the ABA convention.

Chapter 31: Nice Nurses Finish Last

Lest one think that all the employees of the nursing homes are incompetent or cruel, let me state that this is definitely not true. 99% true, just not 100% so. That doesn't mean that the occasional nice and competent nurse is a blessing. The opposite is actually the case.

In this age of managed care, the name of the game is to optimize care. This is in contrast to the traditional medical thinking of maximize the care. Under this antiquated thinking, it was assumed to be in everybody's interest to keep the patient as long as possible. This maximized administrator's contentment in that his beds were full. The doctors were happy because they got paid fee for service, meaning every time they saw the patient they got paid. The patients were happy because it was like an all expense paid holiday, albeit with occasional but acceptable annoyances like an enema or two. The families were happy because they were freed from having to care for their beloved, albeit old, family member, at least for a while. More than a few families went on week long vacations coinciding with their loved one's admission to the nursing home.

This was all well and good until the headlines in the newspapers starting reading "Medicare is going bankrupt" on a fairly regular basis. This was followed by a number of studies showing prolonged institutionalization actually resulted in worse outcomes, changes in the law mandating HMO's and managed care and a rise in the Medicare tax and deductibles. All of a sudden, "crisis" followed "crisis" and things started to change. First, the amount of money available to the nursing homes from Medicare and the HMO's decreased. Next, the ratio of employees to patients at the nursing homes decreased in an effort by administration to keep the bottom line healthy. This was followed by increasing dissatisfaction by the patients and their families as the amount and quality of care decreased. Inevitably, this dissatisfaction was followed by involvement of the legal profession, bringing lawsuit after lawsuit. This resulted in the bankruptcy of almost half of all nursing homes accelerating the reduction in staffing and, inevitably, more dissatisfaction by everyone affected. The legal profession still hasn't figured out how demanding higher standards of others by suing them results in lower performance. I'll explain it to them someday, preferably while I'm performing their annual colonoscopy. It seems that, for some reason, lawyers need at least an annual colonoscopy to allow them to remain healthy and focused enough to enable them to continue their pursuit of the perfect suit. At least that's my recommendation to them.

Acting as an agent for the HMO and also in the country's best interest of optimizing care, it has been my general good fortune to have as unwitting allies the best half wits that minimum wage can buy as employees in the nursing home. The nursing home staff is like a little United Nations, but with all the industrialized nations and literate third world nations declining to participate.

Having a nurse or aide whose name is not pronounceable in English makes for interesting interactions with our mostly deaf elderly patients whose lifelong contempt for these foreigners has come home to roost. Imagine the ignominy of having your entire body exposed to a person of another race, whose sex is subject to debate and whose language you can't comprehend. This stranger then treats you like the rest of your family would like to treat you if they didn't have to restrain themselves because they feel that you're about to kick the bucket anyway and they figure if they could just hold on a little longer to stay in your good graces you'd keep them in the will.

Since there's little reason to treat the patient's family any better than the staff treats the old, demented, smelly, disgusting, wretched patient on his last legs whose relentless demands are starting to get old even before he's moved from the stretcher to the bed on admission, the nurses generally ignore them entirely, causing the family to issue their own set of complaints. Now the administrator has to deal with the patient's family's complaints in addition to the patient's. There's a general tendency to think that the employees in this paradise-like, home away from home, are trained to be courteous, prompt, caring and competent and should show the respect due a patient because he's a patient and a native to this country. It's assumed that the foreigners should all get down on their knees and thank God and each individual American with their every breath that we allow them to wipe our butts. They should be honored that we give them the opportunity to clean up all our vile emissions from every known natural orifice and the numerous manmade ones too that patients tend to have after a nice little stay in the hospital.

However, even if they aren't Native Americans, these foreign interlopers learn quickly and they soon take on all the annoying habits and attitudes that it took the rest of us a lifetime to acquire. (Except for New Yorkers, of course, who are genetically endowed with obnoxious genes which are manifested from the moment of birth.)

Thus, there's an instant mutual dislike between the patient and his caregivers, usually fomenting into active hatred of all involved. There seems to be an inverse relationship between the degree of hatred and timing of onset of this adversarial relationship and the geographical distance of the patient's family from their loved one multiplied by the number of years that the family last saw the patient. Thus, an estranged son from California who hadn't spoken to his father in Florida for thirty years already has his lawyer filing papers while his father is still in the ambulance on the way to the nursing home.

So, how does this all fit in with me? Well, it turns out that even a free stay is not appreciated in a lousy joint. Therefore, the worse the facility and staff, the shorter the stay because staying is just too annoying to be worth the free food. The patients actually demand to leave, frequently before I even see them for the first time. In fact, if they're not complaining it means they need to stay. Other possible explanations for not complaining are: 1. the patient's dead, 2. they're too demented to speak, or 3. they're psychotic and enjoy the torture. But once they start complaining about anything, they've progressed to the point they're well enough to go home. Sometimes, actually, not infrequently, I engage in those little touches that just might tip the balance of whether or not the patient starts complaining. Multiple enemas is one of my favorites, but other contenders include round the clock anything (meds, blood tests, vital sign measurements, etc). These are little tricks I learned while reading about the Nuremberg trials involving the best the Nazis and Japanese could throw at the Allies under the heading "Ve haf vays uf making you talk". As effective now as then.

Everything usually goes along swimmingly. I write a few orders and in no time the patient is miraculously cured, demanding to go home. Every once in a while (mercifully not too often), I do find myself up against a formidable foe: the nice and competent nurse. The patients actually like her and therefore their free stay turns out to be a pleasant experience. It then becomes next to impossible to get the patient to leave because they know their rights and aren't going to be intimidated. I write my little orders but these goody two shoe competent nurses will have nothing to do with nasal enemas or cat food diets. I'm thwarted at every turn. What can I do? I'm desperate! I know, I'll lie! It works for everyone else, why not me?

So I pick a fight with the nurse. I order some stuff I know she won't do and I ask the other nurses for gossip. The other nurses are only too willing to provide me with all the ammunition I need because they all feel threatened by this competent nurse who's always showing them up, always getting the nice gifts from the patients and commendations from the administrator.

So armed with juicy gossip, embellished just right, and charges of insubordination and a difficult personality to get along with, I march into the administrator's office, demanding this nurse be fired, or at the very least, sent to the Alzheimer's wing on the midnight shift. Since I have so many patients and am usually the squeakiest wheel, I have the clout to get my way. Also, the administrators don't like doctors to stand in the lobbies turning blue from holding their breath. They feel it's bad for business. The passersby don't know if it's really stinky inside or the doctor saw something even he couldn't stomach. They rarely consider it to be the obvious, he's throwing a hissy fit. So they turn around and look for another nursing home to dump their loved one in while they are in Europe for a fortnight.

The good nurse, not realizing that bad things could happen to good people, are totally unprepared for the firing that they are about to receive when called into the administrator's office. They even smile at me as we pass in the hallway, me having cast my spell and they stepping into it in a few short moments.

I usually hang out in the waiting room to wave goodbye to the devastated nurse as she's escorted from the building. It's sometimes unclear if she just ignored me or didn't see me through her tears. I always shout a "good luck" anyway.

I am now free to go on my merry way. Unfortunately, in this market where nurses are traded from nursing home to nursing home like hot commodities, no matter how bad the nursing home is, the good nurse inevitably shows up at another one so we have to start all over again. It's easier the second time because I can tell the administrator that "the nurse was fired for cause from her previous job. Oh, you didn't know that?"

It becomes a revolving door. Wherever the good nurse goes, I'm not far behind. Hounding her to the end, never giving her any rest or sense of security. I vow to drive her from the profession, making it safer for those that follow me and giving fair warning to those that might follow in her footsteps.

Sometimes we meet and she'll finally speak: "Doctor, why are you doing this to me? I'm such a nice person, what have I done to you?"

I respond, "I will not tolerate any delay in the discharge of my patients! You make it tolerable for them so they stay too long. You think you must put the patients first, but I've hoped you learned, nice nurses finish last!" Sometimes I ad a diabolical 'Ha!' and flick my head as I turn away. I can sense her hatred as I walk off. So, that's what daggers in your back feel like. If looks could only kill.

Chapter 32: The Enemy of My Enemy Is My Friend

There are bad nursing homes, which, seemingly paradoxically, are really good, for me. Then there are incredibly bad nursing homes, where I myself feel in danger and I'm not even a patient. When I go to these really bad facilities, I make it a point to touch nothing and to disinfect myself when I leave. In some facilities I feel I must have set the world breath holding record for to breathe the stench is surely to destroy various essential parts of your body.

It is against these really awful facilities that I've declared war as enemies of humanity. I really don't care if the patient lives or dies, this is just a job based on volume, not results. It usually makes little difference what I do anyway, the patient will live or die on their own in most circumstances. But it does make a difference to me that I have to work at a place that not only hurts my sensibilities but might also hurt me physically. So for these facilities, I employ my most powerful weapons, anonymously of course. I call in the State. There are a whole myriad of ways to take down the house of cards that skilled nursing facilities are built upon.

Glenn Allen

One of my most potent weapons against a facility is to simply not admit there. This works well for the most part but every once in a while a patient slips through so I have to go to plan B (and C, D and E; I do whatever it takes).

One of my favorite ways to really annoy the facility, and by facility I mean the people in charge of the facility as the inanimate building is almost always totally immune to my efforts, is to "innocently" violate a law. You have to understand, there's no point in violating a law that will either get you in trouble or won't get them in trouble. Therefore, you have to be somewhat selective in what you do and when. The when is easy, do it when the State is there. And if they're not there enough on their own (which is almost constantly), get them there with an anonymous complaint to one of a half dozen 800 numbers the State posts around each facility so they have a reason to be there, thus justifying their own existence, no matter how petty and ridiculous the complaint. I've conveniently placed a half dozen or so agencies on my cell phone's speed dial in case I need them in a hurry. That, in fact, is why my plan is so easy, it takes nothing to initiate a State investigation. As a taxpayer, this has got to be the worst use of my good money. As an instigator (as are at least half of the patients and their families), this works out nicely.

There are various State agents performing what I call state sponsored terrorism. They come in like they are some demigods expecting you to bow down before them. My favorite one is the ombudsman who actually has no power at all but acts the most ferocious. Their performance is both impressive and pitiful at the same time. Their act is all sound and fury but no punch and after the dust clears, everyone's still standing. The only effect is that everyone is now a little more annoyed than they were before but otherwise unmoved in their position. The ombudsman doesn't even know that he was ineffectual, he's off to another facility to spread the misery around.

So what's a good way to annoy someone? At least for me, that's easy, as I'm told by just about everyone from my mother on down that I'm really annoying so this exercise is just a walk in the park for me.

Given our passion for privacy, the State has made a number of laws that try to achieve that. Like it's really possible to maintain dignity let alone privacy in a hospital or nursing home. But the lip service serves my purpose well. So I wait until I'm sure one of the myriad of State investigators (from any bureau, it doesn't really matter) is in the building and I get on the paging system and start giving orders like: "Nurse Jones, this is doctor Ali Karb-dhula al azir and I want patient Smith to have enough enemas to clean her out sparklingly clean. I want her so clean that I'll be able to eat off her colon. She's really backed up and has the foulest smell imaginable coming from her. Can we take her out back and hose her down so she'll stop offending everyone?"

You can imagine how patient Smith must be feeling about now. If she wasn't planning to die soon before, she certainly is now. The State inspector has been listening to this announcement on the PA system and has started to tally up the violations of State law he's just heard and is righteously incensed. So he proceeds directly to the administrator for redress. Now the administrator, if conscious, is either leaving by his/her secret escape route with his bags packed for Rio or is hiding under the desk. If not conscious, which is the case with the majority of administrators in these clueless facilities where I'm forced to do business, he or she is just sitting there unaware of the hellfire that is about to break loose.

So the State inspector enters the administrator's office and calmly asks if the administrator has any last words and would he like a blindfold? The administrator, being the eternal optimist that he'd have to be to continue working in the rat hole he's in, pleasantly replies there must be some mistake and let's work to get to the bottom of this.

So they try to piece together what the investigator thinks has happened. Taking out his notepad, the investigator says "It's really quite simple, one of you doctors used the PA system to give privileged information of a highly embarrassing nature to a nurse somewhere else. I can shut you down for that right now!"

"Before you do anything rash, don't you think we should investigate this a little further?" implores the administrator.

"Okay, but it's going to be a waste of time. I heard what I heard and my mind is made up." spaketh the demigod.

'Oy' thought the administrator (and he's not even Jewish), "Okay, let's start with what you heard."

"I heard this doctor Ali Kazam or someone talk about a patient Smith to a nurse Jones. I want them here now!" foamed the livid investigator, galled that he has to somehow justify his immutable decision that he just pronounced to a person and facility whose existence he was about to cause to cease. Why, they were already nonentities in his mind.

The administrator, feeling pretty low, reaches for the intercom to call in his director of nurses, not so much for her knowledge of the personnel, although that is essential too because he doesn't really know anyone's names except the DON's, but to have someone to whom he can shift the blame. "Nurse Mons Dieu (a fairly common Haitian name he's been told), please come in my office."

"I rrright be dere." She replies in the best English she can figure out. And true to her word, she finds the office in only the third place she looked. "I ham hair." She states as she enters the room.

Even the administrator is taken back from smell of Mons Dieu. He figures his goose is cooked as the only way anyone could smell that way was by not having used any personal feminine products since climbing out of the hold of the smuggler's boat or actually performing the enemas that were the current topic of discussion and forgetting to duck.

The State investigator had to be resuscitated.

After a quick revival with smelling salts, the State's man on site recovers his composure sufficiently to start the questions in earnest. It wouldn't be until later when he goes to the bathroom that he finds not only are his pants on backwards, but also he's wearing a diaper, but that's another story. Even the worst administrator can exact a modicum of revenge occasionally.

"So Mon Dieu, who is this Ali Kazam, nurse Jones and patient Smith?" sneers god's man on earth.

"I am zo zorry, monsieur le interregator, but mon nom ist Mons Dieu, not Mon Dieu."

"Whatever, let's get to the point. Someone messed up good here and I want to know who it is so I can make sure the State is satisfied with the punishment." The investigator couldn't imagine why both the administrator and DON had wry smiles on their faces when he said 'messed up', were they so immature that a semi dirty word would titillate them so? Only later did he realize that not only was he wearing a diaper, but also it had a full load in it. But again, that's another story.

"Monsieur le terror, you must know ve haf no doctor named Ali Akazam or even anything like zat. Not only zat, but ve haf no nurse named Smith nor patient named Jones. If you hurd anyzing like zat, you hurt vrong. I myself hurt nozing uf zee zort. I vunder, vas zere efen a oferhead call at all?"

Mons was beginning to be worth her considerable weight in gold. If doubt could be placed in the mind of the State, there was hope, thought the administrator.

Of course, he thought his DON was just making it up, he had no idea that there were no such people in his facility. I made sure of that. Faking breaking the law is a whole lot different from breaking the law for real.

So, the, by definition, subnormal intelligence associated with bureaucrats began to take its toll on the investigator. It was hard enough for him to keep a thought straight in his mind. To add ambiguity and doubt into the mix threw him into a veritable tizzy so that all the specifics of his open and shut case began to run into a jumbled mess. The only thing remaining in his mind was that somebody did something wrong and he had to fix it. He therefore wrote up a violation notice, to be affixed next to the numerous other ones the facility had accumulated, that the DON was an offense to his sensibilities and needed to wash daily. To make sure, he'd be back for another inspection as soon at the facility called him to assure him she'd complied with the order. The administrator was pleased. He was off the hook and was virtually assured that the investigator would never return because he'd never get the call that the DON was ready for inspection. It also pleased the DON because she was now certain of long term employment as long as she never washed. Things sometimes work out.

Life goes on and so does the facility. I didn't say my methods were foolproof, only meant to annoy people. As time goes on, I expect to be able to fine tune my attacks and use the enemy of my enemy as a useful tool. The British got it wrong though, neither one will ever become my friend.

Chapter 33:
Run Away To Fight Another Day

The American Bar Association meeting was scheduled for early May in Chicago. This was possibly the best place for it to be. It was a large and therefore anonymous city for us to be in. Sandy had spent a decade there last winter and was therefore quite familiar with the city and could act nicely as a guide. Although he was not enthusiastic about going back, he wouldn't be too unhappy in May as the arctic blasts were usually long gone by then.

We had learned a lot in our several outings, mostly about how not to get caught, but also in planning and tactics. We were now about to embark on what would be a national headline, not just local scandal sheet sensationalism. Up to now, no one had put two plus two together to link a series of seemingly random acts of violence against lawyers into a coherent picture of conspiracy. The ABA meeting would change all that. National investigators would be put on the case and supercomputers would be employed to gather data and synthesize patterns that might become discernable with the closer scrutiny. We'd therefore have to be even more clever in planning and execution (pun intended) if we were to live to pull off more eye openers such as we planned for the nation's most virulent lawyers, those active in the ABA.

The ABA, instead of being the organization insuring justice for all, has taken on the trappings of a trade organization dedicated to maximizing employment and income for its members. Thus, it long ago stopped being a service to the public but merely stirred the pot, conjuring up novel theories on how to sue the unwary, promulgating these evil injustices across the country, thus insuring a never ending supply of suits for its members. The only other so called "legal" organization to come even close to doing as much harm in economic terms and societal upheaval as the ABA is the ACLU. The ACLU has found ways to turn the Constitution and the Founding Father's intentions on their ears so as to come up with legal theories directly in opposition to the principles upon which this country was founded. One the most insidious results of "protecting our civil liberties" has been for the population to be forced to live behind barred windows while the criminals have full run of the streets.

It is for this and similar reasons that we three have taken up our crusade. We have no illusions that we would ever be considered heroes by those we were trying to save. Save is what many think Jesus does but they're going to have to wait for the next life to be sure that will happen. We know we're going to be damned to hell by many in this life but the problem for those doing the damning is that it only works on fools who think there is a hell and a next life. We know better. We know that there's only here and now and we're actually living in the hell we've made for ourselves on earth. We're going to do our best to change that and we've dedicated ourselves to that end. The means: kill all the lawyers.

Of course we know the arguments: who chooses who to kill who and why. And if others of common interest join us in this endeavor, what's to keep us from turning on them as the next group to be eliminated. Who appointed us god, judge, jury, executioner, etc?

Our answer is: you pays your money and you takes your chance. If you're unhappy now with the status quo and only seeing it get worse, you've got to do what you've got to do. I expect if you agree with us enough now about the lawyers being the root of all evil, we'd have a sufficient commonality of interests that we'd probably be able to work out our differences in the future. If fact, that gets at the crux of this issue. We would have to sit down and work it out, knowing our lives were at stake if we failed. Under our current system, we'd merely sue, usually at the drop of a hat, and not think a second time of the negative consequences to ourselves as there really wouldn't be any in the short term. The real negative consequences, whether we won or lost, would be the same for both parties: the increased power and pervasiveness of the lawyers.

So, the planning proceeds. The annual ABA convention is the largest gathering of lawyers in the world and brings together the ring leaders in one convenient and compact target. According to their slick glossy advertising brochure, they'll be meeting at the cavernous Chicago Civic Center. As an added bonus to the thousands of lawyers gathered together in one place, the largely Democrat local political leadership will be there with the Mayor giving the opening address. This clearly represents the best time to do the most good as almost all the delegates would want to hear one of their own espouse more practical ways for the lawyers to exert ever expanding control of our every thought and action. After the opening address, they would break up into smaller working groups making it harder to "hit and run". Tuesday, May 18, 9 AM. That would be D-day and H-hour. That gave us just over two months. We'd be ready.

Chapter 34: Fraud and Abuse

In order to make money in any business, you have to have a product to sell and a public willing to buy that product. The same concept, and I emphasize the CON in concept, holds true for health care in general, and nursing homes in specific. No one likes to be away from home and, certainly, no one likes to be sick. Nevertheless, one of those inevitable facts of life is that, unless you mercifully die suddenly, you die a slow, lingering, horrific death until you then die suddenly. At least, that's what the grieving family always says: "Why did grandpa die so suddenly? He was always in such good health all his life until two years ago when, on his 95th birthday, he suffered a massive heart attack followed by those series of a half dozens strokes. But he was going to dialysis three times a week faithfully and never put on his prosthetic legs and try to get out of his bed on his own. Why should he have died in your care in the nursing home? He was only here for six months and refused hospice. He wanted to live! Why did you kill him?"

"Sorry, mam, but we needed the bed." Was what we were all thinking. But Ricky jumped in and said "We're all sorry for your untimely loss, but God moves in mysterious ways and maybe he needed grandpa in Heaven to help with an urgent project and didn't have time to give you adequate notice. If we're lucky, grandpa may be done with the project by Christmas and will be able to rejoin you then."

Ricky is smooth. The family was mollified and left us alone, at least for a while until their lawyer was able to come up with a novel legal theory, like death is optional.

After all, there's nothing like a thankful family to help round out your day and make all your toil suddenly seem so meaningful.

Anyway, back on the point, the business of health care is making money. Providing relief from suffering is merely a byproduct, the so called "hook" to snare the unsuspecting suckers into your money making endeavor. Thus, the need for the marketing director. The front line guy who brings in the patients whose payment goes directly to the bottom line. Normally, most businesses have a certain amount of overhead, so to keep up the pretenses and in accordance with generally accepted accounting rules, the typical nursing home would set up an operation that looked like it was prepared to deliver medical care. The administrator hired staff, set up a facility and ordered supplies and furniture. Unfortunately, the supplies were outdated, the furniture was World War II surplus field hospital beds bought at government auction and the facility was the old field operations headquarters for a toxic waste cleanup site. Also, the only people that the owners hired that spoke any English at all were the administrator and the marketing director. This way the patients and their families were able to be sucked into the evil web by sympathetic sounding personnel who were nowhere to be found to hear complaints when reality hit.

It is therefore clear to the stockholders that they should spare no expense in hiring the right marketing director. Let's look at what they're selling: a run down, rat infested garbage dump with the accumulated germs of ten thousand mortally ill patients from which no patient can ever recover, a staff of illegal immigrants hiding out from the border patrol and an administration hording all cash and selling the medical supplies on EBay that were donated to him from third world countries because they felt sorry for the patients. What type of person can sell this scenario to people who still have a chance to make a clean get away to home? Did I not mention con man a moment ago?

I had the good fortune to meet a true artist in his field at South Florida Rehab, which they abbreviated SFR and we all pronounced "suffer". P. T. Barnum probably had him in mind when he stated a sucker was born every minute. Not as the sucker of course, but as the person who made the suckers of the world shine. His name was Ricardo. He was of a certain hot Latin persuasion but he tried to blend in with his targets so he softened his name to Ricky. It didn't really overcome the problem of his glass eye always looking at you crossed eyed. The real problem was that his glass eye looked more real then the real one and most people were startled when the other eye moved and the glass one stayed still. Handing out twenty dollar bills to the case managers and the powers of attorneys as inducements to choose his facility did go a fair distance though in easing their concerns.

Ricky could sell refrigerators to Eskimos. Any field he chose, he could excel in, as long as it was selling and the buyers didn't look too close. Therefore, he really excelled in convincing drugged up, bed ridden patients that SFR was the place to go for their rest and recuperation.

My favorite example of buyer's remorse is when the patients would beg me to find them a nurse that speaks their language. "Didn't they tell you that if you didn't speak Creole, that was okay, there were a few nurses who spoke Romanian?"

"Noooooo! They never told me! You've got to help me. I haven't had my diaper changed in five days and even my family stopped visiting me. What should I do?" they'd cry.

"I don't know, but when you find out, let me know and I'll come back and do your admission physical." I shout from the hallway. I really wish they'd close the patient's doors so they stop bothering me as I walked down the halls. I must remember to bring that up when I'm out golfing with the administrator next Wednesday.

Back to Ricky. He'd come up with some of the most outlandish promises to get patients to choose "Suffering" over some of his rivals who were actually legally licensed. I remember missing one of my white coats one day. I couldn't imagine who would have taken it until the hospital called me up and asked how I had the nerve to write on all the charts to send all the patients to SFR. It turns out Ricky had helped himself to my coat to give him an advantage over his competition who were trying to stay within the letter of the law, even if not the spirit, and had been getting away with this until he overstepped his bounds just a little bit and started discharging all the patients in the surgical suites to the nursing home. Even then, it might have continued going unnoticed except that on several of the patients, the surgeon was still operating and they objected to having to walk back to their car instead of being driven there by the assistant administrator as was customary at the hospital. I explained that the coat was stolen some time ago and I had nothing to do with it. That should have put an end to the practice of early discharges to the nursing home. However, the administrator at the hospital found he was saving so much money by not having to supply all those expensive lifesaving medications and treatments that he continued the practice by preprinting the order forms calling for a discharge to the nursing home on the second hospital day. This would have worked out for Ricky except that the hospital administrator failed to specify which nursing home the patient was discharged to, so he was back to square one.

Ricky tried spiking the family's drinks with LSD when they toured SFR. The families usually had an impression of great grandeur while under the influence of the LSD, which probably was to be expected as Ricky had them all watching a travelogue of the Taj Majhal instead of actually seeing the facility. This would have worked well except the families were so stoned that they couldn't remember which facility they were touring. Inevitably, when they got back to the hospital and asked the nurses where the Taj Majhal was, they were given the name and address of a rival facility which was called the Taj Majhal. Interestingly, the facility which called itself the Taj Majhal just so happened to have been recently renamed to the Taj Majhal by another adept marketing director shortly after Ricky's initiation of his latest scam. The $50.00 per patient referral fee to the nurses didn't hurt either. It made Ricky's $25.00 fee pale in comparison.

Despite these setbacks, Ricky was quite effective in his recruitment efforts. He would frequently fill "suffer" full. His best day was a 32 patient effort, which pleased the administrator no end but the rest of the staff of "suffer" were distraught as they had only 12 empty beds. Richie came back triumphant from his tour de force at the hospital only to be met by an angry mob at the front door. And that was only the patient's families. Once they had sobered up, they realized what a hell hole they agreed to and wanted to take their loved ones out immediately. But since the doors were barricaded from the inside, all they could do was burn the cars closest to the front entrance. Of course, the closest cars were all parked in the handicapped spaces. That could have been a tragedy but since no cars with handicapped stickers in Florida were actually driven by handicapped drivers, they finally got their comeuppance.

Ricky, beating a hasty getaway, made it to the secret hidden rear doors only senior staff (that is, only those who could read English and could understand what "entrance in the rear" meant) knew about. He quickly slipped inside and tried to make his way unseen to the administrator's office. Unfortunately, he was met by another angry mob, but this time it was the staff. Although he felt he could handle them as he always did in similar situations, usually by shouting "Here comes the INS", he had gone too far this time. He was suffering from a false sense of security as he couldn't understand their yammering as a cacophony of a dozen different languages emanated from the crowd. Most of them were lamenting that the ceilings were only eight feet high and there wasn't a fixture high and strong enough to throw a rope over that would also support Ricky's weight.

One of the aides was taking a night course in English so she could translate for her boyfriend on his job. He was having the most difficult time trying to get across to his victims that this was a robbery and he wanted their money. Half the people would take out their wallets and give him their rubbers, the other half would take off their galoshes and give him those. It wasn't as lucrative as he had hoped so he sent Chiquita to night school. And now it was paying off. Chiquita was acting as spokeswoman for the lynch mob, translating back and forth for both parties.

"Look what you've done, you pig! There are patients everywhere. In the hallways, in the lounges, in the nursing stations. We've even had to put some in the beds but you know how we hate doing that. That means we have to clean the sheets when they leave and we don't have time for that. The laundry room is full just keeping up with all our personal laundry so that our moonlighting laundry business is getting backed up and the customers are getting upset. Do you know what it does for repeat business when they bring in 410 count sheets and we give them ripped, soiled sheets that say 'Not for resale. Property of U. S. Navy"? We all have to make a living and we can't do so if you keep us busy with patients."

"Look, I'm sorry but if you have a gripe, take it up with the administrator." Ricky fidgeted.

"You know we can't mess with the man. He's an officer in the Immigration Department and we can't make any waves." Chiquita looked scared as she mentioned his name.

"Well, that's too bad. I'm just doing my job, like you are." Stated Ricky, feeling a little more secure in his situation, even though outnumbered 20 to 1.

"And what about Mr. Rotundo that was just admitted? You called up to say he was a little overweight and might need a bigger bed. Well the forklift that dropped him off bent a tine and he landed on my brother in law, crushing him to death. That normally would make me real mad but I hated the guy and he refused to pay me the $5.00 I lent him last week. Lucky for you that I got to his wallet first when they off loaded Rotundo and there was $5.00 there for me. Otherwise, you'd be in big trouble. As it is, three of my clients, oops, I mean boyfriends hurt their back lifting him so I'm going to be out a lot more than $5.00 if they don't get better soon. Fortunately, I have a waiting list so you got lucky again. The housekeeping crew finally got him onto the Hoyer lift and he weighs over 500 pounds. Now what are we going to do with him. No one's going to stick their arm in his crack to wash him. We're going to save that job for you and your going to do it now with the fine mop of hair on your head."

The mob had grown from a number of disgruntled employees to include patients and their families. They had been hearing the growing disquiet down the back hallways and went to check it out. They had already been prowling, looking for Ricky and hoped they may have him cornered. As they rounded the bend, Ricky saw the patients furiously wheeling their chairs with one hand while holding torches in the other. The family members followed shortly thereafter brandishing pitch forks in a most menacing manner. "There he is, boys!" shouted one diminutive wizened patient in such a shrill voice that even the rats thought it was horrifying. "Let's get him!" They all charged at top speed, which, fortunately for Ricky, wasn't that fast as the patients were all ancient and most of them ended up spinning in circles as they were wheeling their chairs with only one hand, thus lacking effective directional control.

Just at that moment the administrator walked in. He and a member of the Board of Trustees were returning from lunch at the Club. Even though it was only three PM, they had decided to call it a day a little early as he thought it was best to show up for work at least once a week as there might actually be some work for him to do. The mob dispersed as quickly as it formed. Thus, Ricky was saved. He also received a bonus for the most number of patients admitted on one day. Mr. Rotundo's butt would just have to wait a little longer for washing. He's waited these many years, he could wait a little longer.

Ricky went back to his office. He sat daydreaming and scheming. "If there was just some way I could get referral fees from the Taj Majhal too, I could actually make a decent living. Maybe I'll call their administrator and do lunch."

Chapter 35: Could This Be Dante's Inferno?

Sandy quit his job as a fire installation installer after only one week on the job. He figured that if he didn't know how to unscrew a pipe by then, then he never would. He went on to Chicago April 1st. He rented a car and apartment for two months and attended three trade shows at the Chicago convention center. Bulldog arrived a week later and me two days after that.

Sandy laid out the plans of the convention center on the table. "This is the main auditorium where the opening ceremonies will occur. There are 15 exits, all with doors that can't be locked from the inside so free egress is possible. There will probably be guards at every door anyway so blocking them would require a small army and is clearly not an option. There are overhead fire extinguishers every ten feet but I don't know if they all feed from one source or not."

"Good work so far." I said. "What about jobs?"

"Good news there. I've gone for an interview and they want me back tomorrow. I'll probably be offered a job in the sprinkler department. They also need maintenance people that speak English, so you'll probably be in by tomorrow after your interview." Replied Sandy.

"That's great. And what about you Bulldog?"

"You're looking at the newest gasoline truck driver in the Midwest Gas and Oil Company fleet. I start full time tomorrow."

"Okay, we're on our way. I'm hungry, anyone care to go out for a bite?"

"Sure thing." said Sandy. Bulldog nodded in the affirmative as he was already donning his jacket. Even in spring, Chicago was nippy in the evening.

The next month went by quickly. We all were able to hold onto our jobs but it took quite a bit of dumbing down to do it. If you seem to be smarter than your boss, he's sure to feel threatened for his job and he'll fire you in no time. This is part of the reason for the grain of truth behind the saying 'good help is hard to find'. Of course it is if you keep firing the good ones. In any case, we worked hard, learned our trades fairly well and most important, were able to fill in the fine details of our plans so that it would work as hoped.

May 18 finally arrived. The main auditorium was filled with lawyers whose faces and names were recognizable from the front pages of every newspaper in the country. Ten thousand of them and their spouses, honored guests and local and state politicians had come together for this great moment. The annual meeting where networking was used to gather the latest evil ideas for suing everyone for everything, spreading the plague of their terrible work across the countryside.

Seven AM Bulldog showed up for work as usual. He was to deliver the gas to a local gas station across town. The whole trip and delivery usually took two and a half hours so he wouldn't be expected back until about 9:30. He drove the truck over to the service area of the convention center where I met him about 7:30 AM. The 15 minute trip took twice as long because of all the state police and limousines. I would have been a little anxious were it not for the miracle of instant messaging through our favorite cell phone company and unknowing partner in crime, Nevertel.

Bulldog backed the truck expertly into the loading bay. I was impressed with his clearly well honed truck driving ability. I'll remember that in case it played into our future plans. Jim Freed was with me, not looking as cool as I'd hoped he be, not having trained with us on our numerous previous forays. I hoped that his long years of experience in the police department wouldn't let us down though. We needed him to keep the area clear of intruders. He had a taser, an empty closet and lots of duct tape for those with inquiring minds.

Sandy had previously bypassed the pressure alarms for the overhead fire extinguishing system and rewired the lights on the control panel to show green regardless of any malfunction. There were over two miles of extinguisher pipes in the center but he was able to isolate the main conference hall for us. He had also placed an incendiary device with radio control at each sprinkler head in the hall. It was a tribute to his skill, agility and perseverance as it was no small task as there were over a hundred of them, some 75 feet from the floor. A little vertigo would go a long way in that endeavor.

Freed clicked the call button on his phone giving all of us a little chirp in ours. He saw someone coming through the small window in the loading bay's security door and he wanted us to maneuver towards him for backup.

He took a step back and leaned casually against the hard and unfinished concrete wall, trying to look relaxed as if he was supposed to be there but the wall put several large indentations in his unprotected arms and his face looked strained at best. A couple of maintenance men came out for a quick smoke. They looked at Jim, didn't recognize him, gave him a half nod of acknowledgement anyway and proceeded towards the steps down to the loading dock. Bulldog and I had already advanced to the bottom of the four step landing. As they passed Jim and looked at us they looked at each other with a slightly puzzled expression. That didn't last long as Jim clubbed one on the back of the neck with a heavy tire iron and tased the other one before he could open his mouth in alarm.

We dragged them to the closet and bound the tased one. The other one needed no extra attention, he was dead from a broken neck. Note to self: don't get Jim angry and if do, don't turn your back.

By isolating the great hall, we eliminated one and one half miles of pipe but that still left a fairly large volume of water to drain. That took a good 45 minutes including the half dozen interruptions by uninvited interlopers to our private party. The closet was getting full but we were getting a fairly nice stash of rings, watches and cash which would help finance our activities. Jim was really getting into it. We promised him the first Rolex but, wouldn't you know it, the workmen seemed to have left their best jewelry at home.

The water finally stopped draining except for an occasional drip. It took several more minutes to get things hooked up. Bulldog raised up the gas delivery hose to me, I held it as Bulldog attached the special adaptor so the hose would couple to the extinguisher system.

It was now almost 9 AM, the attendees were largely seated as they didn't want to miss the opening address from the Mayor of Chicago and a former president of the ABA. He was revered by the trial lawyers association as the man who broke the back of the tobacco industry, thus guaranteeing literally billions of dollars in legal fees for decades to come. Many a millionaire was sitting in the audience, owing their good fortune and early retirement to the good life to the man who was about to speak. Only a handful of those lawyers actually remembered the names of more than a few of the plaintiffs who had supposedly suffered at the hands of the "evil" tobacco companies. Each "victim" received a mere pittance from the settlements, hardly enough to bury them after all the legal fees, court expenses and other contingencies were paid for, like the $50,000.00 honorarium and the $1000.00 gavel they were presenting the Mayor today for giving the opening address. None of them had spoken to a single plaintiff after the final settlement was reached. At best, a secretary would pass along a note from one of the plaintiffs that they were upset over something, usually the lack of receipt of any of the settlement money for months after they read about the settlement in the papers.

The record was three years for one lawyer's clients and they only got paid after suing him. Unfortunately, he had already spirited away all available funds offshore and the only assets they were able to get was his 1991 Caprice he left at the airport as he left the country. He had already shipped his BMW and Lexus out and only left the Caprice because CarWorld offered him less for the car than it cost to rent a cab to the airport. Not one other public spirited lawyer ever raised their voice against his actions. The Bar Association couldn't make it go away entirely after 300 of his former clients petitioned it for redress. The Bar was forced to suspend his license for three years but he could ask for reinstatement after attending a Bar sponsored ethics course and giving 50 hours of community service. He's now sitting on the porch of his ocean front home in a carefully researched country that doesn't have an extradition treaty with the United States. He's sipping his 20 year old scotch and teaching three third year lawyer students taking a course in international law. Their assignment: find three other western hemisphere countries without extradition treaties with the U.S. He might want to engage in international travel again if he ever gets bored of his new home.

We started pumping in the gasoline. The truck was a big one, 1000 gallons. We hoped it would be enough. The system was still a closed one so not much gas could be pumped against the building air pressure. We had to stop pumping when the pressure reached 60 PSI for fear of premature rupture of some component of the system. Placing this part of the operation on temporary hold, we turned to the other necessary tasks. Bulldog went to get the car which was parked just around the corner in the only available slot – by a fire hydrant of all things. He drove it back proudly waving the ticket we received. $250.00! Outrageous how the city took advantage of its citizens to line the politicians' and unions' pockets at everyone else's expense. Sandy stood guard with Jim and I turned on the portable TV we brought so we could watch the opening ceremonies in the hall a hundred yards away. Bulldog backed the car in deftly (definitely our driver in the future) and got out, returning to his station at the controls of the gas truck. I placed the TV in the back seat of the car, went to the trunk and retrieved the radio controlled device.

The TV announcer blabbed his usual drivel, the Mayor was climbing onto the podium amidst tumultuous applause by those who owed him so much and by those who would hang on his every word today to be able to learn enough to be able to join the throngs of those who owed him so much.

I signaled to Jim and Sandy to come join me. They gave me the all clear sign. They then chained the door shut so that anyone smart or lucky enough to figure out what was going on couldn't get there to stop it. They joined me in the car, Sandy next to me in the back seat, already fixated on the TV screen before he had his second foot inside. Jim sat up front in the passenger seat. He seemed to have both a calm and resolved look about him as if he finally understood and accepted our ideals and a flushed look of exertion and energy from the physical and mental rigors we had put him through. Despite my earlier concerns about how Jim would act under fire, I was pleased to realize he was now fully one of us.

The crowd was still on their feet whooping it up for their hero, His Honor. I gave the signal to Bulldog. He turned on the pump switch to max, trotted over to the car got in and drove off. As we were exiting the service bay, I pressed the button to lower the garage a final time and hit the radio control activate button almost simultaneously.

As we drove off into the congested streets around the convention center, Sandy and I concentrated on the images we were seeing on the TV. We could see inside the hall where the faithful were still giving a standing applause to their cash cow guru. There appeared to be a series of pops heard above the tumult, followed by a sudden brightening of the images followed almost immediately by a rain of fire and brimstone rapidly engulfing the hall. The cameras continued to roll despite their abandonment by the operators, who, like the rest of the crowd, were momentarily stunned by the conflagration all around them. A run towards the exits became a stampede as everyone, in a primal return to their self preservation instincts did what any animal would do when confronted with overwhelming adversity – they ran. They ran in all directions at once, trampling their neighbors in a desperate effort to save themselves. At first husbands tried to shelter wives but the relentless rain of burning gasoline caused even the strongest to break and any semblance of civilization evaporated even as the oxygen was sucked from their lungs and the flesh burned from their bodies.

Those lucky enough to be closest to the exits soon found their situation hopeless as the fire spread to the corridor and thick black smoke, reeking of the acrid smell unique to burning flesh encircled everyone, making it impossible to see and impossible to breath. The guards at the doors started into the hall to try to help but the few that could retreated the other way. A few actually made it to the outside and fewer still survived the third degree burns they suffered.

The Mayor tried to escape out the back through the stage door but his aides and other dignitaries beat him to it. Unfortunately, no one could see to find the doors and the bodies heaped up inches from salvation. The Mayor, like all but a handful of the audience, met his untimely death from burns and smoke inhalation. The last images seen around the country were horrifying in their starkness. The viewers were spared the worst when the smoke became too thick to see through and the screams finally were silenced when the wires burned out. The people in the hall, those still conscious, continued to scream their final words for another few minutes. But soon, all was silent except for the carnal barbeque that continued until all the fuel, human and gas, were consumed.

As we continued towards the apartment, the wail of the sirens started to drown out the usual street noise. All the pedestrians were staring towards the direction from which we came. The smoke was thickening over the area and clearly something was up. As is our nature, we are all attracted to a disaster. It even takes on a sort of carnival atmosphere and everyone watches in fascination. All is okay, as long as it isn't us that the disaster is happening to.

Chapter 36: What Next?

We made it home without incident. We drove into the parking lot at the apartment house, parking in our assigned spot and got out. Four black men and a TV. If anyone was watching, they might have mused, that's a switch, bringing a TV in rather than the other way around that stereotypes demanded.

We let ourselves in, put our equipment down and started getting undressed. Bulldog, being the most fastidious of us, hit the showers first. He removed the short kinky haired wig and stepped in. Bulldog liked a hot shower and soon the steam was thick in the bathroom. Little whispers of fog escaped from the gap under the door where it meets the floor. He liberally lathered himself with the special soap they use in Hollywood to remove the most tenacious of makeup. The brownish dye reluctantly let go from his skin and his natural color reappeared. Bulldog wasn't prejudiced, but having grown up in the south, he instinctively felt better with the color he was born with than that which his family had always hinted wasn't as good as their own. After being self liberated, Bulldog dried off and opened the bathroom door, allowing the small parade of men to metamorphasize back to their natural state.

Feeling refreshed and allowed to relax in the hotel room for a few well deserved moments, we were ready to return home. The TV was on in the background, broadcasting nonstop disaster coverage, the only part of interest was the final victim tally which would take a few days to sort out. My only regret was that the families would be able to collect life insurance on the evil ones we'd eliminated, a final poke in the eye with a sharp stick to the rest of the world, the true victims of their prior existence.

"Up to ten thousand souls may have been lost in this terrible disaster …" intoned the anchorman.

What he obviously didn't understand was the souls were long ago lost, more correctly, sold, to the devil, and all that was happening now was the empty shells of their bodies were joining their souls in hell.

We did an express checkout so that the front desk didn't see us in our transformed incarnation. We slipped out the back, unnoticed by the passersby and got into our previously packed rental car. The drive to the airport was uneventful. We said our goodbyes, made plans for our next meeting and went to different airlines for different flights to different cities, just in case someone was able to pick up a common thread later on.

Home would be restful. I'd go back to work. A few weeks vacation would raise some eyebrows, not so much due to suspicion of any connection with me and the Chicago fire, but more out of envy that I could take that much time off. The South Seas are a long way off and a once in a lifetime trip demands some time. Being relatively taciturn and not one to bring my private life to work, the questions would soon fade away and I'll be left alone again.

Chapter 37: Hospice

Some patients are hard to kill. Sometimes they need a little push. So I have to bring in some help. I ask a consultant. The obvious choice is an oncologist. They actually use poisons legally! Unfortunately, they don't use an effective dose so the patients linger. They feel and look like shit and just as it looks as if this is it, the oncologist backs off, the patient rallies and they try again. This can go on for months until the patient can no longer take it anymore and they either shoot themselves or take an extra dose of chemotherapy. The oncologist always seems so surprised that the patient didn't make it and they lower the dose on the next patient so they linger even longer. This is actually quite a good system for torturing someone but not very useful for the mass murder needed to take care of the lawyers. So except in a publicly announced effort to deter lawyers from practicing their trade, this just won't do.

However, there is an organization that precisely fits the bill. Hospice. They not only are legal, but also they're virtually suit proof as you have to sign away all your rights without recourse when you start with them. In addition, there are eyebrows raised and questions asked if you SURVIVE their services. They're perfect. And they don't mess around. They administer enough medicine so that if you're still conscious you automatically get another dose. What's more, they have nurses sit with you around the clock so that at the slightest stirring, you get more. If you're too groggy to swallow, it doesn't matter – they either give you a shot or stick it up the butt.

It's actually quite interesting how they do the butt thing. As soon as you sign up, they stick a plastic tube up your butt. The tube is attached to a powerful fan which can blow a suppository halfway to your kidneys from twenty paces so the nurses don't have to worry about getting their hands dirty and deal with that annoying hand washing thing we've led you to believe we're supposed to do. Nor do they have to get close enough to the patient to smell the rotting flesh that we become in the end. (An obvious double entendre, even for the dimwitted.)

There are two major concerns that we have with hospice. Because they use only pure medicinal morphine, they have to be careful not to sign up people looking only for a fix. Also, they have to screen the nurses carefully so they don't skimp on the medication, leaving more for themselves to self administer. That's why they always come in pairs and not singly. I've found that just makes for easier self administration. I even caught one sitting on a pillow covering the patient's head so that they'd have a lot more for themselves. Would have turned them in, too, if they hadn't offered to share.

Hospice works well for any patient but it is just more appealing to use it liberally on lawyers, especially if there's still hope as was the case with Mr. Brown. I met Mr. Brown one day while I was interviewing his roommate, Mr. Slobberly, who was admitted to the nursing home the day before. Mr. Slobberly had suffered a stroke the week before and was in the nursing home for rehab. His biggest problem was he couldn't swallow well and not only tended to drool but also splattered profusely as he spoke.

As I entered the room I introduced myself. "Hi Mr. Slobberly, I'm going to be your doctor here as your regular physician doesn't come to the nursing home. How are you feeling today?"

"I freel otay." He said as he sprayed me with a fine mist and one decent sized hocker. I learned my lesson quickly and backed up out of range.

One of the problems in understanding him, in addition to the obvious speech impediment, was the blaring TV which his roommate was watching.

"Hold on a minute, Mr. Slobberly, I'll be right back." I took the few steps over to the next bed and asked his roommate, Mr. Brown, "I was wondering if you wouldn't mind turning off your TV for a few minutes while I talk to your roommate?"

"Hell, no I won't! Who gives you the right to barge in here and start bossing me around? This is my room and what I say goes! Damn straight!"

"I appreciate your understanding in this matter, Mr. Brown. Thanks for your cooperation." I replied as I reached over and turned off the TV.

I didn't get one step before a set of invectives that boggled my mind started spewing from Mr. Brown. He must have been rehearsing them as they came out in a steady stream, almost lyrically strung together. Within a moment he had turned his TV back on and turned the volume beyond the ear drum rupture threshold.

I turned around, didn't even give him the courtesy of a glance and pulled the plug from the wall. The sound of silence was short lived as Mr. Brown started up verse two on his diatribe, this time adding a little twist. "You bastard! You had no right to do that! Plug it in right now! I'm calling the police! I want your name and social security number. I'm a lawyer and I'm going to sue you! If I didn't have this broken leg, I'd get out of bed and whoop your ass!"

Those pieces of information actually weighed heavily on my decision to take the course of action that I did. I not only noticed he was old and decrepit, but also that he was laid up on his back with his left leg in traction and with a set of steel braces holding his leg together in external fixation. He was essentially a prisoner in his bed and I had nothing to worry about for at least another month. By then, I was sure he wouldn't remember anything about this whole episode. Just in case he did though, I knew I had to come up with a special plan to deal with this situation.

"Get back here, you bastard!" were the only nice words I could decipher as he droned on for a few minutes. I rung the bell for the nurse, gave her an order for some valium IV for Mr. Brown and was soon able to renew my interview with Mr. Slobberly. Mr. Slobberly was run of the mill and no real concern or challenge but I needed to do something about Mr. Brown.

Back at the nursing station, I dialed the number for hospice. "Hi, this is hospice." She answered soothingly.

"Hi there, I'd like referrals please." I replied.

"Hold please." Intoned the pleasant receptionist as the theme song for Soylent Green played in the background.

"Referrals."

"Hi there, I'd like you to see one of my patients, a Mr. Brown. I'd also like you to send over Nancy. Is she available?"

"She's always available for you, doctor. Is this another one of your special cases?" she inquired conspiratorially.

"Never you mind. Just have Nancy meet me in an hour."

"As you wish. Bye."

I went about my business for the hour and right on time, as always, Nancy showed up.

"I'm told you put a special request in for me again. You need the usual?" Nancy winked.

"Actually, this one is somewhat different."

"Different?"

"Yes, the problem is he's not even my patient so I can't write for a consult."

"I see." said Nancy. "There might still be a way to handle this. Let me take a look at his chart."

I handed her the chart and continued my rounds. She caught up with me a half hour later.

"I think we might be able to work this out." Nancy said. "It turns out he has no relatives who might ask questions later. This is what I'll do. I'll ask him if he's in pain and if so, I can stop his pain but he has to sign up with us."

"Okay, let me know how that turns out." I said and returned to my work.

Another half hour later, Nancy caught up with me again. "It wasn't easy but I got him to sign." She gloated.

"Great, how'd you convince him? He needed a lot of pain relief?"

"No, actually it turned out he is a drug addict and when I offered him the good stuff, he was all over it. He broke two pens in his frantic effort to sign up. Problem is, with these drug addicts, they're so used to it that I doubt there'll be a drop left over for any of us." She lamented.

"Oh well, you got to do what you got to do." I resigned myself.

Nancy didn't waste any time in getting started. "I'm back, Mr. Brown. I need to start an IV to administer the medication."

"Good luck. I haven't had an open vein since the Miami Drug Fest in the summer of '95. If you find one, just leave the needle in in case I'd be needing it later." his face a little brighter at the prospect of a new port to ecstasy.

Unfortunately, that optimism lasted only a half hour or so, which was the time it took Nancy to realize it just wasn't going to happen. His veins were so scarred, she not only couldn't start an IV, she couldn't even find a remnant of where a vein had once been. "Well, this isn't working out. How about some pills?" she asked.

"Hell, no!" Mr. Brown exclaimed. "I didn't sign up for some halfway measures! I want the full deal or no deal at all. Hell, if I wanted pills, I could have gone to my grandmother's house and stolen all the damn pills I wanted. She has a regular pharmacy what with her doctor shopping and all. She sells the leftovers to supplement her social security. She's wealthier in retirement than when she was working. And I didn't go through the last half hour of being poked in a dozen places I knew there wasn't a prayer of finding a vein just so I could get some pills. Pills aren't worth the paper they're printed on. Pills wouldn't get a two year old high. The hell with pills and the hell with you. You get me some good stuff or I swear I'll get off this bed and club you with my crutches. Then I'll feed you the pills and see how much pain they relieve for you after the whooping I'm fixing to give you. Why, I'll …" he tiraded on until Nancy finally was able to get a word in edgewise.

"Okay, okay. My bad. Enough already. I've got a backup plan. We can bring in the Hospice 5000 Rectal Blow Pipe. That's got to provide you with the relief you're looking for and so deeply deserve." Soothed Nancy.

"I like the sound of that, whatever it is. Rectal has always done right by me. Let's go with that. How long until I get this blow up my pipe?" Mr. Brown asked with a brightening continence.

"Not too long at all. Luckily, I've got one in the van. I'll go to get it and be right back." Nancy was delighted to get a chance to try my new invention. It was called the 'Hospice 5000 Rectal Blow Pipe'© that they patented at my suggestion. The one she carried came with the optional turbocharged air jet and the extended 20 foot reach so she could administer the drugs from the hallway. It was ideal for patients like Mr. Brown who were really smelly when we couldn't afford being overcome with the fumes from the back flow.

Nancy paged me, "Okay, here's your big chance. He's going for the Hospice 5000."

"Hey, that's great. Thanks for the warning, I'm heading for my car now. Give me five minutes to get out of range." My heart leaped at the thought of literally blowing Mr. Brown to the next world with my invention.

"Whoa there. Slow down big boy. You're not getting off that easy. I need help getting it in, and I mean both in the building and in the patient. I read your manual. It specifically says that the kick start takes about the same amount of strength as it does to start a 1200 cc Harley. I can tell you right now, three of me couldn't start one. So just turn yourself around and meet me in the lobby."

Defeated, I responded "Okay" even as I saw Nancy approaching me from the other hallway. The hallways in this nursing home were actually quite well suited for their job. In this case they served as both a torture chamber and a mortuary, depending on the phase of my treatment of the patients. As we met, I said "Hi Nancy. Fancy meeting you here."

"Funny. Let's go out to car and bring 'er in. I was barely able to load it up with my husband's help. I have been looking forward to using it and I guess there's no better time to do so than with the inventor at my side."

I hadn't been looking forward to using it, let alone lugging it, myself. I had hoped to live vicariously through the misery of others but today wasn't my lucky day.

"Okay, here we are." Nancy said, gesturing at her late model SUV, while she activated the door locks with her key transmitter. Inside stood an ungainly contraption, leering down on us as if it knew what it was designed to do. Actually, I planned it exactly that way when I designed it. It was supposed to give the recipients of it's ministrations a small insight of what lay before them both during and after its use.

"Okay. Let me help." I said. "Just step back and I'll handle it." I pressed a series of buttons on the keyboard and it suddenly sprang to life, lowering itself off the SUV and wheeling itself towards the front door before it stopped and waited.

Nancy was astonished. "How did you do that? I spent a good half hour lifting and prodding that thing up into the van and you just made it get down on its own. I read the manual cover to cover and nowhere did it say anything about self locomotion. What gives?"

"Did you read the part about paying for premium user support?"

"Yes, but I wasn't about to pay a thousand dollars extra per year for worthless user support. It said it had a three year warranty."

"Your choice." I said as I walked on while Nancy was just realizing that premium user support might not be such a bad idea after all.

We bracketed the Hospice 5000, me in front, Nancy bringing up the rear, as it rolled itself into Mr. Brown's room. I had switched into green scrubs and put on a surgical mask and a cap and stayed off to the side so he wouldn't realize I was in the room.

"What the hell is that contraption?" Mr. Brown practically leaping off the bed in a supine, layout position. I gave him a 7.5, leaving him room for the improvement in his performance once we got it fully deployed.

"This is the Rectal Blow Pipe," Nancy replied, leaving off the Hospice 5000 so he couldn't ask for maybe the smaller, 2000, version. "This is what we're going to use to ease your suffering."

"I'm not sure I know what suffering is yet." he said, looking a little leerily at the 5000. "How much of that has got to go inside the rectum. I mean, that's larger than the two liter cola bottle that I'm more intimately acquainted with.

"Now don't you worry, Mr. Brown, I assure you that, despite it's looks, you and the Blow Pipe will soon be the best of friends. All you have to do is turn on your side and we'll do the rest." Nancy looked at me. She had read the manual and knew what an ordeal she could expect inserting the business end of the machine into Mr. Brown. "Any premium user upgrades that might come in handy about this time?"

I gave her a wry smile and said, "But of course, my dear. I do give great value to my best clients. Watch this."

Mr. Brown called out from over his shoulder, "Who that? That's not that doctor I'm going to sue for turning off my TV because if it is I want to have nothing to do with him. Do you here me?"

Nancy quickly stepped in and distracted Mr. Brown, "No, that's not the doctor you don't like, that's just my aide to help me set this thing up for you. It'll go much easier if you just try and relax." She intoned as she turned him back on his side from the partial turn he had already made in an effort to see me. I had ducked behind the curtain as a precaution in case he recognized me despite my disguise. I made a mental note not to talk anymore.

Nancy turned towards me, giving me a look, what's next? I stepped back to the Hospice 5000, punched a few keys and waited as it whirred to life.

"What's that noise?" Mr. Brown being more alert now than he was even after three months of court ordered detox. Of course he cheated daily in detox so that's not really saying much.

"That's just us starting up the Pipe." Nancy explained. "What's going to happen now is we'll insert the drug administration coupler into your rectum where it'll stay securely in place to insure a reliable drug deliver regimen."

What happened next also wasn't in Nancy's standard owner's manual. The Hospice 5000 Rectal Blow Pipe took charge of the entire situation. Its several, heretofore hidden, arms reached out and securely embraced Mr. Brown so that the only part of his body he could move was his eyelids. One hand covered his mouth to muffle his screams as two more spread his legs and yet another inserted what looked like a three pronged grappling hook with fierce looking barbs into his rectum. It was the oversized version so even the 5000 had a little trouble at first. It was meeting a little more resistance than I had expected. I withdrew the insertion arm and went over to do a rectal exam. To my surprise, there were a series of curled up papers inside. I pulled them out, opened them up and started reading them.

As I was doing so, Mr. Brown turned his head just enough to catch me in his peripheral vision. "I thought that was you doc. I forgot to tell you something. My lawyer stopped by and I told him what was going on. He said he knew all about you and asked if he could leave those in there for you. It turns out another one of your patients is suing you and he's been having a hard time serving you. So Merry Christmas, you've been served!"

It was indeed another suit. Damn those lawyers, they're getting too clever! Oh well, after they're disinfected, I'll put them with the rest. In the meantime, I think I'll have a little something extra for that smug bastard, Mr. Brown, here. I repositioned the insertion arm up against Mr. Brown's anus and merely touched a button boosting the power up to 50% popping the hook inside with little further ado. As the arms lessened their hold on Mr. Brown he was almost able to squirm free and gave out what could have been a blood curdling scream from the look on his face but just came out as a gurgle under the hand holding his mouth.

"Now just relax Mr. Brown. I'm about to administer your first dose." I said as I set the electric discharge unit to 25%, about 300 watts.

The Devil Who Walked The Earth

Mr. Brown gave a large jerk within the confines of the arms still firmly holding him. He was desperately trying to free his butt from the Blow Pipe. The barbs held firm and all he accomplished was setting them deeper.

"Now, now, Mr. Brown, let's settle down a bit." I said as I slowly switched the wattage up and changed it to the continuous rather than intermittent discharge mode. I hadn't gone this high before but I figured Mr. Brown was a deserving subject to test the full range of power of the 5000.

Mr. Brown continued to squirm but, much to my surprise, and probably his too, a smile started to break out on his face. I didn't know what was wrong so I started to back down on the voltage to do some trouble shooting. His smile faded and he made some gestures which I took as him asking to turn it back up. I thought about it for a minute and then started to turn it back up. When I got to 50% again, his smile returned and he finally started to relax. As it got to 75% I saw arcing between his thighs down to his toes in a sort of Jacob's ladder type of discharge. At 85% there was a glow coming from his butt like you see coming from the chimney's at night when they burn off the waste gases at petroleum refineries. Since I'd never tested this on anyone before, I took careful notes of setting and reactions. I made a note to limit future machines to a 50% setting with higher settings available by special command override for premium subscribers only.

As I never intended to give Mr. Brown any pleasure, once I finished my notes, I turned off the voltage, rendering the Blow Pipe in its standard manual drug administration mode. The 5000's arm over his mouth withdrew allowing Mr. Brown to talk again.

His first words to me were "Doc, you can call me Isaac. I need another dose right now."

"Maybe a little later, we have to charge her up again." I was surprised that he spoke to me civilly after all that, but to become best friends in a blink of an eye was a little too much. "See you soon." I didn't want to hang around right now. I was anxious to get home to see if these new settings were for real. "Bye Nancy. Good luck."

Nancy was speechless. She spent the next few minutes looking at the index in the manual and then called in her American Express number to my 800 number for the premium upgrade. "Okay Isaac, let's get started."

"Hold on there a minute. I'm Mr. Brown to you until you can do what he just did. In the meantime, while we're waiting for this sucker to get recharged, I want my meds now. Just start them blowing and don't let them stop."

As I slipped out unnoticed, I saw Nancy already working hard at setting up the medication administration hopper at the top of the Blow Pipe. She started the auxiliary power unit needed to turn the turbofans used to blow in the industrial strength narcotics stacked by the door. I hurried around the corner of the blast shield just before the hurricane force winds started to blow. The protective grill work for the intake pipes was already starting to get clogged up with aides and visitors. The cow catcher cleaner unit was working well in keeping the vents open.

"More, more, moooorrrreeee …" could be heard from Isaac as I finally left the range of earshot.

It took a long while, almost a record for longevity for a hospice patient, almost two whole days from the time he signed up to the time he took his last breath, with an almost record amount of medication being administered, but we were finally successful. But I'm always sad when a lawyer dies and his screaming and agony ends.

As they carted off Mr. Brown's carcass, I breathed a sign of relief. Once again, I congratulated myself in aligning myself with hospice. They were real life savers, only my life, actually, in a pinch. I was somewhat disappointed to see the grin on Mr. Brown's face though even though he never got up past 50% again. Oh well, back to Mr. Slobberly. Let's see how he's getting along. We already have the 5000 set up in his room so it would be convenient if it turns out he needs it too.

Chapter 38:
Training a Monkey Is Easier

The major part of my work as a hospitalist, more precisely a SNFist (pronounced sniff-ist), as I'm currently stationed in the skilled nursing facility aspect of institutionalization, is trying to get patients strong enough and steady enough to leave the nursing home. (I don't care where they go, just so long as they go). My first roadblock in the discharge process is usually encountered when I introduce myself and tell the family that their loved one is in a nursing home. They indignantly state that is not so, they're in a rehab facility. I usually allow them their shallow victory, largely by ignoring them and concentrating on talking to the patient, not the assembled entourage of strangers who show up calling themselves family.

I call them strangers for several reasons, not because I don't know them, but because the patients don't know them. They usually hadn't seen their loved one for years and only spoken to them, if ever, rarely. In addition, the patients are usually so demented that they wouldn't have a clue who these people were even if they lived with them, which a fair number actually did. The only thing they have in common is the hope on the family's part that they are mentioned in the will. They showed up now to assess how soon they might be partaking in the presumed largess of the patient. Tending to their investment as it were. I can always tell who was standing to get the most by their anxiousness to pull the plug.

Those with the least to gain always wanted everything to be done. Why? First, to spite the other family members who were in line for the lion's share of the inheritance in an effort to delay their good fortune as long as possible, even though they knew the end was inevitable, and second, to make the patient suffer longer for not being as generous to them.

Why should anyone's actions and motivations in death be any different than they were in life? The patient's will continued to show the same favoritism that they had shown all their life. It makes no difference how much love and effort a child shows to their parent, the parent will continue to favor whoever fits in best with their concept of the world. Note to self: don't try to change attitudes, it won't work. Do what you've got to do and not expect anything in return. Mental sanity tip for the day.

Getting back to the patient's interview, I try to explain to the patient and the 1000 critics that surround them that our goal is to get them home as soon as they're capable. The chorus immediately arises that they're **entitled** to 100 days at the insurance company's expense. I explain to them they have a maximum of 100 days only if needed and only a rare patient needs that long, most need only a week or so. The next words out of their collective mouths were that they're hiring a lawyer and would hold me personally responsible if anything happens to the patient ever, for the rest of his life!

My usual response is I'm from the Jewish American Indian tribe, the so-sue-me tribe. It also reinforces the conviction that my efforts to kill the lawyers are indeed the only moral thing to do. That will also eliminate most of our politicians, those devil's helpers who came up with the concept of "entitlement". There has probably not been a more subversive word in the English language than that. It has allowed countless millions to take the socialist path mandating that others must do all for them as they're "entitled" to food, shelter, medical care, respect and whatever entitlement du jour the liberals come up with on an ongoing basis. It has sapped our individualistic spirit leaving only a minority of us not on the government dole, thus ensuring that anyone advocating a return to self-reliance won't have a chance at the ballot box. Well, we'll see about that. A few more displays of antilawyer counterterrorism on my part and we might have them reeling and begging for mercy. Going to a lawyer should be a last resort, not a preemptive strike to get your way even if it's wrong.

Finally the family leaves and we can get down to real work. If we're lucky they stay away but, as was noted above, if they're spiteful to each other, they're spiteful to the medical profession too so we have to put up with their crap for the entire stay. One of our prime motivators to get patients out of rehab is to get the families out too. Their very being there backfires on them if they wanted a long stay because we'll shorten the stay just to get rid of the more obnoxious ones. There's an unwritten collusion between the physicians, nurses and physical therapists to shorten stay and lessen goals if the families upset us. I guess we can be spiteful too.

The real work of the rehab is rehab. That is to say, getting the patients well enough to go home. We actually achieve that goal on occasion, but we are usually quite surprised when that happens. Not because we don't care or don't try or aren't competent or shorten the stay on purpose or any other reason ascribable to the medical team. No, the reason we usually fail is the quality of protoplasm we're presented with to work on. There's just nothing there. Yes, there's a body but usually neither the body nor the spirit are willing. We are given the broken down heaps of humanity and expected to work miracles. And woe to us who fail to raise the all but dead, the family's lawyer will be in contact with us shortly.

I have always considered it a financial and social failure to plan if anyone ever shows up in the rehab. Here you have a bunch of paid "workers" (and I use that term loosely) who look at the clock hourly to see how much money they've made so they can go out and do what they want. The nurse's aides, the ones closest to the patients, are the worst. They're usually foreign speakers getting paid the least amount of money and have no American work ethics at all. They come from countries where human life is cheap and where siesta is almost a religion. They eat the patient's food, rob them blind, ignore the call bells and then lie about it all. More than a few good nurses have found their tires slashed or their cars keyed after trying to discipline one of them. The patients treat them with the disrespect they so largely deserve but then wonder why they aren't getting the service they feel they're entitled to. Duh.

I estimate that over 90% of my patients, the average age of which is 85, are so severely demented that they neither know where they are nor why they're here. Half of those don't even know who they are. If you ask them to raise their right arm, a good reaction by the patient usually prompts me to say, "No, the other right arm." The usual reaction however, is no reaction at all by the patient. Either they are unconscious, so demented they can't possibly understand what you want or have had a stroke and you asked them to move the side that they don't know even exists anymore. So raising anything is actually a good response. Is it good enough to get them home alone eventually? Probably not, but that's not our goal. Our goal is to get them out of rehab. They can go to assisted living facility or they can home with help, or heaven forbid, to a loved one's home. That's always sweet, when a patient stays with a family member. Now that family member has to work for their inheritance. More often than not, the relative who takes the patient home, unbeknownst to him/her is the disinherited one and doesn't realize what a sucker he/she is until it's too late. What that does is set up a legal battle by the heirs, guaranteeing more work for the lawyers. That's actually okay in a way because the very people threatening to loose the lawyers on us get a taste of their own medicine. Unfortunately, it just further enriches the lawyers, makes the inheritance fall short of expectations and makes the heirs look elsewhere to make up for the perceived shortfall. Bingo! They're back suing us. What a surprise. Our only defense is good records. Copious, self serving and usually falsified records. We're no dummies. If the courts are going to rely on written evidence over verbal testimony, we're going to do everything we can to bulletproof ourselves.

This leads to hours of paperwork and minutes for patient care. Thus the call bells go unanswered as we're too busy justifying our efforts to actually touch a patient. An aide eventually shows up, turns off the bell and walks out. The demented patient is too slow to realize his last best hope to get to the bathroom is gone for at least another half hour. It really didn't matter though as he'd already made in his diaper before he called anyway. He was just calling because the poop was getting cold and uncomfortable. It'll get even more so by the time the next shift's aide shows up. Apparently, each patient gets only one call per shift. But even that's not true. There are three shifts, two of which will answer the call bell at least once per the shift. The third, the night shift, doesn't want to be awakened from their sleep so they turn off the alarm center at the nurse's station and sleep all night long.

As I walk down the hallways in the mornings, before housekeeping has a chance to flush out the built up nighttime waste with it's accompanying stench, I contemplate holding a breath holding contest between the rehab docs and the best swimmers the world can throw at us. I'm willing to bet we'd win hands down. I myself have been known to make entire rounds lasting over half an hour without having the courage (or death wish) to take a single breath. I was thinking about bringing in my scuba gear for longer rounds but thought twice about it as I became concerned that the nurses might mug me to get a chance at a breath of fresh air.

So I decide to get to work. I try to pick up a chart but it's missing. I ask a nurse to help and she says it was checked out to MDS, one of the myriad of committees set up to lawyer proof the charts. She goes to get it and I pick up another chart. A short time later she returns with the chart and I put the second one down to review the first one that I wanted to start with.

Let's see: patient lived at home alone, walked independently, no significant medical problems except for high blood pressure. Neighbor called police after she hadn't seen him in several days. Found on floor, unable to speak and brought to the hospital. He was dehydrated and had a bladder infection but no other problems were found so he was sent to the SNF for rehab. Adult protection services surveyed his apartment and found it to be a pigsty. They've placed a hold on him so he can't leave rehab without their permission.

I called the family, a long distance number, of course. They said he's sharp as a tack, totally independent and has never had any medical problems. They last saw him three years ago and spoke to him over the holidays six months ago. They fully expect him to return home alone once he's feeling better.

Okay, time to see him. I call up the physical therapist and say "Let's see him together". We meet a minute later and go to room 101D. No patient. Not in PT either as the therapist just came from there. We go back to the nursing station. No nurses. I overhead page for a nurse to come to the nursing station. In the meantime the therapist goes back to the gym, I'm to call when I find the patient. Fat chance, I can't even find a nurse. I pick up the second chart and start to review that one again. A nurse finally materializes. I'll never know how they disappear and reappear like that but the experienced ones are real good at it.

"Would you please find me Mr. Jones?" I ask.

"What room is he in?" she replies.

I had forgotten the nurses don't know the patient's names. "101D".

"Oh, you mean Mr. Demento. We moved him to 105W yesterday."

"But the chart says 101D. Why wasn't it changed?"

"It wasn't changed? Oh, that's probably because the ward clerk was off yesterday."

"And no one else could change the label? Union rules? Both arms broken? They don't allow you anything sharp like a pen to write with and crayons are too messy and anyway they didn't have a color you liked?"

"Oh doc, you're so mean."

"And you're stupid and ugly. I guess we never can change."

"You can French kiss my ass!"

There, she did it again. She dematerialized before my eyes. If I could just get one to like me, maybe they'll show me how they do that. "If you can still hear me wherever you are, your slip's showing and your nose is shiny."

Nothing like breaking them down psychologically as my sport for the day. I call back the therapist. She's with someone and will be there shortly. I return back to the second chart and continue reviewing it. The therapist shows up, we go to room 105W. No patient.

"Oh, that patient" exclaims the therapist in recognition of who I'm seeking. "He's in the gym."

"Grrrr" I mutter under my breath. We walk to the gym. There's the patient in the corner. Will miracles never cease? He's tied into a wheelchair. Drool dripping from one corner of his mouth. I introduce myself to him. His response: drool welling over both corners of his mouth. I turn to the therapist working with him. "So how's he doing?"

"Max assist in bed mobility, transfers and nonambulatory. But he has good potential."

"Bless you my son, may you have as good potential."

"Doctor what a terrible thing to say. You want me to be like him?" she indignantly replied.

"But you said he has such good potential. You made me believe he'll be walking again before the session is over. Have I misinterpreted your words? Have I offended you in some way by wishing you as well as this patient with good potential? Where have I gone wrong, I beseech thee, tell me the error of my ways?"

I wouldn't have believed it if I didn't see it with my own eyes. The therapists are now able to dematerialize at will, just like the nurses. We do live in miraculous times!

Undaunted, I began my interview. "Hello Mr. Jones, how are you today?" No response other than a blank stare. "Okay, if that one stumped you, tell me, who are you today then?" He just opened a third front in the drool war, it now made a full frontal assault over his lower lip. Fortunately, I remember what mom said and always wore my goulashes. "Mr. Jones, if there's anyone in there, move any part of your body." No response but I might have achieved sensory overload so I rephrased the request: "Mr. Jones, lift your right arm." I studied the left arm for signs of the slightest activity, but no, there was nothing.

The therapist said "Look, his leg moved!" but upon closer inspection it was just the cloth twitching as a drop of saliva hit it.

"It appears to me there's not only not good potential, but there's no potential whatsoever. I'm transferring him to custodial care."

"But he just got here, please give him a chance. Let us work with him a few days and if nothing happens he's all yours." Implored the head therapist.

"I'm afraid not." I said as I pulled out my black hood and scythe. "He's condemned to enter the other world, the place of no return. The place where the entrance sign says 'abandon all hope, ye who enter here'. As you can plainly see, he has advanced Alzheimer's. He is beyond the care of mere mortals. Yes, he's going to Cacophony!"

All in the room shuddered, they knew what this meant. Cacophony, the wing of exile, the wing of tears. The wing way in the back of the building, where many have gone but from where none ever have returned. Even nurses have been known to disappear entirely once exiled there. Of course, those nurses had Alzheimer's themselves so when they lay down to sleep during the night shift, they were undressed, placed in hospital gowns, had their names placed on the doors and they were never allowed to leave again. At least not vertically. There was a constant parade of hearses out the back door. Nature's way of recycling. I wonder if they changed the original name of this nursing home from soylent green before or after the movie came out?

Alright, let's get on with the next one, I thought to myself as I finished entering the order to stop therapy and consult hospice. That'll teach the family for being strangers. They thought they knew their "independent" relative. They didn't have a clue. All to do now is wait for the nasty call that I wasn't giving their loved one a fighting chance. My response would be the same as always, come on down and take a look for yourself. If they did come down, they'd first accuse me of drugging him, until I showed them he was on no meds. Then they'd want him back to the hospital to find out what was wrong. I'd explain he was just in the hospital and what's wrong is he's old and worn out. Have another kid if they wanted a newer version. Then they'd say isn't there anything we can do. Of course, would be my reply, let's call hospice. If I wasn't fired on the spot, that represented a breakthrough for the family and the patient inevitably would end up in hospice and be gone shortly. If they did fire me the patient would suffer greatly and the family would agonize greatly without the benefit of hospice before he'd die shortly. Hospice is the way to go. In any case, once transferred, they were out of my hair and I'd move on.

The head therapist pulled me aside one day and asked me to explain how I knew someone was demented and if advanced, hopeless.

"There's a number of ways to tell, my dear," I said overtly paternalistically. "Let's go see a few and you'll soon see how easy it is. I have a number of simple rules. I have to keep them simple so even I can understand them. Let's go into this room here to start with." I said turning into a room with one of my many patients in it. "Hi, Mr. Smith, how are you today?"

"Fine," replied Smith, seemingly appropriately.

"Do you know where you are?"

"Yes." Replied Smith, looking at me somewhat perplexedly as if I had just asked the stupidest question in the world.

"Well fine, Mr. Smith, where are you?" I asked knowing the answer would come to him in about the same time it took to get a nurse to do things right around here (never will happen for those of you who still have hope).

So the therapist and I waited while Mr. Smith's remaining two brain cells met and greeted each other like they had just met for the first time, which in reality is the way Alzheimer's works on a macro level. I had already found a chair, knowing that this was going to take some time. The therapist began to rock on her heels to try to maintain balance while still remain stationary. After a few minutes Mr. Smith appeared to have moved on to a new set of problems, possibly going over the presentation he was going to give before the Nobel committee regarding his latest project. I gently coaxed him back to deal with the problem at hand. "Mr. Smith, are you still there?"

"Yes."

"Good, do you remember I just asked you a question?"

"No, how did you get there?" He looked as if I had broken into his home and was holding an ax over his head while he slept.

"Oh, I've been here for a little while. I was wondering if you knew where you were."

"Yes."

"Oh, goody. Where are you?"

He developed that same, far away and never coming back look he had the last time I asked him where he was. "Well, this is where we came in so we can go now." I said turning to the therapist. "Shall we alight?"

"Okay, but that's one patient that you selected, what does that prove?" she asked.

I took her to the chart rack, pulled out Smith's and showed her the PT notes indicating he was oriented and a good rehab candidate. "If I'm not mistaken, you just indicated he's severely demented and can't even tell where he is or remember who walked into his room a minute before. If you were not a trained professional, say a family member, you would never have pressed him for a specific answer because you would project your abilities on him and would be content with that answer. Not only that, you would never have confronted him with such a question and therefore you'd never know there was a problem until very late in the disease. You certainly wouldn't have picked it up from a different state during a holiday greeting call. That's why the distant families never know there's a problem and are so surprised with that diagnosis. Suffice it to say, he's not a rehab candidate, he'll need 24 hour care and you need to direct your therapy towards that goal and not independence. And you should listen to me when I tell you something medical in the future."

As we were walking down the hall, one of the elderly female residents stops her wheelchair in front of me and says, "You're so handsome." I thank her and continue walking.

"That is another example of how you can tell dementia. Nobody except an outrageous extrovert with theatrical tendencies would ever stop anybody and say such a thing. We'd all think such things, but never would say them. Not until the frontal lobes atrophy as they do in Alzheimer's and we lose the socialization rules we learned as children do we start saying what we think without filters. That particular thing happens to me a lot. It shows two other problems with aging – loss of good judgment and failing eyesight as I'm not handsome but I do wear a white coat and a good bit of good will goes with that. The demented patient knows something's wrong, they want help and associate a white coat with help so they imbue me with characteristics that I don't have. The usual response is for complete strangers to come up to me as she did and say what she said."

"That's a mouthful. Anything simpler?"

"Do you know what time it is?"

"Sure," she says as she's looking at her watch, "it's 11:30 AM."

"There's your simple lesson. I asked you a question and you immediately looked past the literal question and proceeded to answer something that wasn't asked but implied. I only wanted to know if you knew the time, which by the way you didn't and had to look at your watch to find out after you answered in the affirmative, so the correct answer was 'no'. But you took it upon yourself, as a good citizen usually does, and in an effort to be helpful, lied about whether or not you knew what time it was. You then made an effort to mitigate that lie by finding the answer to a question I didn't ask. You didn't intend to lie but you didn't think it was reasonable to stick to answering the simple question. You went out of your way to give me an answer to a question I didn't ask, as if I was entitled to an answer to a question you asked yourself but nevertheless you felt you were obligated to answer. In this case I couldn't have cared less about what time it was. The point being, you went multiple steps beyond the question, got yourself caught in a lie in the process, spent time on a project that I didn't care about. In fact, I'm somewhat resentful that you trapped me in your own little project that had only a passing relationship to me. The only good that might come out of this is your understanding my point that demented people limit themselves, involuntarily, I might add, as I'm sure they'd prefer to be normal like you, to answering the question in the simplest way possible. If you ask them if they know what time it is, they inevitably answer 'yes' and leave it at that. Just like Mr. Smith did when I asked him if he knew where he was. He didn't, of course, but that's irrelevant to making the diagnosis. The diagnosis can be made with one question. 'Do you know' and then inserting whatever topic you care to. Demented people always say 'yes' even though the real answer is always 'no' but normal people will proceed as if the next question was the one asked: 'what time is it?', for example."

The therapist almost staggered down the hall, "You promised a simple answer. Do you ever listen to yourself?"

"Not if I want to maintain my sanity. But I don't care if you do or not."

"Well I do and I promise I won't be asking any more simple questions of you. And lord help me if I ever ask you if you know the time!"

"Ta ta, young one. Do have a good time in your merry make believe world of trying to return brain function to the dead. Do let me know how the experiments turn out, won't you."

She turns and walks away, making a somewhat rude gesture as she does.

"As much as I do enjoy our talks, I look forward to your sign language lessons even more. Don't get caught under any dead weight."

She made another, even ruder gesture.

"Oh goody, some more sign language. This is my lucky day. By the way," I called after her, "I hope you enjoyed the shipment of monkeys I sent you so you'd at least have some potential to work with."

Chapter 39: Phone Orders

I am part of a large group of physicians covering nursing homes in several counties. Whenever I'm on call I get a huge number of calls, most a useless waste of my time, and don't have time to engage in small talk. The nurses, after having suffered through the process of admitting patients and verifying orders with my group for years now, usually have the process down pat. Not infrequently though, we meet up with a nurse from one of the following categories: too stupid too procreate, brand new and scared of her shadow or passive aggressive with pronounced antisocial tendencies. Nurses from any of those categories present insurmountable problems to the efficient use of our time and maintenance of our sanity.

My wife has started to keep a list of some of my better attempts at coping with these inferior life forms. Every so often she reviews them with me. For those who know her, review is one of her favorite pastimes so I get my wit and sarcastic humor thrown back at me often. Most of these episodes occur in the evening when I'm trying to relax. The shrill trill of the phone alone is enough to get me on edge, so I'm primed to give the hapless novitiate on the other end an earful if she's not perfect. And as my wife often likes to remind me, none of us are perfect.

I return my first beep of the night. Ring, ring.

"Hello, this is Rat Mouth Rehab. How may I help you?"

"Wing two." I respond.

Ring, ring, ring. "Hello, this is Nurse Bumpkin, how may I help you?"

"I'm returning your call regarding a new admission."

"Oh good, doctor. I'd like you to verify orders on a new patient." She says demurely.

Must be just out of school I think to myself, she's not yet developed an attitude. Wait a minute, maybe she's just leading me on, going to pounce on my first misstep. Got to be careful with the one's you can't pigeon hole from the beginning. "Okay," I reply, "Name."

"John Bezoar, B . e . z . o . a . z."

"Social security number."

"1-954-555-5598".

"Are you sure? That not only seems like too many numbers but I recognize it as your facility's phone number as I just called it." Must stay calm, wife watching TV and can't disturb her. It's too late, she's turned my way, must have heard a little edge in my voice. Oh no, she's taking out her pad. Is this to egg me on or does she sense the inevitable. Well, I just have to control myself to frustrate her, but this nurse, in two sentences, has already got me primed.'

"Oh doctor, you're right, it is the facility's phone number. You've got to forgive me, I'm a new graduate and this is my first day on the job." She pleads.

"Alright, but let's try to be a little more careful. Try again, what's the social?" I'm all sweetness and light. Maybe she'll let her guard down so I can really zing her shortly.

"Okay, here it is: 555911411."

"What insurance?"

After a short pause she replies, "Managed care."

The tea kettle inside my head is starting to whistle ever so slightly. I can feel the pressure of the steam building up behind my ears. "Yes, I know it's managed care. They're all managed care, but which one?"

"Medicare?" she offers.

"No, Medicare is the only insurance that's not managed care. This time actually look at the chart and read it. Don't guess. It's in there somewhere."

A pregnant pause. She finally answers again, ever so hesitatingly, "I can't read it, can you help?"

"Of course, my dear. Hold the chart a little closer so I can read it better."

"How about now?" she offers.

"No, it's still too far and not clear."

"Well, how about now?"

"Nope, can't make it out either. Can you bring it any closer?"

"I can't, it's already touching the phone."

"Do you have it against the ear piece or the mouth piece?"

- "The ear piece."

"Ah, that's where you have it wrong. It needs to be against the mouth piece."

"Is that better?" she asks as she moves the chart lower. Her voice is somewhat muffled as the chart is now blocking direct sound to the mouth piece but she could hear me better as the ear piece is now unblocked.

"Oh yes, that's perfect. I see the social security number and insurance perfectly. Thank you my dear, you're a gem. By the way, would you be so kind to ask your supervisor over so I can tell her what a good nurse you are and how helpful you've been?"

"Yes, I'll get her right away and thanks for your patience and help."

"It was nothing, my dear, nothing at all." You have to remember that the typical nursing home's equipment was probably hand manufactured by Alexander Graham Bell himself. Video phones are just science fiction to them. I have a few moments to contemplate how I am going to play this. Do I ask that a pike be stuck up her butt and she be displayed on the nursing home's front lawn as a warning to the other nurses? Probably not. With the nursing shortage and all, they probably couldn't spare her. What's more, if I remember Calvin and Hobbes correctly, that would probably violate some sort of zoning code. How about if I ask for her to be exiled to the back hallways from which no nurse has ever emerged? That would satisfy me but the DON probably wouldn't go for that either. The only real option is to spread the news of the videophone that we just perfected. Maybe that would shame her into quitting but that'd be unlikely as shame has probably been banished from her in nursing school. It's becoming clear she'll be staying at this nursing home for the six months it took to qualify for her signup bonus after which she would be moving on anyway to collect her next signup bonus at the next nursing home. In the background I could hear her excitedly telling the supervisor how good she was about holding the chart up to the phone for me so I could read it personally and how pleased I was. A loud "Oh, my God" was audible even without the benefit of a phone.

The supervisor picked up the phone and before I could say a word my dilemma resolved itself. "Dr., I'm so sorry, please forgive us. We'll try to get you a better nurse in the future. It's her first week on the job and she has a lot to learn. Please let her live."

"Okay, bye." Click. Well, that was easy. I wonder if it's legal to keel haul a nurse if you're beyond the three mile limit?

My wife just looked at me in disbelief. She had just witnessed a first. I didn't yell or demand a vital organ from either the nurse or the administrator. She took my temperature but that was normal. I actually liked that part but I can never tell her as I'm sure she'd stop if she knew. I now buy rectal thermometers by the gross so we always have a fresh one handy. She used to put a mirror under my nose to see if I was still alive but she stopped that technique some time ago as not seeing my reflection was just too disconcerting for her.

My biggest dilemma now was deciding whether or not to call back as I hadn't actually verified any orders. What the heck, I'll let them call me back if they want as I already received three more beeps during the short while I was on the phone with them.

Next call in my beeper: Lyselle at Nuts to You Nursing Home, extension 150. I dial the number. Incredibly they answer on the eighth ring. "Hi." I say, as pleasantly as I possibly can, which I'm told is passably nice. "Extension 150."

"Hold on." The voice at the other end droned

The phone rings a few times and someone answers. "Hello, north wing."

"Are you Lyselle?" I ask, hope against hope that this might be a short and efficient call.

"No." the disembodied voice responds.

"Well, may I have her please?"

"Who?"

"The nurse I asked for."

"Who did you ask for?"

"The person you said you weren't."

"I wasn't paying attention. Who did you ask for?"

"If you weren't paying attention, how do you know it wasn't you?" I asked incredulously.

"I know it wasn't me. Who do you want?"

"What's your name? Maybe I want you."

"I don't give out my name over the phone."

"Well, how about just your first name so I can check and see if you aren't indeed the person I'm looking for."

"No."

"How about if I guess your name, would you tell me if I'm correct?"

"Maybe."

"Okay, let's give it a try. Is your name Lyselle?"

"No."

"Would you be so kind as to look for Lyselle then?"

"No. Stop bothering me and next time call the right extension for the person you want."

"What is Lyselle's exten…" Click.

Responding to my next beep, I get a nurse who speaks only Creole (although she says it's English): I have a patient.

I say: Great, why are you calling me?

She: Because I have a patient.

Me: I'm so glad that you are so happy about having a patient that you are obviously making random calls to announce it to the world.

She: But I am calling you to tell you that I have a patient.

Me: Yes, I understand you have a patient, but how do you think that makes me feel? You have a patient, are clearly gloating about it and I'm left out in the cold without a patient of my own. That's pretty cold of you to taunt me like this. I think I'm going to hang up and call my mother for comfort.

She: No, don't hang up; this is a patient for you.

Me: It is? For me? Are you saying that just because you feel guilty about making me so sad?

She: No, I call you to tell you I have a patient.

Me: There you go again. First you tell me that you have a patient, making me feel sad, then you tell me it's for me so I felt better ever so briefly and just when I felt I could safely take the gun away from my head, you snatch the patient from me like an evil Indian giver. What type of fiend are you? Oh, what's the use? I might as well end it all now. Goodbye, cruel world.

She: No, don't go, this patient is for you.

Me: No, it's too late, I've gone too far, I'm over the precipice and there's no putting the toothpaste back in the tube. (loud noise by hitting books on desk).

She: Oh my god!

Me: Ouch, I can't believe I missed so badly at so close a range. Look, I'm going to have to hang up the phone while I pick up the gun and reload. I seemed to have winged myself and I can't use my left arm anymore so I'll need my right hand for a little while.

She: No, don't go, I have a patient.

Me: All the more reason for me to finish the job. But okay, I won't hang up. How about if I just lay the phone on the desk so we can still talk if we shout so we can hear each other? (moderate clunk as I put down the phone) (I shout) can you hear me now?

She: A little bit.

Me: What? Talk louder.

She: I can barely hear you.

Me: Great. Now just wait a minute while I pull back the hammer with my teeth. (loud noise) Damn, let it slip and it shot out the left side of my cheek. Took a few teeth with it too. Sorry if I'm not able to talk so well anymore. You'll have to forgive me as I've forgiven you for living in a country where English is spoken by everyone but you. There, I've got it this time. Well, bye now, enjoy your patient. (loud noise). Damn, missed again. Look, I've just shot my other arm off. Could you have someone pop by and finish me off. I only have three bullets left and

I'm not sure that'll be enough to finish the job. Better have them bring a club just in case. Got to go now, the blood's dripping towards the electric plug and I don't want to get electrocuted. I'm told that's really painful. Bye again. (click.)

On to the next SNF. Ring, ring, ring, ring, ... I lost count after 12 but I'm sure it was up in the twenties by the time they finally answered. I didn't really care as I was spending my time usefully on the computer while listening on speaker phone.

They finally answered. "Hello, Manor of Death Care. How may I direct your call?" the receptionist intones pleasantly.

"I'd like the second floor nursing station please."

"Certainly." She replies.

Ring, ring, ring, ring ... This time I only count 15 rings before they answer. "First floor." the nurse announces.

"So this isn't the second floor like I asked for, is it?"

I must have seemed a little annoyed as her response was "Maybe when we get a building lift it will be, but for now the answer is no. Would you like the second floor?" she growled.

"Would I get it if I said 'yes'?" I replied.

"Maybe."

"Well, let's give it a try. Can you switch me to the second floor please?"

"No." Click.

Okay, they can call me back too. Next one. Ring, ring. An answering machine picks up on only the second ring. So far so good.

"You have reached the Rehab of South Florida. The world's best and most exclusive center for getting better. We as carefully screen our patient's financial statements as we do their pedigree. Rest assured, the person in the next bed won't be a homeless person with AIDS. If you know your party's extension, please dial it now. For 'Millionaires' Wing' press 1, for 'South Pacific Island Wing' press 2, for 'We Never Let Our Addicts Go Cold Turkey Wing' press 3. If you haven't heard your category, you've called the wrong number. Try the county flop house down the street and make sure you don't call us back again. Even if you do, you won't be able to get through as we'll have put caller block on your number by then."

I looked at my beeper. It said "call Nurse Paprika about patient Smythe. He has a malignant hang nail and his pedicurist is tied up on the other wing. What should they do?" No extension or wing name. Now I'm reduced to playing phone roulette. I'll have to dial numbers randomly and hope I hit the right one before they get annoyed and block my phone. I knew a doctor that happened to once. When he went there to make rounds the next day they had his car towed and the door interlock system caused the revolving doors to lock in mid revolution. All the patients and their grandchildren took turns farting and burping into his air supply until he passed out. He was found naked that night in the median of I-95 and arrested for indecent exposure. He's now the head doctor at the VA in Minot, North Dakota because they wouldn't let his type cross into Canada.

I press 1 and hold my breath. "Hello." the nurse answers.

"I'm looking for Nurse Paprika." I reply, somewhat cowed by the only institution that can have my citizenship revoked even though I'm a fifth generation, native born American.

"She's on the 'Cold Turkey Wing', you dip wod. Shape up or we'll see to it you never work anywhere ever again. And don't you think we can't unblock your feeble attempt at blocking caller ID with that ridiculous *67. You're in the computer, honey boy and we know where you live."

It was encouraging to know that in an emergency I could call there and have my location pinpointed precisely in seconds and not waste my time with 911. "Well thanks very much for the transfer, Nurse Crachett." I said, but only after I was placed on hold. I wonder if they could hear and record me even when I'm on hold. They're so good, maybe they can even read my thoughts over the phone. Not wanting to take any chances, I tried thinking like one of the nurses causing my mind to instantly go blank. Can't be too careful around these people. Note to self: never call here again. Send John the gimp and have him do his falling down act. Sue them into oblivion. Worked before, can't hurt to try again.

"Cold Turkey Wing. Here, you never have to do without. How may I help you?"

"I'm returning Nurse Paprika's call."

"This is Nurse Paprika. Who are you calling about?" she torted.

"Who did you call about?" I retorted.

"I called several doctors. Who are you?" she resnorted.

"I'm calling about Smythe. How many patients do you have?" I purported.

"Just one, but you can't be too careful with the privacy laws and all. I even have to get a consent form signed every time I wipe his ass." she cavorted.

"Ah ha! You said Smythe was a he! That's highly privileged information. If I let him catch wind of your indiscretion, it's curtains for you and your whole house of cards. Now let's see what you can do for me." I heehawted.

"P-p-please don't tell anyone, I'll do anything that you want." she pleaded.

Glenn Allen

As I ran out of rhyming nonsensical words, I felt this episode drawing to a close. "I really don't want anything except for you to leave me alone and don't call me again for a week. If Smythe wants something, just follow your corporate bylaws and charge him cash according to the fee schedule, escalating based on recency of banning by the FDA." Click. I won! That was always my toughest home. Boy, do they play rough and for keeps.

Another five beeps. This is really getting old. I looked at the numbers, deleted all but the one I liked the best then turned off the beeper as I had enough for the night. The nurses will just have to either figure it out themselves or call the medical director at two AM to confirm the orders. That's what he's getting paid for anyway.

I next called back the SNF I deigned worthy of receiving my call. It wasn't really my favorite so much as it was the least worst of those that had beeped. Ring, ring, ring, ring … Twenty eight rings. A new record! Actually, the record potentially was a lot more but I usually hang up at twenty five as I just couldn't take it anymore. I was feeling charitable tonight so I just let it ring. The truth was I was in a really tense session of internet Doom and forgot that the phone was actually ringing until the voice on the speaker phone startled me. I thought at first that the enemy had outflanked me and was relieved to realize it was the maniacal voice of the charge nurse and not one of the demons in the game. I put the game on hold and addressed the nurse: "28 rings. That's got to be a record for you too. Did I wake you from sleep or were you just gouging yourself on some poor patient's food?"

"Up yours. That's my business anyway. What do you want disturbing me like this?"

She really should try out not so much as a voice but as a sound effect for Doom. If I could just record her while we're on the phone, I'm positive I could cow some of the other players into submission.

"I'm returning your call."

"On who?"

"How many did you call about?"

"Just one but I want to make sure we're talking about the same piece of fetid meat." She said affectionately about her favorite patient. She wasn't usually that complimentary.

"Oh, I'm sure we are. By the way, how are all the rest of Satan's spawn? Have any family reunions recently? I understand you're having a field day in Iraq."

"I'm really looking forward to harming your new car." she said longingly.

"Revenge doesn't become you, at least not until you move to a new city with a name not pronounceable in English. So, what do you want?"

"Mr. Peabrain needs something for his shaking and his blood sugar is low."

"How low?" I asked with some trepidation.

"Twenty." she answered with great disinterest. Probably wanted to get back to stealing office supplies.

Whoops. "How long has he been shaking?"

"About 45 minutes." she replied with a 'Come on, get on with it, I've got things to do' style yawn.

"When did you check his sugar?" I asked, crossing my fingers.

"About ten minutes ago."

Yes! He's been seizing with hypoglycemia for almost an hour! Brain sizzled to a crisp. Can transfer him to the hospital and save myself a trip to the facility until they get another admission as he's my only patient there currently. "Tell you what you do, my dear. Call both the morgue and rescue and whoever gets there first can have him."

"What happens if he's still shaking and the morgue people show up first? The last time this happened they refused to take him because he was shaking so bad they couldn't get him in the bag."

"Take them aside, give them a few cups of coffee and see what happens. Whatever you do, don't let any sugar sprinkle onto him or it may raise his sugar enough to stop the seizures. Better yet, just use artificial sugar so we won't have to risk it. By the way, when is his next dose of insulin due?"

"In about an hour."

"Tell you what, give it to him now to make sure he doesn't miss it if he's in transit when it's due. Don't want to take any chances."

"I'm way ahead of you," the nurse replies gleefully. I've been having my student nurses practicing their injections techniques for the past half hour. I figure if they could hit him, they could hit anyone. Only one nurse stuck herself and she started shaking about 15 minutes ago."

"Great, if the morgue doesn't take Mr. Peabrain, it won't be a totally wasted trip as they can haul off your student nurse. It would be a pity though if they couldn't take them both. A waste of taxpayer's money for them to have bought that extra wide cab just to service your home and then leave almost empty handed. Why don't you look around and see if anyone else is imminent. If so, just have them wait around a little longer. Anything less than three at a time from your place is a downer for them. Well, let me know how things go. Call back in the morning. Bye." I turned off my beeper and thought to myself, "That was easy. Now I can get back to uninterrupted DOOM."

Chapter 40:
Out of the pattern

I needed to get some night currency work in so I went out to the field where I keep my plane. Boca's a relatively quite, single runway field and is usually user friendly.

It had been miserable all day and continued on as a drizzly night. The clouds had lifted just enough to make it VFR (visual flight rules) but every once in awhile a low cloud would inch by. At those times the drizzle became rain and the preflight took back seat to finding a dry refuge. Finally, ready to go, I taxied out on the ramp, made the call to ground and proceeded on to the run up area.

All systems go, called the tower. "Uh, Boca Tower, this is 3527 whiskey, number one runway 5."

"3527 whiskey, you have ground, switch to the tower, 118.425."

Oops. "Boca tower, this is 3527 whiskey, number one, runway 5."

"3527 whiskey, say intentions."

I recognized his voice, it was the same one for ground! The same one for ground made me switch to tower, what a jerk. I'll show him. "Intentions."

"Uh, 3527 whiskey, did you plan to do any flying tonight? Because you might become disappointed real soon."

"Boca tower, this is 3527 whiskey. I might have misspoken. I had hoped to do three stop and goes to update my night currency."

"3527 whiskey, you can't do stop and goes here. You'll need to taxi back to the end and get clearance again. You're cleared for takeoff, left turns."

What a stickler! There's no one around and he's going to make me taxi back. "3527 whiskey, cleared for takeoff, runway 5".

Take off was routine but the clouds were in the way at pattern altitude and I lost sight of the field intermittently. What the hell, I'm in MVFR (my visual flight rules) and I say I'm okay. If it's good enough for my instructors, it's good enough for me. Anyway, they have me on radar and they'll just have to keep planes away from me.

"3527 whiskey, you need to extend crosswind for incoming traffic. I'll call your downwind."

"Okay, you'll call my downwind 3527 whiskey." Now he wants to send me to Pahokee. Moron.

Minutes later, he finally calls, "3527 whiskey, multiple planes landing, turn downwind and I'll call your base."

"Hokey dokey, big eye in the sky."

"Uh, 3527 whiskey, did you copy?"

"3527 whiskey, you'll call my base."

The clouds were a little thicker then even MVFR allowed for, but, hey, they've got radar and they're calling the shots. I just wished that my attitude indicator would stop spinning, it was making me dizzy. Fortunately, I only included it in my scan incidentally as I was really most interested in the Hobbes meter, the instrument that determined the time in flight and thus the cost of this trip.

"3527 whiskey, turn base now."

Well it's about time, what'd you do, forget about me? "3527 whiskey, turning base." Lo and behold, there are the runway lights, maybe this guy knows what he's doing.

"Boca tower, this is 3527 whiskey, runway in sight, would like to be cleared to land."

"Hold on 3527 whiskey, I don't have a visual on you yet."

"Boca tower, I'm practically over the threshold, request permission to land."

"3527 whiskey, still don't have you but if you see the threshold, cleared to land."

"3527 whiskey, cleared to land." The landing was picture perfect and I started to turn to the taxiway. It might have been the fog or just the darkness of night but I didn't remember a Hotel taxiway. Didn't matter, turned onto it and called ground."

"Boca ground, this is 3527 whiskey. Request permission to taxi back to runway five."

"3527 whiskey, permission denied. Try contacting ground on 121.9."

Even for Boca and this idiot of a controller, that was a strange request as ground was 121.8. "Boca ground, this is 3527 whiskey, I'm just a little confused. Here I am talking to you yet you want me to change to a different frequency. If you don't mind my saying so, that doesn't make any sense."

"3527 whiskey, unable to help. Have a nice night. G'bye."

Staring dumbfounded at the mic didn't seem to help so I switched to 121.9. "Boca ground, this is 3527 whiskey at Hotel. Would like to taxiback to 5 for another stop and go."

"3527 whiskey, we've been waiting for you. Stay where you are. Fort Lauderdale Executive ground, out."

I guess that explains all the blue lights that seemed to be moving towards me. I was sort of surprised at taxiway lights that rotated and moved. Taking out my cell phone, I called home. "Do you have the bail money ready? No, the Broward County Jail, not Palm Beach this time …"

"Sir, put your hands where we can see them and step out of the plane!"

"…Gotta go. Bye."

Chapter 41: Respiratory Therapy (Or: You Have a Great Looking Pair of Lungs)

Every SNF has their share of really sick patients. Those, who by all rights, should have been dead long ago. Unfortunately, we doctors try to play God and interfere with the natural course of things. We keep people alive artificially, with no reason for doing so other than we can. After a while, we've kept them alive for so long that they start to rot as their organs start to shut down, one by one. You can easily tell when it's been too long when they start to smell like they've been left out of the fridge for a few days too long.

One of the prime instruments of our unnatural acts is the respiratory therapist ("RT"). The RT is charged with making sure the lungs continue to breathe, even though everything else has shut down. Their role model is the pacemaker. The pacer doesn't know whether a patient is dead or alive, all it knows is that the heart didn't beat in the last second so its job is to make it do so. The pacer therefore will put out an electrical impulse every second forever, or at least until its battery runs down. It's not unusual for a body to be exhumed years later and the coroner finds the pacer is still working. That's what the RT's professional credo is: first in and last out, we never stop working. I'm convinced it's just their professional society's way to insure full employment for the worldwide glut of RT's.

The RT's are licensed and empowered to be far more hands on and engaged in active intervention and invasive procedures than just about any other health care personnel other than doctors. They can intubate a patient in the throes of death, change tracheostomy tubes, administer all sorts of inhaled medicines and change the settings on ventilators and do so virtually unmonitored. In their hands lies what quite frequently is the power to administer, quite literally, the last breath of the patient in their charge. A whim or a askance remark will influence whether or not the patient gets to see the sun rise again or have their eternal spark snuffed out. Usually, the patients, if conscious, realize how dependent they are on maintaining the good will of the RT. It's most commonly the family who feels they can tread all over the RT with absolute impunity without concern for consequences. They haven't figured out it is unwise to antagonize the person with their finger on the trigger of a gun pointed at them.

I, on the other hand, have figured out how important it is to have the RT on my side. With just the vaguest of hints, I can have three months of an unsatisfactory doctor patient relationship resolved overnight without the slightest indication to outside observers that more than nature had just taken its course. A smile always crosses my face when a disagreeable patient is tagged, bagged and dragged out of the building feet first.

The RT's also regularly have their way with their patients. I remember walking in to a patient named Sam Johnson's room one day and saw the RT, named Nellie, kneeling on the bed, straddling her legs on either side of his chest. She had her shirt undone and she was doing a shimmy with her ample breasts in his face. Mr. Johnson, it turns out, had really upset Nellie and she was taking advantage of his critical coronary artery disease, recent heart attack and severe heart failure to stimulate him into an untimely demise. It was indeed working. The telemetry monitor was showing ventricular tachycardia although Nellie had muted the alarm so all appeared normal to any passerby.

I blurted out "Whoa, Nellie!" I couldn't help myself, it was the best I could think of on the spot in what was clearly an emergency situation. I panicked and knew I'd pay for it later. "What in God's name are you doing?"

Nellie didn't miss a beat. "I'm saving your hide." She called back breathlessly. "Mr. Johnson here was writing a memo to his lawyer to sue you and everyone else, so I decided to help you out." Her shimmying was starting to even get my attention. I unconsciously moved to stand in front of the telemetry monitor to prevent any unwarranted distraction. It's not every day that you get to admire a coworker's efforts up close.

"I'm getting a little tired and Mr. Johnson has stopped moaning. Would you mind stepping back from the monitor so I can see if I can stop?"

As she turned directly towards me, all I could think of was 'Whoa Nellie!' again.

Stumbling over the cord, I deftly managed to disconnect the telemetry monitor. Dusting myself off and looking as suave as I could, I managed to unplug the light and trip on the call bell before I restarted the monitor.

A nurse came running in at the call bell, saw the situation and turned around, yelling, "It's all right, it's just Nellie administering last rites to Mr. Johnson, and the doctor, well, he's just being a guy. Call off the code." Turning towards me, she said "Next time get a room." Glancing at the straight line on the monitor, she added "Actually, it looks like you have one now."

Blushing quite brightly, I looked at Nellie, then the monitor, then again at Nellie and said "I guess we're done here." as I backed out of the room. "And thank you." I offered as a last gesture of a grateful nation.

"Bug off twerp! Next time have the decency to buy a ticket, like all the rest."

In a quiet moment a few days later, I was able to sit down with Nellie and just talk to her. "I really do appreciate what you did for me with Mr. Johnson. I'm just curious, why and for how long have you been doing this with patients?"

Nellie thought about it for a while. "I guess it all started back in training. I was just a student and they had me bag my first patient. I fumbled putting the bag onto the tube, got my finger caught for a moment in between them while I was attaching the setup. The patient kept getting worse and worse and no matter how hard I tried, I couldn't seem to squeeze the air out of the bag sufficiently. Finally they called the code. As I was cleaning up, I noticed that the band aide I had on my finger was missing. It was then that it dawned on me that the problems I was having during the code occurred because my band aide had fallen into the tube and all I was doing was pushing it further and further down into his lungs the harder I squeezed. I guess I've just been trying to capture the same thrill ever since. Now, you're not going to tell anyone are you? Because if you do, you wife will be getting a call from a certain sex kitten asking if her little snooky-poo can come out and play."

"I think we understand each other well enough that we can rest assured our secrets are safe with each other." I assured her quite sincerely. Note to self: contact hospice re special job.

"Okay then. I'll be seeing you." She cooed. 'I wonder if Vinny and Guido are in town. I might have a little job for them' she thought to herself as she smiled at me while looking deep into my eyes.

'Forget hospice, I hear Vinny and Guido are in town. I might need them real soon.' I ruminated to myself as I stared deeply down her blouse.

Turning back, Nellie added, "By the way, that was masterful what you did with Mr. Brown." 'Oh my god, I've got to call Vinny and Guido right now!' she startled herself into realizing, her pupils dilating widely in the process.

'Oh my god, I've got to call Vinny and Guido stat!' I jumped up in my chair in a full fight or flight response. "Why thank you. I appreciate that coming from a true expert." I answered back as I was punching in #1 on my speed dial. 'Damn, it's busy.' I said to myself as I glanced over at Nellie in heated conversation on her cell phone 'This is not good.'

Things lightened up quickly as I saw Nellie hang up, glance in my direction and then speed for the emergency exit. "Alright, having Vinny and Guido on retainer is turning out to be worth the expense. Bye Nellie, nice knowing you. Be reading about you soon.' I hope it's not hard to train a new RT. Good ones are hard to find.

Chapter 42: Ripples in the Pond

In the aftermath of the great Chicago fire, the remaining big players in the trial attorney's guild held a conference call and arranged for an emergency meeting to be held in New York in two weeks. The editorials overwhelmingly expressed outrage that some madman could commit such a heinous mass murder. The right to redress grievances was firmly entrenched in the founding of this nation and attempts to stifle that right shall not be tolerated. There was a smattering of sentiment though, usually tucked safely away towards the end of the vitriolic diatribe against the senseless murders that allowed for just a smidgeon of doubt that maybe the trial bar had gone a touch too far. An understandable, if not actually justifiable, rage might have been engendered by what might be perceived by some as the Bar's excesses. Nevertheless, those types of thoughts could never justify the carnage. Yet, perhaps, there should be a look at the laws that allowed for the above mentioned unjustifiable rage to develop and certain revisions in the worst of the laws might not be unreasonable.

As one could imagine, even the slightest suggestion that the Bar brought this on themselves was outrageous and was totally unacceptable in the extreme. A flurry of lawsuits were threatened and some even filed against those newspapers that had allowed that seditious rhetoric to be published. In solidarity with their legal brethren, a few judges even allowed the cases to proceed despite the first amendment rights of the newspapers to absolute freedom of speech. A Justice Department inquiry was opened into possible criminal activity of the newspapers for such clearly inflammatory writing possibly leading to the aide and comfort of criminals. One just didn't want to get in the way of the trial attorneys.

Somewhat unnoticed was the smattering of advertisements in the Wall Street Journal for legal practices for sale. Advertisements for lawyers to join firms also took a slight up tick.

Chapter 43: Let's Get This Done

I put down the paper, turned to Sandy and Bulldog and said, "Okay, here's our next big opportunity, but we have to work fast. There's going to be another big meeting of what's left of the leadership and we need to get them. The cracks in the establishment supporting them are starting to show. Just read some of the editorials from the more conservative papers calling for a fresh look at our civil liability laws. Here's one stating that our 'national productivity has long been hampered by the constant barrage of lawsuits, driving our businesses and jobs overseas, threatening our entire economy and our way of life.' Hell, our way of life has been the constant fear of suits for decades now. Another one says 'The US has 5% of the world's population and 90% of the lawyers. Maybe we're out of whack here.' We won't win in the media but it doesn't hurt to have some public opinion on our side."

Bulldog, reading from the Times, "And I quote 'The perpetrators of this heinous crime should be taken to a public square, saturated in gasoline and immolated on national television for all to see as a deterrent for anyone else that might want to harm our legal system.' I wonder when the prohibitions against cruel and unusual punishment, not to mention summary, extra judicial executions were waived when their ox was gored."

"When money's at stake, the trial attorneys know how to protect their own." Sandy chimed in.

"I have a plan that'll be relatively low risk but we need a little info first. Obviously security's going to be so tight a fart couldn't leak out. So we have to be invited in. They're going to need food so we need to find out who's going to cater…"

"We're going to poison them!" Bulldog broke in.

"Exactly! However, we won't use a fast acting poison so they'll be on our tail immediately but something more befitting the vile stain they've left on this earth. We're going to use a chemotherapeutic agent, Adriamycin. It's a red liquid so it will make a great looking punch. Mixed with liquor, you won't even know it's there. We can make it concentrated enough that even a four ounce drink will do you in."

Sandy, looking a little befuddled as the only nonmedically trained member of our group, asked "What does this stuff do and why won't it be traced back to us?"

"Normally it is used to kill cancer cells, but after taking a certain amount it causes intractable heart failure. The heart failure doesn't come on suddenly though, it might take weeks to months, long after the meeting so it'll take a while for investigators to put it together. In the meantime, they'll be dying off right and left in a slow and excruciatingly painful manner. The only possible cure would be a heart transplant which is almost as bad as the disease itself and will bankrupt all but the richest of them. Hopefully, their HMO's will deny coverage altogether citing self inflicted wounds or self destructive behavior leading to their own problems. I've got here that leading terrorist manual, the PDR. Let's see, page 2198, Adriamycin. Okay, it says 50% of people receiving 550 milligrams per meter squared (mg/m^2) of body surface area will get heart failure and 100% receiving $1\ gm/m^2$ will do so. We'll need to do a few calculations on the terrorist's best friend, a pocket calculator. Let's assume the average fat ass trial attorney's surface area is 1.5 meters square. Using the $1\ gm/m^2$ figure we'll then need 1.5 grams to be sure that'll do 'em in. The average drink is 4 ounces and there's 28 milliliters or ml per ounce, so that makes the average drink 112 ml. Therefore we need 1.5 gm of Adriamycin in 112 ml. If the punch bowl holds 2 gallons which is 8.8 liters, we take 8.8 liters divided by 112 ml and you get 78 drinks times 1.5 gm which finally equals 117 grams of Adriamycin needed for each complete filling of the punch bowl. Let's say we fill the bowl twice so we'll need 234 grams. I'll find out what that costs and buy me some right away. Next, as a show of solidarity with our legal brethren, we need to find a caterer to offer to donate the punch to the gathering. Being the blood sucking, cheapskate bastards that they are with a sense of entitlement exceeded only by the welfare leeches that abound in our society today, they couldn't possibly turn down free food, let alone free booze, now could they. Just to make sure that we get them all, we'll throw in free Hawaiian Punch, you know the red stuff, laced with our special addition, to take care of the teetotalers, if there are any. Any questions?"

Sandy still looking a little unclear, "Why don't we blow them up, burn them, shoot them? Why do we let them linger?"

"Exactly."

"Exactly? Oh, you mean you want them to linger?"

"This time, yes. We've knocked them off in a variety of ways but always quickly. We now want them to suffer, loudly and publicly. They may present sympathetic figures in their death throes but they also represent one of the horrors of living – a long, slow agonizing death due to an incurable condition. The message won't be lost on those who try to carry on. We can kill you, or, worse yet, we can let you live. This should be the beginning of the end for the trial attorney's bar. Once they get the message, our demands will be taken seriously. We can fine tune the results we're hoping for: the end of all the senseless lawsuits with their lottery mentality and no consequences for their pursuit. Also, I think we'll throw in that the criminal defense lawyers are next when they defend the indefensible. Basically, we're asking that the lawyers try the case first in their mind and only if there's a clear and legitimate case should they pursue it. If not, the lawyer and their client will both be held responsible. I think most people will like it."

"I know I do." Chimed in both Sandy and Bulldog almost simultaneously.

"Great. Okay, Bulldog, with your gift of gab, get to work on the catering angle. Sandy, find out when and where the meeting will be and who do we contact to make the offer of the donation. I'll get the drugs. We have two weeks to get this done. See you back in a week."

Chapter 44:
The Last of the Worst

Finding a caterer was no problem for Sandy, he was a known gourmand and threw a few parties in his time. Any of several were willing to pitch in, thinking it their civic duty to do so. Also, having the plaintiff's bar on your side couldn't hurt when the inevitable ptomaine cases arose. They didn't see the irony that those cases arose with alarming regularity and that the constantly rising cost of liability insurance was slowly driving them out of business. Sandy found so many that were willing to donate that he actually was able to put together a package to cater the entire meeting for free. The attorneys definitely couldn't turn that down. At the same time it diluted the attention that would be paid to any one source of poisoning. Just hope they all had their liability premiums paid up because with joint and several liability, the estates will be hot on their trail. That is to say, even though only one of the caterers would be at fault, and even then unwittingly, because the cause of the poisoning could never be found, they'd all be held liable. Maybe if that little nuance was fully explained during the trial, the public would finally wake up to the fact that they were being subjugated by the attorneys. Nah. They'll never figure it out.

All Bulldog had to do was read the paper and surf the net. All the info he needed was in the public domain.

I contacted several wholesalers, using a few false names and ID's I picked up over the years, and I got all the Adriamycin I needed.

Since things were falling into place so easily, we just spoke on a conference call, being careful to use the code words we agreed to the week before and finalized our plans to meet in New York next week.

There were thousands of members of the Trial Attorneys guild and various hangers on and peripheral players left but only the top 250 were invited to the meeting. The Waldorf hosted them, clearing out the top two floors of other guests to allow for better security. The Waldorf, not wanting to pay for the whole shindig exclusively, quickly agreed to the other caterers' offers to help out. Big error, Waldorf, see you in court.

John Jamison, the acting president of the Guild was one of the first to arrive. He drove up to the covered entrance in a white limo, flanked by two plain black cars. The black cars discharged their passengers first, four large, well armed and well trained guards in each. They professionally surveyed the canopied area. Satisfied that all was well, four went inside to look for anything untoward. The other four formed a human wall around Jamison and escorted him in as they got the nod from one of the others already inside.

Mr. Reilly, he only went by the last name, always proceeded by 'Mr.', was in charge. "Mr. Jamison, follow close to me, don't look around, don't move outside of our box."

Even if Jamison was inclined to do otherwise, he couldn't have broken out of the box with half a dozen of his attorney friends. He felt he had chosen the security agency well and felt a modicum of comfort in their presence. And if something went wrong, fuck 'em! His estate will add a security agency to its portfolio. Jamison had built up a small empire of companies he had bankrupted and taken over as judgment satisfaction. Jamison felt himself more than lucky, he felt chosen. The minor illness that prevented him from attending the convention in Chicago was quite a stroke of luck. It spared him from the same fate of so many of his colleagues which he considered as another but inevitable step in his preordained rise to the top of the Guild's leadership. The ascendancy to President of the Guild would greatly enhance his prestige and allow him to demand even more outrageous fees from his clients. He was next in line for the president's job in the Guild anyway. There were a few challengers, some of whom were actually calling for reform, but they were all gone now leaving the road directly opened for his coronation. This meeting would confirm what all already knew and he'll press on with new authority to make sure the government changed no laws to jeopardize his money making machine. Better yet, they'd find the perpetrators and it would turn out they were some anarchist group calling for the overthrow of the government. The country and government would have to support the Guild unquestioningly then as they faced a mutual and deadly enemy.

"Clear, one." Whispered Mr. Jones in his communicator from the elevator and another clear came from three. No name, just a number. He really wanted to stay low key. Being high visibility in this field did not equate to longevity, so everyone tried to blend in to the background. With most of the agents being over six feet tall and over 200 pounds, that took some doing. Only the best survived long enough to be well paid for their efforts and this crew was well paid.

Once safely ensconced on the top two floors, most of the delegates would be able to rest and do the work they came to do – reestablish the hierarchy of the Guild and press their demands for action and protection to the Federal government. A separate working group was assigned to draw up the lawsuit to ensure that they got their way. The more aggressive of the lawyers were demanding four full time Secret Service agents, the same agency that protected the President of the United States, for each member of the Guild, but cooler heads prevailed and reduced the number to only two. Woe be to them that tried to block this demand, they'd be tied up in court until their grandchildren's wedding if they didn't comply. "Nobody messes with a trial attorney" was their secret motto, "and lives to enjoy their wealth" was the second, never spoken part.

The rest of the delegates arrived within a few hours and they were able to sit down for the first of their free catered meals as a group for supper at 6 PM. Tony and his famous ribs was first up. A spectacular crystal fountain with five swans spewing an enchanting red nectar of the gods emanating over the three tiered bowl looked almost too good to drink. But the extra salt we made sure was cooked in the ribs made thirst an undeniable urge and imbibe they did. A second filling of the fountain was necessary with Sandy being happy to oblige. The regular man had gotten a sudden illness that could only be cured by an evening at the track with his new found stash. Sandy, being the standup fellow that he was, was glad to step in and help out his caterer friend. After all, it was he who set this whole thing up and he couldn't let them down. Using the vials I had given him, Sandy carefully measured out the right proportions and refilled the fountains with great alacrity. He was having the time of his life, knowing he was helping bring about the end of the last of the worst people on earth.

Chapter 45: Friday Rounds With Mandy and Reggie

Friday, finally, I sighed resignedly to myself. It's been a tough week. I was getting a little slap happy. I needed a boost to get me through this last day until I could recharge my batteries over the weekend. How could I ever achieve a sustainable lifestyle with all the sniping from all sides in a relentless assault on my psyche? It was like a thousand Chihuahuas nipping at my heels. I couldn't take a step without someone else wanting a piece of me.

"Doctor!" an insistent voice from the rear called to me.

Now what? It was only 9 AM and I was already quite irritable. "What?" I said a little too harshly as I noticed the administrator, Imeverso Winey, hurrying to catch up to me which he had to do at almost a full run to overcome my New York Olympic walk.

"I'd like to ask you about Mr. Hank Eron." He said.

Hank Eron had been there for three weeks already and was quite a pain in my side. I hated patients who lingered. I hadn't been able to get rid of him yet as physical therapy said he still had 'potential'. 'Potential' is all he had and he must be saving it up for some future burst of activity as he hadn't used any of it up in actual performance. He remained bedridden except when four people manhandled his lard butt into a wheelchair. Once there, one of them had to dedicate his life to him by standing right next to him at all times to hold him up lest he fall forward and break his nose again. Strokes are a terrible thing for a mind, but once you had one, you can never go home again. His estate is still thinking of suing, but so far, a slightly bent nose in his 96 year old craggy facial features is actually an improvement in his looks. They're waiting to see if he has any complications so they can sue for real money. So far he's hanging on and his heirs are getting a little ansy to get on with it. They hunger for the good life bought at his expense and paid for by the hapless nursing home for having the misfortune of admitting a hopeless patient at the end of life. Still, if he were just to fall again and break something important, or better yet, develop a bed sore on the tip of his nose, they could be in for real money. He was now able to be held up by only one person instead of two so physical therapy recorded that as progress. They held out for another month of observation to see whether or not a small Philippino aide could be assigned to hold him freeing up the one they call Gorilla who was currently assigned to hold him. "What would you like to discuss about Hank Eron?" I asked Mr. Winey, knowing full well he wanted me to rescind the discharge order I had just written. They were desperate for patients and even coveted Mr. Eron for the extra thousand bucks his continued stay would bring in now, even if it cost him a million bucks in a few years when the suit was settled. Mr. Winey knew he wouldn't be here in a few years so he didn't really care what happened then, it was too far in the future to try to contemplate. All he wanted was to bring in the quarter in the black so he could hold on to the tenuous thread that kept the CEO from kicking his ass to the road and bringing in the next hapless administrator, who just so happened to be the CEO's brother-in-law.

"I was wondering if you wouldn't consider giving him some more time. I'm told he's making good progress and I'm sure the family will appeal if you discharge him now when physical therapy is reporting such good progress and great potential."

Of course they're going to appeal. The facility wrote the handbook on how to appeal and it was given to each family upon arrival along with a complimentary one hour inservice on the appeals process. All of this occurred during a catered evening meal at a local two star restaurant, secretly bankrolled by the local nursing home association for all patients' families, followed up by a 15 minute daily reminder by the social worker to every visitor to the facility. An appeal was inevitable, so I just discounted that argument in my discussions with any nursing home personnel.

"And what progress might that be?" I asked incredulously at his bald faced lies and gross exaggerations. "Are the nurses not having to empty his drool bucket quite so often? Is Gorilla now able to hold him up for fifteen full minutes before his arms give out? Has the bleeding slowed down from his nose?" I noticed a perceptible twitch of Winey's right eye lid which always tipped me off that I hit on the answer Mr. Winey was most afraid of me discovering. "So, it's the reduced bleeding, isn't it?" I asked as Winey reached for his eyelid when the spasms became unbearable, shaking his entire head. "Well let me tell you why the bleeding has slowed down. It's not that his nose is healing. It'll never heal as long as his sniveling little rat fink relatives are around because all they do all day long is pick it so it'll keep bleeding so they'll be able to get a larger settlement from their suit. It's slowing down because he's running out of blood and he's becoming anemic. He's not eating and he's becoming dehydrated. I estimate he's got another two days to live if those loving relatives of his keep up their 24 hours nose picking ritual. And then I'll be rid of him and the family can finally file their suit. I'm discharging him just in case their boney little fingers get tired or worse yet, they realize that the longer he lives, the larger the settlement might be and they stop their nefarious acts and try to make him live. So to preclude the possibility that he lives and lingers more, I'm discharging him to custodial care and you can keep him alive for as long as you want. I don't want him to go away mad, I just want him to go away." Actually, that sentiment applied as much to Mr. Winey as it did for Mr. Eron.

"I know how you feel about giving your patients a fair shake, but I wish you'd just keep a few around so we can make a few bucks more. My job depends upon it. Maybe I could make it worth your while."

Now he's talking my language. "What do you mean worthwhile?" I asked him with a half cocked head and a squinty eye that worked so well for Clint Eastwood.

"I mean maybe we could come to some arrangement whereby we both could benefit."

"You already said that. Could you be any more evasive?" I loved the part where the cat holds the mouse by the tail and sort of tweaks it with his sharpened claw. Not so much to hurt the mouse but as to watch the pendulum effect as the mouse twirls around upside down from its tail, swinging nearer and farther from the cat's terrifying teeth as the cat watches on with amusement while it's gastric juices were gearing up for a little snack.

Mr. Winey looked around to see who might be listening. It would have been have easier to count who wasn't as all activity stopped in the nursing station where we were having this discussion, as if E. F. Hutton himself was there about to give an insider tip to whoever was lucky enough to be within earshot. "Um, how about we talk in my office when you have a minute?"

"Sure, see you later." I had to decide what to do next. The issue before me was similar to that purportedly posed by Winston Churchill to an annoying lady at a dinner party. Apparently, Mr. Churchill went up to this lady and asked her if she would go to bed with him for a million dollars. She allegedly responded, after thinking about it for while, that she would. Mr. Churchill reportedly then asked if she would consider ten dollars at which point she drew back and asked in righteous indignation, "What sort of woman do you think I am?" To which Churchill replied "We've already established that, now we're just haggling over price." Had I already established what I was in even entertaining his apparent proposition? Even worse, had I previously established that years ago when I joined the HMO? In any case, what should I do now? Everyone could always use a few extra bucks, assuming that's what he had in mind. Was what he had in mind worth my while though? I was a doctor and made a doctor's salary. He was a nursing home administrator. What might seem like a large amount to him might be chump change to me. I'll have to think about whether or not I'm interested before I decide whether or not to see him. I really liked tormenting my patients and their families a lot. It was a feeling anything less than an outrageous sum of money couldn't buy, and I doubted he had that kind of money. Maybe if he threw in the director of nurses as a love slave to sweeten the deal. We'll see.

All the while that we were standing in the nursing station discussing the pros and cons of Medicare fraud, there was an insistent ringing in the background. I couldn't quite place it so I turned to Madme, the charge nurse, and asked "What's that ringing? Is the ice cream truck in room 203?"

She got a little chuckle out of that, but said "No. That's the new call bell system. All of the electric ones are broken so we gave each patient a little bell to ring. You know, like they have at service departments so you can get the attendant's attention."

"Okay, well she's got mine. She's been ringing for ten minutes already. Isn't anyone going to answer it?"

"Oh yes. I'll have an aide take care of it now. Oh, Wilma, will you please see what 203 wants?" Madme asked.

As I worked on the chart I kept glancing to 203. I wondered aloud "Is that 203 by the door or by the window? Do you think the aide will be able to figure it out merely by the ringing noise? God help us if they're both ringing. What will she do next?"

Madme leaned over and said "Don't be so harsh on the aides, they do their best."

I replied more alarmed than ever as it was several minutes since Madme directed the aide to 203 and the ringing persisted. "Oh my God! What if she can't find 203 in time?" I exaggeratedly relaxed and continued "I guess the ringing will just stop if the aide is too late." But alarm returned to my demeanor "But what happens if the roommate takes up the cause in sympathy and in remembrance of her lost roommate. Will the ringing never stop?"

"Please don't worry, we'll take care of it. Wilma, where are you? Go to 203 and find out what she wants!"

Wilma seemed to be doing a moon walk to the employee's lounge. This might take longer than I feared. Drastic measures were called for. I uttered the words every nurse dreads to hear "Why don't you go in and see?" I asked both naively and as a provocateur.

All activity stopped again in the nursing station, although sometimes you need time lapse photography to see any movement at all in the most active of times. They all stared at me like deer caught in headlights. Had I the temerity to ask that the 'Code' be violated: No self respecting nurse shall engage in any hands on patient care. That's why they invented aides! As quickly as it started, there was an apparent collective realization of the absurdity of my suggestion and they all passed it off as a bad joke.

Ring, Ring, Ring, Ring, Ring, Ring.

This was getting old. I reviewed my options. Looking around, I noticed that the aides were on eternal break. The charge nurse was still in tears about my crude request. The rest of the nursing staff were huddled in a corner trying to decide if I had gone too far and whether or not now was the time to unionize to prevent any possibility that my suggestion might be taken seriously by the administration. In the meantime, half the janitorial staff was keying my car in a sympathy action while the other half emptied the bed pans into an open window. It wasn't so much open as broken by one of their mop handles which was left sticking out of the windshield like a pin in a voodoo doll as a warning against such outrageous behavior in the future.

It was time for cunning and swift action. I stood up, leaned over the desk and called into 203. "What do you want?" I yelled. The staff stood there in stunned silence again. The nurses started furiously to write out slogans on their picket signs. I was an interloper sticking my nose into their business. If they wanted to know what the patient wanted they would ask and lord knows, they weren't about to ask.

"I've been on the bedpan for half an hour!" the voice yelled back. "I want off!"

Not an entirely unreasonable request I mumbled to myself. On the other hand, if she was going to rely on me to help, she'd drown in her own dung before that happened. I had to think. "Ah ha!" I said, turning to Madme. "You've seen that Mission Impossible episode where they put foam in the alarm so when they cut the wires, it wouldn't ring? Well, let's try shooting some whipped cream in there right now." I figured that would hold her until I could finish my charting and could leave.

"No can do." Explained Madme. "It's against health department regulations to have food in the patient's rooms. Might attract ants and vermin." She said reasonably.

"Well, that certainly takes the mystery out of what they call institutional 'food'." I replied.

Madme caught on slowly, but she did catch on and started to glare at me. To try to sooth her feelings, I came up with another suggestion. "How about we tie a string to her forefinger and run it through a pulley in the ceiling and attach the other end to the bell? That way, every time she reaches for the bell, it would pull the string and lift the bell just out of her reach. This would serve the dual purpose of silencing that annoying noise and helping her with her physical therapy program as she tries harder and harder to reach the bell. A perfect plan if you ask me!"

Ring, Ring, Ring, Ring, Ring, Ring. "Get me off this bedpan, now!"

She obviously had realized someone was listening so now she's taken to ringing and yelling too. "How about I replace her vocal cords with a duck call? Would that help?"

Madme's eyes brightened. She liked it! She could use the same pulleys they used to keep the food trays out of the patients reach and could have synthenesia with her duck hunting trips she took as a child. Problem solved. Now I could move on to the next problem to solve.

As I passed the nursing office on my way to the next ward, I heard Marcie, the Dean of Nurses, ask Myrna, the assistant DON if she had a pen. I poked my head in and looked around.

"Did I hear you need a pen?" I asked with a smile.

"Yes, you did. I can't seem to find mine." Replied Marcie.

"Well, I'll be glad to lend you my disimpaction pen." I offered.

"Your disimpaction pen?" Marcie looked somewhat perplexed but Myrna gasped in disbelief, making wave off motions with her hands as if pleading with me to go no further. "What's that?" she asked.

Taking no heed and throwing all caution to the wind. I went on to explain "It's the pen I use to disimpact things."

"What sort of things?" Marcie asked, not quite catching on yet. Myrna appeared virtually apoplectic in the back of the room. It looked like she was going into grand mal seizures, but I wouldn't fall for it.

"Just about anything that needs disimpacting." I continued in an almost professorial tone.

"Like what?" Marcie seemed interested in learning more as she clearly had never heard of a disimpacting pen before.

"Well," I said, tasting the tip to help jog my memory, "This tastes like Mr. Jones' butt from today but I also sense an essence of Mrs. Smith's colostomy correction from last week."

Finally, getting it, Marcie jumped up and escorted me unceremoniously from the office, ending up with a perfect two point toss. Landing on my feet, as always, I waved back and thanked her for her help.

Conveniently, there was a phone right there where she could call 911 as Myrna sounded like she was drowning in her own vomit.

I appreciated the turbo boost down the hall as the stench down that stretch of the hall was particularly foul that day.

Arriving at the next nursing station, I finally had time to sit down and review the cases with case management and physical therapy. Victoire was quite a good therapist and knew how to play ball. We were able to come to reasonable terms for discontinuation of therapy and rarely disagreed. I only had to give her my John Belushi raised eyebrow on one side look once a week or so. That would usually turn the tide and I'd get my way. The case managers were much easier. They'd practically bend over backwards to try to please me. As sport, I kept making it harder and harder to do so, giving them goals like "I want all my patients discharged within two days before I even see them." When they actually did that for a fair number of patients, I then upped the ante and told them I wanted them discharged while still on the stretcher that rescue brought them in on. When they actually diverted an ambulance while still on route from the hospital to the nursing home, even I got a little sweaty. I let them know that I really did want to actually see the patient, even if all the discharge arrangements were made beforehand and I had to scramble to see them before they left. It turned out there was a practical reason for this – I didn't get paid unless I actually saw the patient so discharging them before they made it in the door, as desirable as it may be, wasn't financially feasible for me. So I went over the physical therapy evaluations and the case manager discharge plans and started on my rounds.

One of the insurance company case managers would usually accompany me to help soothe the patients and family's ruffled feathers as I made my equivalent of "Sherman's march to the sea" "total destruction in my wake" rounds. And to take the occasional bullet that particularly rabid families might aim at me. They usually would aim at the heart but fortunately, that would fall harmlessly into the void where the heart was surgically extracted from the case managers when they were hired by the HMO's. An overall convenient situation for me. I hated breaking in new case managers, which was necessary every so often if they had inadvertently left a remnant of heart in the chest cavity and it started to grow back before they could reoperate in time.

We had wandered over to one of the forgotten back wings of a particularly large SNF. They called the wing Cacophony, which I'm sure you would readily agree was a particularly apropos name if you ever had the occasion to take even a casual walk down the hall and listened to the various wailings of the inpatients echo seemingly endlessly over the hard plaster walls. With a little imagination you could possibly hear the laments of the earliest patients still reverberating as the thought of sound proofing had obviously escaped the architects back in the 40's when the building was constructed. I pulled out a chart and was sitting there reading it, trying to mind my own business when I heard a Munchkinlike voice call over the counter top. I had been the physician to one of the actual, honest to God, original 1939 Wizard of Oz Munchkins and would recognize that quality of voice anywhere.

"I want ice cream!" the voice demanded. "I want ice cream!" it repeated more insistently.

I looked around but none of the care givers charged with meeting the needs of the denizens of this ward seemed to have put in working batteries in their hearing aides.

The voice repeated a third, fourth and fifth time: "I want ice cream!"

I couldn't take it any longer, and against my better judgment, I stood up, looked over the counter and saw an ancient lady who stood no more than four and a half feet tall. She was normally formed but just tiny. Feeling the slightest bit of pity for the wizened, old but petite, hag standing there in front of me, I asked in one of my nicer voices, "Can I help you?"

She looked up at me, and with venom I'd expect from someone who actually knew me, she said "I don't have to look at you!"

Somewhat taken aback, but still in a relatively good mood, I responded: "I don't have any mirrors in my house for that very same reason." Sitting back down, I muttered to myself "How low have I sunk that I now feel compelled to match wits with demented patients?"

In sotto vocce over my right shoulder, I heard Mandy whisper to Reggie "And usually coming out on the losing side of the contest too."

Startled by those words, speechless for one of the few times in my life, all I could do was to take out my memo book and write, note to self: assign Mandy to discuss end of life issues with Mr. Nevell Givup and his family. His family had told me if I ever ask them about hospice again, they'll punch me out. Maybe I'll send Reggie too. I thought I had heard her snicker.

The garden gnome kept on whining, "I want ice cream!"

Seeing that this could go for longer than I'd care to tolerate, I turned to the nurses and said "Couldn't somebody drug her up and take me out of my misery?"

They responded in unison "Your whim is my command". I taught them well.

Getting back to the business at hand, I closed up the chart and turned around. "So, what's keeping Mr. Dindin here?" I asked Mandy, the HMO case manager.

"He says he likes the food here better than his wife's and he's not going home. He feels she's been trying to poison him and he's been surviving on the K rations he stole and shipped home during World War II when he was a quartermaster." She summarized from the social service notes.

"He's eating fifty year old K rations and he thinks his wife's cooking is going to kill him?" I asked incredulously. "And he likes the food here that the roach union has been picketing against since their walkout last year in the dispute over the facility's double bagging the wound bandages making it too hard for them to get into? That food? Is he insane? Never mind, I think I just answered my own question. Why was he originally admitted?" I generally asked Mandy to do all the reading so I wouldn't have to touch anything. Most of the germs in the SNF were incurable. It was probably too late for me anyway but I didn't want to take any unnecessary chances. I would have levitated into the building if I could.

"It says here he was admitted for heart failure, pneumonia, pulmonary embolism and acute leukemia." Read Mandy.

"What a wuss! They're all outpatient diseases! Okay, let's go see him." I fumed. I hated seeing patients that I might actually have to examine. Why couldn't they all be on hospice like they should be? It's just a matter of timing and with me as their doctor they've got to sense it's going to be sooner than later.

I opened the door to the overwhelmingly nauseating smell of anaerobic infection from his multiple stage 4, down to the bone, beds sores. "Mandy, would you be so kind as to open the windows so we can get a little cross ventilation?"

"Those windows are hermetically sealed because the waste water processing plant is back there and the prevailing winds normally come right through here." Reggie, the SNF's case manager replied.

"I'll take that to mean no. Yes?"

"Yes. I mean no, I mean ... I'm not sure what I mean." Reggie was easy to fluster.

"I'm sorry, what do you mean? It really doesn't matter. We're all goners unless that window is opened." At which point, I took one of the lunch biscuits and hurled it at the window, which even though was Dade county certified hurricane proof, was no match for an institutional biscuit. It shattered into a hundred pieces allowing the waste treatment plants essence to waft throughout the room. Rapidly realizing the error of my ways, I yelled "Everyone out, now!"

Reggie, farthest into the room, paused for a moment and asked "What about Mr. Dindin? Shouldn't we rescue him?"

"If you value your life, keep moving!" I must have said that with such urgency that Reggie dropped all pretense of caring about anyone but herself and hurled herself through the door that I was rapidly closing. She got out before she collapsed from what turned out, luckily, was only a sublethal dose of treatment plant fumes, patient anaerobic stench and poop in Mandy's pants as she thought she had breathed her last too. As we furiously stuffed rags around the door to stem the fumes from emanating any further into the ward, we finally felt it safe again to breathe. The stale stool and urine smell permeating the ward smelled like an old friend in comparison. It was a close call that we barely survived.

"Next time I get the bright idea that I should examine someone, knock me unconscious and tie me up until I swear it's out of my system." I implored Reggie and Mandy.

Mandy replied "You can count on me. In fact, I think I'll take some practice shots as soon as I finish shoveling this crap out of my pants." She looked around, holding a handful of poop and not finding a socially acceptable place to dispose of it, she just streaked it across the wall behind her. It blended in perfectly with all the other patients' finger painting efforts as they self disimpacted as they walked in the hallways.

At least she had the good taste not to sign her work as did many of the patients and a few of the administrators. "Excuse me while I go into this room for a moment."

I wasn't quite sure what she had in mind until I saw her put each of her fingers into the patient's mouth. The patient then proceeded to suck them clean using the primitive suck reflex which was one of the last signs of human mentality to leave as the brain dissolved into oblivious demented mush. She then opened the container holding a patient's false teeth and used the canines to clean under her fingernails. Brilliant, I thought, as I scribbled another note to myself about proper hygiene in a pinch. Mandy came out of the room, saw my perplexed look and said "Oh, don't look at me like that, you know that's how I clean myself everyday, so knock it off."

"Yes, but I always thought you used your husband's teeth. Won't he be suspicious that you're seeing someone else?"

"No, and we've called a truce. So, let's move on."

"Alright, if you say so. By the way, I guess the discharge plans for Mr. Dindin have taken care of themselves, unless he's become immune to the toxic waste from next door by gradual desensitization by smelling his own odors. Make a note to have maintenance fix the window."

Reggie made a note and gave it to the charge nurse, who looked at her with incomprehension as if it was her responsibility to keep the ward up. She turned to her LPN who wasn't about to be saddled with another chore. She turned to the aide who spoke in a tongue that wasn't even registered with the United Nations cultural diversity registry, didn't have a clue what the LPN said but when given a piece of paper thought for sure she was being given some garbage and threw it away. She missed the can of course but she liked to keep the floors littered and muddy to help remind her of her home town. She was quite proud of the little bit of country she had created for herself here in the big city, so far from those who would truly appreciate her handiwork.

We moved on to the next ward. The screams of the thousands of former, and, I suspect, most of the current residents, fading as we turned the corner.

"Well, that's the last of our patients – they're either all dead or in hospice. It's Friday. I've had enough. I'm going home. Call me if anyone needs anything that I might care about giving them. Bye." If I have to engage in patient care I'll never get any work done, I thought to myself as I walked briskly out of the building. It was almost 11 AM and I still had to pack for the Keys.

Reggie looked horrified, as if I had just stabbed her in the back and thrown her to the wolves. She now had to face all those angry families on her own, with their insatiable and usually irrational demands which she now had to tackle all by herself.

Mandy packed up her books, started whistling, jumped up and clicked her heels once. "I've got me an early weekend. Yippee!"

Chapter 46:
We Offer the Best Care Here

A fair amount of negotiable nonnegotiable demands were promulgated at the Bar Association's meeting and duly disseminated to the media and sympathetic government officials. Implementation had to wait for legislation or executive order but the points were made and most of the uninformed and naïve assumed that the mere demand equated to fact.

John Jamison was elected president of the Bar. His publicist made it clear to the world who was in charge while at the same time being quite vague as to how to have a face to face with the newly crowned president. Jamison was no fool, he saw what the shadowy adversary could do and wasn't about to follow their fate. So he hired a body double and made it next to impossible for someone other that a longtime and trusted associate to meet him in person and only then if they were blindfolded and escorted by his security team.

A lull ensued after the hastily called Bar Association meeting. The police were co-opted almost in their entirety by mayors and governors, most of whom were attorneys, in an effort to find the culprits responsible for the mass murder of so many of their fellow lawyers. A certain urgency was felt by those politicians, not so much to avenge the dead but to try to avoid the same fate themselves. They too were no fools, they knew to the man that politicians and lawyers were virtually synonyms in the mind of the general public, no less a crazed and dangerous adversary as they were now up against.

The lull of course wasn't so much a lack of action on our part as an irreducible minimum amount of time necessary for incubation. We were patient.

The first signs of problems started showing up several days after the Bar's concluding meeting. Three of the biggest drunks in the Bar all became ill with 24 hours of each other. The symptoms were nonspecific, nausea, vomiting, malaise, weakness and diarrhea. They persisted and progressed to the point that all three had to be hospitalized on the same day. Routine labs in the ER revealed marked lowered white count and platelet count. The biggest souse's white count was down 800 hundred from a normal of over 4000 and platelets were under 5,000 whereas normal was over 100,000. He died the same day as admission from an intracranial hemorrhage, before the other symptoms became apparent. His estate filed suit against the hospital and all his doctors a week later.

The other two lingered for a week before they too died. They had the added pleasure of losing all their hair, developing huge festering bed sores before finally bleeding out through their bowels. The smell of partially digested blood mixed with diarrhea prevented even the most devoted family member from remaining in the room with their loved one for more than a few moments. Both their estates filed suit within a week adding loss of companionship and pain and suffering to their claims along with punitive damages which would have bankrupted a medium size country if their claim was granted in full.

The rest of the Bar's attendees all became ill over the next few months, even the teetotalers, to some degree or other. A few more died of acute shutdown of their organs as the first few did but most developed an insidious and progressive set of symptoms including extreme fatigue, shortness of breath and swelling of their feet. Of the 250 attendees, 50 died within a month and all the rest developed the above symptoms.

The diagnosis was fairly obvious, even to the med students who were assigned to them when the cheaper of the Bar members received their medical care at the local teaching hospital. CHF – congestive heart failure for one and all. The CDC – Center for Disease Control was tasked by the politicians to stop everything and get to the root of this enigma. How did 250 of the country's most prominent lawyers all come down with the same problems at the same time?

A fairly elementary preliminary epidemiological answer was propounded: they all had a group exposure – possibly a virus, but with a 100% penetrance and no collateral victims, a virus was unlikely. More probable: poisoning. This was an especially likely answer given the criminal activities preceding this event.

This pronouncement, widely disseminated by all the media, sent a collective shiver down the back of the politicians and lawyers alike. No politician had even been obliquely threatened this entire time, but they had a guilty conscience and feared they were next. The National Guard was mobilized in every state except Alaska. There, the overwhelming sentiment was actually supportive of the events as they were unfolding and the Republican manufacturer turned governor felt a little bit of glee. He had been all but bankrupted by the endless frivolous suits that all productive citizens were subjected to and had run on antilawyer platform. He not only felt vindicated but now was so vocal in his support that the governor of California, a dyed in the wool union activist liberal called for an investigation of his fellow governor as a possible suspect in the murders. Failing that, at least he should be considered as a coconspirator after the fact for giving aide and comfort to the criminals. And if that didn't work, he'd find a thousand ways to finish the job that the civil lawyers in Alaska had started. The governor of Alaska not so jokingly suggested that Alaska might succeed to finally be able to "form a more perfect union" as established in the Constitution, the first lawyer free zone of freedom in the world.

John Jamison, the now reclusive President of the American Bar and not of the United States of America as he had to be constantly reminded of in the more conservative press, no longer could be taken care of at home. His trophy wife of three years abandoned him, not so much because he was no longer able to work and bring home a seven figure salary, he had ample reserves to keep even the most extravagant wife happy, but because of fear that whoever it was doing such a good job of knocking off all the lawyers might come to her house to finish the job. She didn't want to be anywhere nearby him when that happened. She heard the phrase collateral damage too often to be ignorant of its meaning. Likewise, even the most desperate undocumented alien knew that being that close to the media spotlight was a sure one way ticket back to unpaved streets and abject poverty. So Jamison had no one to help and he needed help badly. He filed one more suit before leaving for the nursing home, he demanded that the government find him a heart donor or he'll bring the government to its knees.

In his heyday, there are those who believed that Jamison could do just that, but now he could barely talk without gasping for air. Those who didn't know him wondered where he got the chutzpah to make such a demand and such a threat. Those who knew him realized that even in his final days, he just couldn't help himself, it was in his nature.

A little story gained some prominence in the media to explain this to the uninitiated. A frog and a scorpion met at a bank of a river. The scorpion wanted to get across and asked the frog to help him. The frog said to the scorpion that he was afraid that the scorpion would sting him and he'd die. The scorpion assured him that he wouldn't possibly do that because if he did so while they were crossing he'd drown and die and also he would be too grateful to do so when they got to the other bank. With this reassurance, the frog agreed and the scorpion crawled on the frog's back. The frog started to swim but as they were about halfway across, the frog felt a terrible sting on his back couldn't swim anymore and start to sink. With his last breath, the frog asked the scorpion why he stung him and the scorpion responded just as he was going under "it's my nature".

Thus, everyone to the man, for the first time in America, finally understood that if lawyers exist, there were going to be suits. It didn't matter what the issues were or whether or not any issue existed at all, it was just what lawyers do: they sue.

With that simple story, and the generally better business climate and generally improving sense of well being, America actually was feeling a little better about itself everyday. The shrill cry for justice in the liberal media was starting to become somewhat muted as their circulation and viewership started to shrink. The conservation media could barely keep up with demand for its newspapers and its speaker bureaus became so popular they had a waiting list of years. The number of suits dropped precipitously. Those who did sue made sure that their position was a popular one with their conservative advisors. They made sure that the suits were well publicized in advance so as to try to justify themselves, both lawyer and plaintiff, in an effort not to become a statistic by the unknown "lawyer avengers" as we were being called in the papers.

John Jamison was brought by ambulance to a local and nondescript nursing facility. He checked in under an alias. A doctor was assigned who didn't know who his patient was. All he knew was that a middle aged gentleman with idiopathic end stage congestive cardiomyopathy was admitted and expected to die shortly. Dr. Aventura introduced himself to Jamison, established as good a rapport as one could with a breathless reprobate and kindly announced that "We Offer The Best Care Here".

Jamison tried to spit on him but was so weak all he could manage was a weak gurgle and some drool. Dr. Aventura, not knowing the (criminal) intent, dutifully wiped Jamison's lips with a paper towel from the bathroom, having no soft facial tissues handy. His lips were rewarded for the doctor's kindness by a superficial abrasion due to their being left paper thin by the Adriamycin overdose. Jamison saw the blood on the paper and immediately tried to threaten the doctor with a suit but was only able to get out a breathless "I'll ..." before falling back in bed too fatigued to finish the sentence with a "get you for this". Dr. Aventura took it as a thank you, nodded and left, pushing the call bell on his way out for the nurse to come in and clean up his mess.

Chapter 47:
If You Attack the King, You Must Kill the King

There was dissension in the ranks. A new administrator, May-oui, was just hired, continuing the revolving door that goes along with virtually every job in the nursing home industry. I call it the shifting sands of loyalty whereby virtually every position has a 300% turnover every year. What with low pay and even lower moral, I'm surprised whenever anyone stays anywhere for a year. I don't even bother learning anyone's name because they're just not there long enough to make it worthwhile and it just clogs up my mind with too many useless facts.

Anyway, one Monday morning I walk into one of my better SNF's and find the only two worthwhile people in the place were upset. One was the case manager, the other the charge nurse. They've proven their worth a thousand times over and whenever I can help them, I go out of my way to do so. This was shaping up to be one of those times.

"So what's getting you so upset?" I asked Bouncy the nurse.

"They've hired a new administrator but from what we've heard, it's a package deal with her live-in lover, Sadass, as social worker. Even though it's against all company policy to hire attached people, it wouldn't be that bad except that I know the social worker and she's a lazy pig who thinks she owns the place because her boss is her lover. This means we're all going to have to work twice as hard to get our work and her work done and she knows there's nothing we can do about it."

"We're screwed!" chimes in the case manager. Her name is Thrszcycxx but we call her "The Chief" for short. That upsets her a little but even she can't pronounce her name the same way twice in a row. We took pity on ourselves and made her name something recognizable in English.

"Why don't you do something about it if it upsets you so much?" I asked.

"What can we do? She's the new bosses' lover. We can't just go up to her and say we don't like your taste in women. Also, she's not even here yet. We can't say we think the new social worker is going to stink based on rumors we heard. No, we're stuck with her for as long as the administrator's here." laments Bouncy, who's not living up to her name just right now.

"Maybe so, but how about the administrator's boss, Candyass. I understand you've discussed problems with him before. Won't he help?" I offer helpfully.

"No, he's the one who hired her. How would it look if he fires her right away? It would be an admission that he doesn't know what he is doing. Although that's actually the truth." replies The Chief.

"Okay, how about just waiting and seeing what happens? You seem to be caught in a bureaucratic nightmare, so why not play their game. Every time there's even the slightest annoyance with Sadass, write her up. Send the original to May-oui and a copy to Candyass. After a while, the weight of the load will have to break something. So either Sadass or your ass will get the boot. You'll both be in great demand so you won't be out of work long." I said in my most hopeful voice.

"Easy for you to say, but it's us who'll have to put up with her until someone, and it'll probably be us, has to leave but we like it here and don't want to leave!" they chimed in together so characteristically that I call them "The Bounce" whenever they do that.

"Well, let's just see what happens and I'll help you if I can." Usually I can too, but this will have to be a double header because it wouldn't do to get rid of one without the other. Both the administrator and the social worker have to be fired. If not, the remaining one would sabotage me at every turn which I wouldn't want to put up with.

Over the next few weeks, every time I walked into the building I got an earful of the incompetence and insolence of Sadass. Sadass got things so twisted that they started speaking to her only in palindromes so even if she got it backwards, she'd still get it right. It was becoming intolerable for all of us but so far I had no stake in this war, until today that is. It was another glum Monday, miserable as the rest of the work week loomed and twice as bad for the number of patients whose needs pileup over the weekend.

It just so happened that The Chief had taken off the previous Friday and had tried to explain to Sadass how to help with one of my discharges that was scheduled to leave on Friday. Sadass blew The Chief off, saying that "the ship will continue to sail without you being here for one day". That might be true for all other activities that The Chief is not involved in, but that ship crashes onto the rocks if The Chief was the pilot and her relief didn't show up when The Chief left her post. The bottom line was, my patient didn't go home. Now what you have to understand is that my job is the discharging of patients. I don't give a damn if they are carried out or walk out. I only care that they leave. So when they don't leave it makes me see red. Red ink, too, but definitely red. After evaluating the facts as presented, I then called up May-oui and asked her about the situation. She first said she herself came into the building on Sunday to check it out. She tried to lay the blame on The Chief by her not answering her beeper. Unfortunately for May-oui, The Chief was standing next to me and reminded me she was out of town and everyone knew it. I said to May-oui The Chief was out of town and everyone knew it so she couldn't blame her. Next, May-oui said the equipment orders were submitted too late on Saturday and they couldn't get the equipment on time. I replied that I ordered the equipment on Friday when I was there. May-oui retorted it was ordered too late on Friday then.

Gotcha! I thought. "But I left the SNF before noon on Friday so if anyone ordered the equipment too late it was Sadass, which is the basic premise of this discussion."

"Well, it wasn't a big deal and I'll look into it to see what we can do in the future." clicked off May-oui.

"So there you have it." I said turning to The Bounce, "Just as you feared, dead end's ville."

As God is my witness, as these words are leaving my mouth, up comes a pleasant, well dressed middle aged man who says "Hi Doctor, I'm Crimea River, I'm the corporate vice president and I was told I couldn't leave the building without first meeting you."

Sneaking a quick peak up towards the heavens, I gave Him a little wink. As I shook Mr. River's hand I asked "Do you have a moment to talk to me?"

"Of course." Crimea says, not realizing he's been hooked and was now being reeled in.

"Great. The Chief, do you mind if I use your office for a moment?" The Chief being too stunned to speak, simply nodded in the affirmative.

"So Mr. River, I just wanted to say how nice your facility is. I consider it the premiere facility in the entire two counties I'm responsible for. The people that work here, by and large are the tops. Everything is going along swimmingly and I love to bring my patients here."

"Well, that is good news and I'm glad we're doing a good job for you." smiled Mr. River.

"There is just one thing that's of a small concern to me."

"Oh, and what's that?'

"Well, as you know I'm in charge of all of the admissions for all the SNF's for just about every HMO that exist in these environs. That equates to over ten thousand patients per year and the reason they have entrusted me with this responsibility is because my team does a good job for them. And I include in my team not just the doctors who work for me but the SNF's we work at. They also entrust me with choosing which SNF's those are. For me to choose a SNF, they must be able to handle my patients efficiently. Unfortunately, an incident occurred in this facility just yesterday which gives me pause."

"That doesn't sound so good. What happened?" asked Mr. River. I could hear him adding it up 10,000 patients per year times $250.00 per day times an average length of stay of twelve days equals $30,000,000.00 per year that I control. No small time operator he's dealing with.

"What happened was your social worker chose to ignore your case manager's request to make sure the discharge went well, saying, and I quote 'the ship will continue to sail without you for one day'. Well, the ship crashed and burned and no one seems to care except me and, of course, the patient, who wanted to go home but couldn't. This falls into a category of something less than kidnapping and false imprisonment but something worse than good client relations. And it cost the people who hired me hundreds of dollars which they don't care to donate to your company's party fund. And I'm not even going to touch on the personal relationship that the social worker and administrator have. I'll just say that I understand nepotism is frowned upon in most corporate climates. Anyway, I thank you for listening to me. I'm sure I'll be able to work something out but I just needed someone to vent to. Sorry you came along at the wrong time. I hope the next time we meet will be under more pleasant circumstances."

"So do I, Doctor, so do I." Crimea was a genuinely nice guy. I hoped the seeds I planted would eventually take sprout.

I went to see another patient. This one was a new admission so it took a good half hour to finish it up. When I came out of the room, Bouncy was waiting for me. She had a look of both terror and awe on her face. "I don't ever want to cross you." was all she could say.

The Chief soon caught up with me. "What did you say to him?"

"Him who?" I asked, totally stupefied.

"You know, Mr. River."

"Oh, you mean Crimea. A really nice guy. Nothing really, had a nice little chat, exchanged a few pleasantries and went our own ways. Why, what's up?"

"Well, Mr. River took me and Bouncy aside, asked us what we thought of Sadass, which didn't take long because we told him we didn't think much of her at all and the next thing you know May-oui and Candyass were in Sadass' room with her cleaning out her personal effects. They escorted her to her car but that's where she has to sit for the rest of the day as she came in with May-oui and has no way home. I don't know how you did it but you did it! What's really scary though is it took you five minutes to do what we couldn't in five weeks. It's spooked Bouncy big time. She came out of office to say what she said to you and she's locked herself back in there. None of us could have imagined let alone have ever seen such raw power. You know how we simple people's lives have a familiar pattern which allow us to make some sense of our existence permitting us to live with some semblance of order so we don't go crazy. Well, you just took that whole order, turned it upside down and shook it. It's going to take some time incorporating the fact that there are people out there who can play with the rest of us like pawns." The Chief was college educated and it showed.

"What about May-oui?" I asked with some trepidation. "Is she still the administrator?"

"Unfortunately, yes, she still is." bemoaned The Chief.

"That's too bad, but I'm going to have to live with it. Anyway, what happened with Crimea and me was he realized which side his bread is buttered on. It's real easy to understand. Karl Marx said it best: 'All of politics is an economic struggle'. I boil that down to the capitalist phrase: 'The bottom line is the bottom line'. Once you understand that money is everything, the Green Party not withstanding, you will understand virtually everything in the world. There are a few other, relatively minor, motivating factors, one of which is revenge. So if Sadass is gone but her lover May-oui remains, I need to watch my back and you need to help me, because she's going to be looking to get me. As the Romans found out and the British were so fond of saying, 'If You Attack The King, You Must Kill The King'. I attacked the king but she continues to live. I'm in trouble. But don't worry, Crimea River will be back soon and I might be able to finish the job then."

Chapter 48: Nursing Homes: An Uplifting Experience

Every once in a while I actually have to show up for work. It just wouldn't be right to keep calling in orders from the islands without seeing my patients for weeks on end. I do so with trepidation though, as who knows what evil lurks on the hands of men. Or on nurses, door knobs and the very air you breathe in these last bastions of pestilence we call nursing homes. Saddam could have saved himself billions if he would have been able to find a way to collect and distribute the effluent from the nursing homes without all his agents succumbing to those very toxins before they finished the job. The mortality rate in the nursing homes is quite high as it is, so maybe we're doing Saddam's job for him anyway.

Nevertheless, my rare visits to the nursing homes are usually greeted with abject silence as the early warning system in the parking lot allows sufficient time for the staff to hide in their most secret spots. Unfortunately for them, I can usually see the toxic green cloud escaping under the doors where they're hiding so I can easily find those I need most without too much difficulty.

"Come on out now, Nurse Levine, I know you're in there." I called calmly to the soiled laundry cart.

"Oh, I'm so glad you came along when you did. I had fallen in and couldn't get out. I could have been there for hours." Cooed "Nursey", as I called her.

"Bull. We both know you were hiding from me and you jumped in there on purpose. Look, your flesh is only starting to fall off around the edges. You couldn't have been there more than a few minutes. Go get detoxified and we'll make rounds." I said, a little sterner than I meant to be.

"How did you know I was in there?" asked Nursey as she applied the embalming solution to the more putrefied areas of her skin. That was the only thing they've found strong enough to kill the super germs they've been brewing in nursing homes since the invention of penicillin wiped out the sensitive bugs leaving only those germs mean enough to bathe in antibiotics and laugh in its face. Even so, they lost an average of one nurse or aide per week to bugs that haven't even been identified yet. They have an open account with Federal Express to ship the bodies directly to the CDC at their Devil's Island isolation unit. They've had to move out their smallpox and anthrax research units to make room for the dangerous stuff.

"By the way", said Nursey, "when I was down there in the laundry cart, a man came by and asked if I wouldn't mind giving you these papers. I said sure." as she handed me some papers that were dripping with the same green ooze as she was.

I took them gingerly, holding them at one corner with a doubled over paper towel as far away from me as I could while I watched them drip on the floor, causing a buckling and dissolving of the ceramic tile unfortunate enough to catch the effluence. A slight sweat started to break out as I knew what they had to be, and sure enough, it was another 'Notice of Intent' to sue me. This one was a little different from the rest as the Plaintiff was my mother and the attorney was my sister.

They were suing that I caused a birth injury, that is, I was born, and my continued existence caused ongoing emotional distress. Actually, now that I think of it, it was just the standard complaint. Oh well, I'll file it with the rest. That reminded me, I needed to pay for the larger storage bay as the amount of legal work was increasing by 50% per month. Oh well, such was the cost of doing business. Speaking of business, I needed to stop day dreaming and get back to the business at hand.

I tried never to get too close to anyone at the nursing homes, thus avoiding the endless hand washings necessary to try to eradicate whatever was the incurable bug du jour. That extended to the patients also. Especially the patients. They acted like a septic tank. All the germs that the home had to offer eventually ended up in every patient. The reasons for this were quite clear. First, they brought in their own resistant germs from the hospital. Second, they were placed in and on suboptimally cleaned surfaces. That could have been avoided if the administration hired help that used soap at home, but minimum wage didn't go as far as it did in the 1930's. Third, the nurses and aides were so understaffed that washing their hands between patients was out of the question or they'd never have time to do their work. Fourth, I had a few special vials that I had been collecting and adding to over the years, taken from incurable raging infections, that I'd administer judiciously to patients and staff that I didn't like. Nothing like a helping hand(ful) to get things moving.

If the patient was there for as little as a day, he became an incubator for a dozen lethal germs. After three days, the CDC started an investigation, and after a week, the survivors were sent for DNA typing so resistant human beings could be genetically engineered to try to save the human race. I didn't even shake hands. Long before SARS, I wore masks to work. I even used SCUBA apparatus at the more vile institutions.

"Well, Nursey, let's see our patients." I stated resignedly.

"You have four to see today. Would you like me to open the charts for you?" she sneered as she added a barely audible "candy ass" under her breath.

"That won't be necessary, Nursey, I didn't forget my gloves today."
"Bitch" I breathed out almost imperceptibly. I used to feel a little self conscious wearing pink Playtex full arm double thickness gloves, but all those who scorned me had long since been incinerated with their ashes sent to Mars by the National Security Council.

"First we have Mr. Gayfellow. He came in with a fever several days ago and has been fully cultured. Here are the results." Whistling out "as if you give a damn." through her eternally clogged sinuses.

"Why thank you Nursey." The chart rubbed against my arm making a noise that sounded as if 'slut' could be perceived through the ethers. "Well Mr. Gayfellow, how are we feeling today?" I asked as I reviewed the lab results.

Mr. Gayfellow was an emaciated, 30ish white male who didn't look as good as his grandfather did despite these ten years in his grave.

"How do you think I feel, you pansy, with those pink gloves on? And they call me effeminate. Afraid to touch me, are you? Well, take a step closer so you're within spitting range and you'll shortly know yourself how I feel. By the way, what do the reports say or do you need to find someone who can read, jackass."

"I see that you seem a little upset, Mr. Godawfulfellow." I observed from a safer distance, taking a step or two backwards. That made good sense to me in case he did get up a sufficient head of steam to lean out of bed and I did indeed become within spitting range. As an after thought I lifted my mask over my mouth and nose as an extra added precaution. "What's not to your satisfaction?" I asked, and Nursey was right, I didn't care, but I had to put something down on the chart to let people know I actually saw the patient.

"That's Gayfellow, you pig. And I'll tell you what's wrong. I was admitted here almost a week ago, no doctor has seen me, and judging from what I've seen so far, none still has. I have this terrible fever, can't eat, no one has cleaned or changed me and I'm sure I'm going to die but fear that no one in this hell hole is going to even notice until the stench from my carcass scares all the roaches out of my room."

"I" putting my hand over my mouth coughing out a 'can't' "feel your pain. I'm sure the staff will do better in the future after I talk to them. And let me assure you, I paid good money to buy the diploma I would hang in my office, if I had an office and the print shop would get on the ball already. But that's beside the point. Let's talk about you and your misery." I said with a little gleam in my eye. "According to the culture results, you have a syndrome called, not inappropriately in your case, HAGS."

"Okay, I'll bite, what's that." seethed Mr. Gayfellow.

"HAGS is a combination of four infections: herpes, AIDS, gonorrhea and syphilis."

"Oh my God, he said he was treated for syphilis, that turd. I hope his butt falls off. So, what are you going to do for me, besides pity, which, by the way, I haven't seen much of as of yet?"

"Mr. Gayfellow, we're going to put you on a special diet consisting of pizza and crackers." I replied as I started backing out of the room.

"A special diet, is that going to help?" he asked somewhat perplexedly.

"Not really, but it's the only food we can slip under your closed and locked door." were my last words as the door shut between us. "Okay Nursey, that went well, be sure to check on him in a few days, we wouldn't want to drive out the roaches. They're the only things that keep this place clean since you fired housekeeping in the last round of budget cuts. Who's next?" I was feeling better as I escaped with my health intact and having exacted a bit of revenge at the same time. It's not that I'm prejudiced against certain patients. No, I dislike them all equally. I'm still working out a payment system where they can just send me money and I can guess their disease by the numbers of their bank account. Until that happy day, I'm stuck actually seeing, if not touching, them.

"Our next patient is Bella Donna. She's a 400 pound train wreck with just about every disease imaginable that you'd expect from obesity. Hardening of the arteries, had both legs amputated above the knee, two heart attacks, a stroke, diabetes, renal failure and is blind. She's also demented, tried to get out of bed and broke her arm. She's here for rehab."

"Of course she's here for rehab, everyone's here for rehab. What an incredibly stupid thing to say. Do you do that just to irritate me?" I lashed out.

"Yes." She glared back.

"You don't like me, do you?" (you shriveled up old hag) left unspoken between us.

"Not really." she responded honestly adding to herself (although I do like it when you're away).

"Too bad. By the way, I heard what you said and I've decided to send all my patients here because I've deemed you the most likely nurse to knock off my patients. I'll be here every day from now on to document your efforts for the World Court's crimes against humanity trials next year. Keep up the bad work. They need a good laugh in Hell. Okay enough of this levity. Let's go see Ms. Donna. Have legal see if we can sue her for emotional distress for her having two first names." We marched off together down the hallway. I had to be careful to avoid stepping on the roaches because they were now represented by the custodians union.

We had to push our way into her room. The door was partially blocked by her exuding blubber, now almost filling up the room. Nursey yelled down the hallway "Hey, who's been feeding porky in here. I told you do not let her lick the other patient's trays when you collect them. That's what we have the roaches for. Don't let me catch anyone doing it again."

Jerks. "Let's get some reinforcements in here to keep this door open so we can get out."

Two fairly corpulent aides waddled down the hall, eventually making it to the room. Just so the time wasn't a complete waste, I took that opportunity to read the chart. I didn't want to make a habit out of it and told Nursey so. Her laughs of mirth and scorn have become indistinguishable over the years.

"What took you so long, you fat blobs?" demanded Nursey.

"Union rules, we don't gots to walk faster than the custodians do and them roaches is on a union slowdown order. Something abouts demanding a better quality food. In any case here we is but I can tell you now, we aints going in that room until she releases Weezey. She went in there last week to tell her she weren't going to allow her to help clean off the trays and we haven't seen Weezey since. We thinks we gots her located under the third stomach fat fold be we can't risk a rescue operation. Ms. Donna has threatened to redirect her farts at us if we try to rescue her or stop bringing her the trays. That would kill Weezey instantaneously. Our best hope is that Weezey gathers enough slime to slip out of there and makes a run for it. We've told Ms. Donna that she's breaking union rules by not letting the roaches do their job. But you know how it is. The National Labor Relations Board may take months to decide and with the Republican majority, it's not clear the union's going to win this time. The local exterminator's union has actually broken ranks with the national union and has filed an amicus curiae brief on behalf of Ms. Donna. They figured if they could win this case, they'd all be able to gets their jobs back here. Heck, it'll support a dozen of them for a year killing off all the roaches and vermin if they wins back this contract."

Good, that gave me enough time to finish the first page which contained the insurance information so I can now bill her. Glancing past the partially opened door, being held by the two aides and Nursey, I hailed Ms. Donna. "Why how are we today?" I cheerfully called.

"You making some crack about my size or are you looking for Weezey too? Cause if you're looking for Weezey, forget it. I'm never letting her go. You got to keep them trays coming forever and I'm making a new demand. I want you to replace my window with a chute and have one city sanitation truck offload it into my room daily. The EPA will probably give you a grant for saving landfill room. You'll need to increase the deliveries once I hit my stride."

The aides were losing their battle. The door slowly was being closed shut by Ms. Donna's ever expanding girth that grew perceptibly as we were talking. The solution to the dilemma became clear. Once the door could no longer be opened, we couldn't bring her any more food. Sure she could live indefinitely on the roaches that formed a constant trail under her door. If we could just hold out long enough for the Labor Board to rule against the roaches and let the exterminators do their job, Ms. Donna would die of starvation. That is unless she was able to live off the photosynthesis from the fungus growing under her panuliculi. Maybe we should block off the windows and stop the sunlight, but no, I think most of what's growing in there was anaerobic and hadn't seen the light of day for decades. We'll just have to wait and see. Of course, Weezey will have to be sacrificed, but all wars have their casualties.

Next, we moved onto Mr. Bon Chance. "Tell me about Mr. Chance, Nursey."

"Mr. Chance was admitted here a few days ago because he couldn't take care of himself at home. We've been waiting for test results from the hospital and they just came in yesterday. We tried to reach you because they were critical results but you apparently didn't get our beeps."

"Probably not. I've put a block on pages from this nursing home. All you guys ever call about is problems with the damn patients and I just couldn't be bothered anymore. In any case, here I am. What have you got?"

"One more double entendre like that and you'll regret you were ever curious about what I've got." sneered Nursey.

"Get over it, you overestimate yourself and underestimate me. Everyone knows what you've got and, believe me, no one cares. (You shriveled up old hag) I smiled back at her. "Just give me the results."

"Here." (You pompous ass) she grinned.

"Let's see, potassium 1.7, sodium 177, BUN 223 and CD4 2. Okay, I got it. Let's see Mr. Chance." We knocked and walked in, all in one motion. Every once in awhile we were lucky enough to find someone in a compromising situation, but not today. All we saw was one of the groundskeepers watering him with a small bucket, but with the degree of dehydration he had, a garden hose wouldn't have been enough. "Get out and do something useful, you toad!" screamed Nursey.

Mr. Chance made a feeble effort to sit but to no avail. "No, not you, you prune. You, groundskeeper, whatever your name, you, yes you, get out!" Nursey repeated at the top of her lungs.

The groundskeeper, Jose by his name tag, shrugged his shoulders, dumped the rest of the bucket over Mr. Chance and walked out.

Nursey glared at him as he left, "You'll never work in this home again! Now look what he's done! He's got the entire floor and bed soaked. The last time we got water anywhere inside the building it took two months and a ton of algaecide to get the mold under control. What're we ever going to do?" she said, bemoaning her fate. Half the aides called in sick last time, saying their asthma acted up in moist environments.

"Why don't you just get rags and clean it up?" I innocently asked Nursey.

The ice is still frozen in Hell from the look she gave me. "Why don't you suck an egg? I'm not bending over to do any cleaning, you want me out of the union? And you know the roaches have water related activities explicitly excluded in their contract, so we're just going to have to wait for it to evaporate."

"Alrighty then. Let's move on to Mr. Chance. Hello, Mr. Chance, how are you today?"

Other than a bit of gurgling from where the water splashed into his nose, there wasn't any response.

"Well, Mr. Chance, I have some bad news and some worse news. Which would you like to hear first?"

Gurgle.

"Very well then, I'll give you the bad news first. According to these lab reports, you have only one day to live. The worse news they've been trying to reach me since yesterday. Oh well, have a good day. Be seeing you." I said with my best bedside manner.

Turning to nurse Nursey, I asked "Do you know the difference between babies and bowling balls?"

"No." she answered somewhat perplexedly but, knowing me, also guardedly.

"You can load one with a pitchfork." Over the noise of her throwing up I added "Have the pitchfork ready, you'll need it soon."

"Uggghhh, blaaaaaaah." Was all that she could manage as she was doubled over in the throws of dry heaves?

"You know it's rude to interrupt me while I'm talking?"

"Uggghhh, blaaaaaaah."

"When you compose yourself, we'll finish the rounds."

"Uggghhh, blaaaaaaah."

"Fine, have it your way, I'll be back next week to see the rest of my patients. I expect your mess will be cleaned up by then." My expectations were well founded, the roaches were already hard at work on Nursey's new mess, as if they needed more work. I've finally gotten to Nursey I mused on my way out.

The other patient was just bed sores and it would take the maggots a few more weeks to clean them out anyway, as long as their union didn't strike for harder beds again. They already had all the work they could handle and they really didn't need to drum up more business with harder beds anyway. They had lobbied for and won beds make of bricks but they really wanted granite to overcome any last ditch resistance by the body to bed sores. It was just their nature to do so on general principles so we'll see how the Labor Board rules on that. In the meantime, they were on a work slowdown and would only eat down to the fat and not all the way to the bone as their contract called for,

Stepping out the door, I was at last free from another uplifting experience in the nursing home.

Chapter 49: The Medical Director

Driving away, I remembered I had to call the HMO medical director to get him to stop paying for Mr. Bon Chance's care. He had no rehab potential and there was nothing left to do for him but wait until he died. He had no family and no money, so all that was left to be done was to transfer him to custodial care. But that could only be accomplished through the medical director. So I placed the call.

"Hi there, Slobrew. I need another letter. You know, the one where we dump their carcass under a bridge and let the wolves have a feast."

"Who is this?" he demanded.

Oops, I forgot they started taping the conversations. Click.

That was dumb, but I'll just wait a while and try again later.

The car ride from nursing home to nursing home was usually pleasant, a good place to catch up on phone calls and listen to continuing education tapes. The worst part of driving was the other drivers. Living in south Florida, all the worst drivers in the world seemed to funnel down I-95 and with no outlet at the bottom of the state, they just seemed to accumulate until there was no more room for anyone else. So driving was like an eternal game of bumper cars but without the rules and courtesy of an amusement park.

And these old geezers played for keeps. I had read in the paper this morning about a parking lot incident where a spry 85 year old name Moishe fought with a feeble 90 year old named Hymie, in a case of road rage in slow motion. The eyewitness reports stated it all started with Hymie zipping into a spot that someone else was backing out of. Meanwhile Moishe had spotted the opening from the next row over and sent out his wife, Yenta, to hold the spot. Hymie couldn't see Yenta because the steering wheel hid the only sector of vision that was still functional from his macular degeneration. His car glanced off Yenta but didn't knock her down as her 62 inch waist cushioned the blow nicely, but it did displace her enough to allow him into the spot. The problem was he was so close to the car next to him on the left that he couldn't open his door. Despite setting the supercharged, 140 decibel, rotatable omnidirectional horn on death blast straight at the neighboring car, shattering its side windows, the empty car failed to move over for him. By this time, Moishe was rounding the row, incensed that Hymie had taken his spot and now enraged as he thought Hymie was honking at Yenta.

Yenta had taken refuge a few cars over, having kicked Hymie's car breaking her toe in the process. She had turned off her hearing aides due to the noise from the horn and paid no attention to the rest of the action.

Hymie was stymied by the nerve of the car next to him not moving over so he decided that the only way he was going to be able to open his car door was to back out and reposition his car, a novel and unprecedented approach unequaled in his recollection (that according to later reports of his landlady, was only a few minutes at most).

Moishe, misconstruing the proceedings in the worst light, as was his wont, decided to block Hymie from backing up with his car. Hymie, not bothering to even look, repeatedly tried to back up without success. In doing so was so battering Moishe's car that, as unreasonable and

The Devil Who Walked The Earth

cranky as he was, even Moishe knew when to cut his losses. Hymie, being unaware that there was a car behind him, couldn't figure out why he couldn't back out. He tried turning around to see but the seat back was too high to allow a clear field of vision. Thus, see nothing, he kept rocking the car from forward to reverse as he remembered doing up north when he was stuck in the snow, pushing the accelerator to the floor whenever he was in reverse. Moishe finally was able to back up enough to get out of Hymie's way. On Hymie's next attempt to break out, he accelerated all the way to the next row, lifting his rear fender up over the hapless parked car's bumper, impaling his car on the Mercedes hood ornament and, with his rear tires up in the air, couldn't get free.

In the meantime, Moishe saw his opening and slipped into the now vacant spot. He got out of his car, reached in the back and pulled out his walker. He then wheeled himself over to Hymie's car as quickly as he could push his walker. Just as he got there Hymie was finally able to open his door. The door swung open fairly rapidly, as it was angled downhill, hitting Moishe in the stomach, causing his dentures to fly out of his mouth onto the ground in front of Hymie. When Hymie finally activated his walker, he was standing right on the dentures. Since Moishe hadn't cleaned his dentures in months, they were covered with a sort of green slime, making them slick as the snot he preferred to swallow rather than spend good money for tissues to dispose of it in a somewhat more savory manner.

Hymie slipped on the dentures, fell backwards onto the adjoining Jaguar's hood catching his Depends on the figurine ornament. As he slumped to the ground the Depends came undone, pulled out from under his pants and fell over onto his head. There was a full load in them which covered up his mouth and nose causing him to suffocate to death from a kind of atomic wedgie. Witnesses stated that they thought there would have been time to save him but they couldn't find anyone amongst the dozens of witnesses who seemed to remember how to do mouth to mouth resuscitation.

No charges have been filed so far but a ticket was given to the parked car for having broken windows.

I remembered to call back Dr. Slobrew an hour after the first attempt. "Dr. Slobrew, I have a case I need to discuss with you to see what you think." I stated solicitously. No reason to upset him as the only way I could divest myself of unwanted and undeserving patients was for him to agree with me that they indeed weren't worthy.

"Alright, tell me about the patient." Answered Slobrew sweetly, as if he was playing to the tapes, which, in fact, he was.

"Mr. Bon Chance is a 95 year old male with severe dehydration, unbelievable electrolyte abnormalities and a CD4 count of two. He's a resident of a long term care facility and has advanced directives that state do not resuscitate. Physical therapy has declined to pick him up, his family has sent in a mortician for preneed cost estimates and his priest has administered his last rites. I was wondering if you'd be willing to make him custodial for terminal care?"

"Welllll, let me see. You say he's dehydrated. How dehydrated would you say he is?" drawled out Slobrew.

"He's so dehydrated that they had to reconstitute the vial of his blood they took in the nursing home with a quart of water in the lab just to get it fluid enough to get it to flow through the tubing in the testing machine. He's so dehydrated that the Park Service denied him a pass into Death Valley because he was a risk to the cacti. He's so dehydrated ..."

"Okaaaaaaay. I think I understand. He was low on water. Okay, let's see what else. Oh, yes, you say his electrolytes were abnormal. I was just wondering which electrolytes we're talking about and how off were they?" Slobrew was on a roll, even if uphill.

"All the electrolytes were off, very off, that is, of the one's that could still be detected in his body. Just for my own edification, how many electrolytes do you think there are in body?" stopping just short of asking whether or not he actually went to medical school.

"You're the clinician, it's not up to me to second guess how many electrolytes there are. I'm sure you're taking care of them all in your best medical judgment."

(What?) "Yes sir, I am. I've dedicated my professional life to taking care of electrolytes and my entire medical career has been leading up to being able to meet the challenge that Mr. Chance has presented me here today. Unfortunately, I have to report that I'm a complete failure. I've failed Mr. Chance in not keeping his electrolytes within normal range. I've failed as an American in letting one of our own slip away. I've failed as a child of God. In fact, God's now banging on the door for Mr. Chance and I've barred it and stuck cotton in my ears, refusing to let him take Mr. Chance merely because his electrolytes aren't normal. I throw myself on the mercy of the world and both demand their harshest judgment of me yet beg for their mercy. I …"

"Okaaaaaay, I guess the electrolytes are off. We'll just push that issue aside for now and move on to the next issue. Oh yes, his CD4 count is two. Are you telling me he can still enjoy listening to CD's but you're not sure if he has four or two? Is that how you see it?"

Slobrew is an idiot. "No Sir. I'm not quite saying that, but close. What I mean is that the subset of white blood cells that help fight infection are a tad low and that he'll have a bit of a problem trying to fight off a cold and the like. Just to put it into perspective for you, a normal CD4 count is over 1000. His is two. We diagnosis immune deficiency when it drops to under 500. His is two. You get full blown AIDS when it's under 200. His is two. The body starts to rot from the inside when the CD4 count is under 50. His is two. The only thing keeping him alive is that the remaining two cells are holding hands but they're starting to slip. I hope that helps with your understanding of this issue."

"Okaaaaaay, so what you're saying is he has only two CD's left and his life's not worth living without more variety?"

"That's just exactly it Sir. His life's not worth living and he wants to die. His family wants him to die, his priest wants him to die, the mortician wants him to die, God is waiting at the door and wants him to die."

"But you've spent so much time and effort on him that you don't want him to die." 'Noooooooooooooo' I scream silently into the phone. "So you see the dilemma I have here. Everything points to him dying except you think he can be saved if we just get him a few more CD's. Have you checked with social services? Do they have any spare CD's they can get him?"

Slobrew, you're retarded and a menace to mankind. If I could reach into this phone I'd strangle you by your own intestines. "Not quite the conclusion I was hoping for Sir. Let me put it another way…"

"Not quite now, son, I have to empty the old bladder. How about if we get in touch again in a day or so? That'll give me time to find a way to lighten the blow to you if you can't save Mr. Chance and that'll give you some time to rustle up some CD's. Be talking to you real soon. Bye."

I'll kill him, I'll kill him, I'll kill him. But first I'll do Mr.Chance.

I didn't get the chance to do Chance. I got a beep stating he passed on. The issue was moot but the point wasn't. Slobrew had to be forced to actually make a decision. I decided to call him back the next day.

Cheerful as always, Slobrew answered the phone, "Helllllloooooooo. Hooooow arrrrre yoooouuu?"

"I'm fine Sir, how are you?" I asked back.

"I'm jussssst fine. Soooo, what can I do for yooouuu?"

"I was wondering whether or not you were able to ponder the fate of Mr. Chance? Let me start off by saying I'm now reconciled to his death and can live with myself in good conscience that I did everything I could do for him and he's lived a good and long life but it's now come to an end. Therefore, I stand before you, hat in hand, begging you to let him go and issue the denial of benefits letter." A fine speech, even by my standards.

"Weeelllll, as you know, I've been putting a great deal of thought into this one, taking into account the efforts you've put into this case and your eloquent plea for more time yesterday. On the one hand, his clinical status appears untenable. On the other hand I can understand your disappointment and request for more time. On the other hand, I have a duty to my employer not to waste money engaging in futile medical care. On the other hand, you tell me it may not be futile. On the other hand, those who know him best, his family and priest are asking him to die. On the other hand, it may be that they have ulterior motives, such as inheritance, causing them to push for his demise. On the other hand …" Slobrew ruminated on but I had to interrupt.

"Sir, you have so many hands in the pot, I was wondering if this is a medical job or a hand job?" I spurted out in frustration.

"Weeeeeellllll, putting it that way, I've decided to defer to your better judgment and not issue the letter yet. The time's just not right. He still has a chance. I hope you use this extra time to your best advantage. I've gone out on a limb for you on this one."

Slobrew, my hero. "Sir, I just got a beep as we were talking, Mr. Chance has finally expired." I said, setting the trap.

"Even so, I'm not sure that extra bit of clinical data should influence my decision. Why don't you get back to me in a week and we'll reevaluate the case on its merits. I might be forced to act then if there's no change in his condition." Slobrew sounded proud of his Solomon like decision.

"That's an excellent idea, Sir. Your counsel has been most enlightening. If I can't handle it from here, I shall return for further discussion. In the mean time, I have been energized and will address his case with renewed vigor. Thank you for your indulgence. I'll try not to burden you with such mundane concerns in the future. Fare thee well, O great one!" As

I was reaching to hang up the phone I could hear Slobrew saying, "On the other hand …" Click.

Okay, enough wasted time with the medical director. Time to move on to the next nursing home.

Chapter 50: Off To the Races

At the nursing home, Nursey was trying to make final preparations for Mr. Chance. He hadn't been pronounced dead yet so she had to find the house doctor to do so. She called over to the other wing to see if he was there.

"What? We're busy." snarled Beasty, the affectionate name we gave to the septuagenarian monster guarding the west wing as if she was the sole heir to its glory and power.

"Doing what, Beasty? Biting off visiting grandchildren's heads?" Nursey asked sarcastically.

"No, you denizen of a lesser ward, we're resuscitating Mr. McFarto, and I can tell you, we can barely breath with the stench he's making in there. We've had to revive Dr. Kabala twice so far, having passed out from the smell."

"Well, when you've finished with the doctor, send him down here so he can pronounce Mr. Chance and we can get him to the morgue before he gives McFarto a run for his money."

A pause long enough for both Nursey and Beasty to realize what was going on. If there are two patients needing the morgue and only one spot, they both needed to get there now or the other one will be stuck with a stiff for who knows how long, adding to the already sewer like stench of their hallways. Neither had the courtesy to say goodbye before they hungup. Beasty just threw the phone in the general direction of the cradle. Time was a-wasting.

Nursey called for her aides but they, of course, were nowhere to be found. There was no time to waste in the usually futile effort to find help when she needed it so Nursey, in a Herculean effort and a new personal best, single handedly cleaned and jerked Mr. Chance, shroud and all, from his prone position in bed to a waiting wheelchair. She tore off down the hall to the elevator bank to make the two story descent to the basement morgue.

Sensing that there she was falling behind, Beasty pushed Dr. Kabala onto the bed, unlocked the wheels and had the aides and nurses grab the four corners of the bed, racing down the hall to the same elevator bank that Nursey was rapidly approaching. Dr. Kabala, true to his oath, continued one man CPR the whole time.

Nursey got there first, exhausted but still with presence of mind to position the wheelchair in front of the elevator door, assuming a commanding lead in the race. Whether or not Beasty planned it, they were unable to stop the bed in time to prevent her entourage from crashing into the wheelchair. Mr. Chance went sprawling onto the floor, the wheelchair folded up as if for storage next to him.

The elevator door opened, Beasty wasting no time on sentimentality, let alone common courtesy, left Nursey there alone with Chance on the floor. She commanded the bed into the elevator, but because of the relatively low door opening, shedded 180 pounds of useless load as Dr. Kabala was knocked on his head and fell off the foot of the gurney onto the floor. This effectively ended the heroic efforts at CPR and sealed McFarto's fate.

Stunned but still conscious, Dr. Kabala was lifted from the floor and pressed into service by Nursey to help her get Mr. Chance back into the wheelchair and down the stairs. Dr. Kabala not yet back to his senses thought Mr. Chance was Mr. McFarto and resumed CPR, standing on the foot rests, tipping the chair over and down the stairs. Chance and Kabala bounced off the first landing, rounded down to the next one and almost came to rest when Nursey caught up with them and gave them a kick creating just enough momentum to keep them tumbling down to the next landing. She gave them a second shove and they rapidly reached the bottom floor. She propped the door open with Dr. Kabala, repositioned the wheelchair and lifted Mr. Chance into it again.

Dr. Kabala came to long enough to see there was CPR still to be done. He jumped on the wheelchair, started mouth to mouth with Mr. Chance and had all the water sucked out of his body in less than a second.

By this time, Nursey was getting up a good head of steam heading to the morgue, just one door away. Just as she was passing it, the elevator door had fully opened and out charged Beasty and her crew.

There was no way Nursey had come this far to lose the race. She barreled down the hall, smashed into the door, which fortunately was a swinging door and crashed into the open slab at the morgue. The sudden stop jolted both Mr. Chance and Dr. Kabala into the opening and Nursey slammed and locked the vault after them.

In the meantime, the swinging door swung back with such force that it knocked over the gurney, spilling all its content and attendants onto the floor. The only people left standing were Nursey and Beasty.

As Nursey sauntered by Beasty, stepping over the carnage and swinging the key by its chain on her right forefinger, being careful to keep it out of Beasty's reach, Nursey said, "Looks like you have a little cleaning up to do. And oh, is that a call bell on your side I hear ringing? I do believe it is! See you at seven at the check out clock. Oh, and by the way, when Dr. Kabala finishes pronouncing my patient, you might want to ask him about yours. He should be regaining consciousness right about now."

Beasty took solace in the fact she had beaten Nursey three out of the four last times they had this race. Oh well, after cleaning up, back to the rat races.

Chapter 51: A Day Out With the Inlaws

My in laws live in Middle America. It's not so bad as long as you don't dwell on the "live" in that thought. Their requirements are simple and usually easily accommodated. Unfortunately, we have one insurmountable obstacle to perfect relations: Stinweeds.

Stinweeds is Middle America's vain attempt to achieve the convenience of fast food but do so at exorbitant prices. They produce a White Castle size burger but without it's taste and charm and sell it for dinner prices. Instead of a dime or quarter as it should cost, they rip you off with an $8.00 price tag. But of course that comes with a napkin, a plate, and if you ask for it, some ketchup. Even if you ask for it, they don't serve it with any taste.

Nevertheless, there are some people who have lived such a sheltered life that they don't know any better and keep going to Stinweeds time and time again.

That's fine for some people, but not me. It's not that I'm special or entitled to any special consideration. Au contraire, it's just that I'm normal. And want to stay that way. I don't know what hold Stinweeds has over the natives but it must be powerful as the place is always packed. I didn't want to be turned into a Stinweeds zombie so I had to come up with a plan.

On our latest (and probably last) visit with the in-laws, the first thought, of course, on everyone's mind (except mine) was a trip to Stinweeds. Despite my usual protestations, I was dragged along against my will. I had several choices. Resist with all my might but that meant I could end up having no food at all that day and just maybe no nooky that entire week. I could go along peacefully but that would be an admission of defeat which wasn't my nature. So I chose a middle ground, I went along but issued vague warnings the entire trip there and during the entire interminable wait on the round-the-corner line that I was going to turn each and everyone of their lives into one living purgatory (I didn't want to go too far in my threats – I needed a ride home).

My pleas for mercy fell on deaf ears, drowned out by the sound of their drool dripping from their greedy lips and hitting the ground in a loud staccato of anticipatory gustatory delight as they anticipated the feast awaiting them.

We finally were shown to a cramped booth with décor right out of the 50's. Judging by the wear and tear of the plastic seats, it was probably the original material from the 50's. The gaping holes in the seats from unmended tears and loss of stuffing made it clear why there were signs as you walked in that issued a height requirement for a child to sit alone. Too short and they'd be sucked into the gap never to be seen again. That could also explain the brisk white slaver trade thriving out the back door. All the lost kids had to be removed lest the fine aroma of the food might be affected by the multitude of unchanged diapers emanating from the crevices in the seats. It looked as if Stinweeds had thought of all contingencies.

The waitress finally acquiesced to come over to our table. The look on her face made it clear that this was just a temporary job until she was discovered by the local beauty parlor. Obviously, tips either were of no concern to her or she thought that they were her birthright and had no relation to her job performance.

"So, what'll it be?" she spit out while admiring the fine polish job that adorned at least two out of the five fingers on her right hand. The other three fingers were obviously being punished for some slight against her sensibilities so she made them go out in public undressed. Or maybe they were protesting the choice of purple, green and orange that were applied in alternating layers on the other two fingers without removing the prior layer first. Regardless, I was able to regain her attention by spilling a half filled glass of water left over from the previous diners on her feet. She jumped back from the shock of the wet feeling but at least she was spared the icy sting of cold water as unfortunately, the monthly shipment of ice cubes from San Francisco was late that month.

"Hey!" she exclaimed. "Why did you do that?"

I could only give her a Who? Me? look as I put down the glass I had in my hand in as nonchalant manner as I could manage while still keeping a straight face. "I'm sorry. Were you talking to me? I was just looking at my watch to see if we'd have time to eat breakfast before it was dinner time. I wasn't paying any attention to you. Can I help you?"

Her stare was a combination of hate and befuddlement. Could I possibly have done this to her by mistake or was I just covering up? Either way she counted this time as putting her closer to the stated corporate goal of wasting a minimum of twenty minutes of patron's time before actually doing anything for them. In more ways than one, my time was nearly up. "Look buster, I don't know if that was an innocent mistake or on purpose, but either way it was a mistake that I don't look kindly on. What if there was something toxic in that glass, like the water we serve here? I could have been injured severely. I'm going to put a workman's comp claim in just in case."

"You're absolutely right! Imagine if some of what you serve and call food here was actually ingested by some poor unsuspecting customer and that customer, having taken a bite of that food and realizing his error, in a final attempt to save himself tried to take a sip of water. And what if some of the food in his mouth regurgitated into the water before he slumped to the floor. Then I come along and spill that contaminated water on your feet. Just think of the personal health consequences to you and your progeny! Oh, the humanity!"

"I don't know what your game is but if you're trying to sweet talk me, it's not working."

I don't know if the perverted neural connections that allow people to reason like the waitress also serve as a disconnect between their taste buds and conscious thought so that they could eat at Stinweed and live to talk about it. It was clear that I had entered a parallel universe where people who were congenitally stupid seemed to be revered as gods.

"Why thank you kindly for the complement. Before the day's over, I see us riding off into the sunset together."

"Hrummpphh." seemed to emanate from her body. "Look wise guy, are you ready to order?"

"Very much so." I smiled my reply.

"Well, what do you want then?" and I'll make sure we don't have any, she smiled back.

"Tell you what. We'll play a game of 20 questions. I make a guess and you tell me if it's on your menu. If you don't have the time or stomach for losing, you can throw in the towel now and just get us menus. Or, even more fun, this can be the moment your whole life has been leading up to and for the first time in public, try to read the menu to us out loud to show the world that all that reading practice has finally paid off. But that might not be a true test of your reading ability as you might have the menu memorized. No, try this, try reading every third word on the menu to us and we'll pick out the words we like the best and you can have the kitchen make that up for us."

"If you wanted menus, why didn't you just say so? I've got to go back to the kitchen and get them." Muttering vague curses as she turned her back to us. I called out vocce dolce "Don't forget to stir the cauldron while you're there, you witch."

Having been here before, I was prepared for the legendary Stinweeds service. I took out a large candy bar and proceeded to ruin my appetite, quite possibly saving my life. A good ten minutes later the waitress returned with the menus. "Hey, you're now ahead of the game, you got another 10 minute head start on the delay for your next customers. Way to go. You might get into the Stinweeds hall of fame at this rate."

Twenty minutes later, she returned again. She was going for the record. The other waitresses were starting to take notice. A few of them held up signs: 8.5, 8.8, even a 9.2. Good, but not good enough. She'll have to try harder. But what could she do? If we got up and walked out, the timing would have to start over again. She had to hope that we hung in there to the end. Another 30 minutes before we were served would put her into the records, beating a 15 year old record set by Mr. Stinweed himself on his last day on the job. He might have been able to extend it even longer but his disgruntled customer took matters in his own hands and threw a glass of water left over from the adjoining table on poor Mr. Stinweed. His weak heart couldn't take the fear of what might be in the water and he died of fright on the spot. The customer was convicted of assault with a deadly weapon and involuntary manslaughter. He was just grateful to the judge that the 10-20 he got was still less than the wait for his meal at Stinweeds. Maybe our waitress did have a justified fear of the water.

"So, I trust that you're ready to order." She snarled.

"Just one question before we start: Are all your sandwiches as skimpy and tasteless as your hamburgers?" I asked innocently.

She froze in place. In all her days as a waitress, none of the customers ever had the temerity to belittle the hallowed Stinweeds fare. She couldn't decide whether she should assault me verbally or physically. As these thoughts and consequences of her actions circled inside her brain, she became paralyzed by indecision. This just wasn't in the Stinweeds manual. It was inconceivable that anyone could possibly risk being denied Stinweeds food or barred from the premises, for surely, this type of irreverence would have those effects. Starring at me in blind rage for close to a minute, she suddenly turned on her heels and quickly walked back to her coven for support. A gasp was audible from the growing ranks of her admirers. The scores quickly were changed to 1.3, 1.5 and 2.4. How was she going to salvage the record? A cheer arose as the waitress' busboy emerged from the kitchen, pad in hand. He was going to take the orders! They were elated to realize a new record was being set. A tag team! Brilliant! This was going to go down in the annals of Stinweeds as the best day in their history.

Just as he was reaching our table, ready to resume where the waitress left off, I finished off the candy bar, declared I was no longer hungry and told the rest of the table to get up and let's go. Being Midwesterners, they had to be polite and accede to their guest's wishes. We stood up as a group marched out and didn't leave a tip. The waitress came running out of the back screaming, "Where's my tip?!?!" but to no avail. The outside door closed between us and we were gone. She turned to the judges. They hung their heads low, put up three zeros and returned to their neglected tables. The funny thing about it was that the other customers didn't notice anything out of the ordinary. They were just glad to be in Stinweeds. Whether or not they actually were served was beside the point.

We, on the other hand, decided it had become too late for lunch and went off to get barbeque for supper. It was an all you could eat place and boy, were we hungry.

Chapter 52:
Attack of the Killer Fruit,
Or:
Who's Eaten Gilbert Grape

Nursey, for all her strong points, had one fatal weakness. A neurosis, as we call it medically. She hated fruit. It didn't matter the race, religion or national origin, and it goes without question the sexual orientation with a name like fruit, she hated them all equally. There was no question of prejudice, she despised them all. Perhaps it had something to do with a deep seated suppressed memory from her childhood involving a rogue pomegranate. Perhaps it was a later in life acquired distaste. Whatever it was, she lived in mortal fear of fruit. She developed an urge to throw up at the very thought of them and did so quite readily when they were in her sight.

This, as you might imagine, played more than a little havoc on her personal and professional life. She would make excuses like she was always having morning sickness and kept cranking out the kids as a cover. But she knew that she couldn't stay pregnant forever, she'd have to come up with a new solution eventually. For now though, that was her story and she was sticking to it.

Unfortunately for Nursey, fruit is universally appreciated and as such is ubiquitous in our daily lives. Her constant efforts to avoid them led to somewhat embarrassing moments for her but amusing to the rest of us. Just the other day she was stopped dead in her tracks by a peach that was sitting on the nursing station counter. At first she assumed her usual doubled over throw-up position but was able to suppress the actual regurgitation by staring at the floor and yelling at the top of her lungs for housekeeping to remove the horrible object immediately or she'll take away their brushes they use to clean the toilets. Housekeeping, remembering the last time they had to do without their brushes, charged to the rescue and whisked away the offending object. All it was was an old rotted peach I picked off a patient's tray. I got a good chuckle, confirmed that what the social worker told me about Nursey was true and had another weapon to use as I saw fit. The only down side was that I probably saved a patient from ptomaine, but what the heck, there would be another meal served that night, probably just as lethal.

On the other hand, there are people out there who absolutely love fruit. One comes readily to mind, Mrs. Mangoe. Mrs. Mangoe, it turns out, was a long term resident of the nursing home ever since she had a stroke a year and a half ago. Following the stroke, she was no longer able to swallow so she was given a feeding tube. The feeding tube, also known as a PEG, is a surgically implanted rubber tube that is inserted into the stomach through a puncture wound in the mid abdomen while under anesthesia. The whole procedure is monitored internally via an endoscope – a three foot long ¾" tube that's inserted through the mouth and passed through the esophagus into the stomach. It has a bright light at the end so the surgeon can see where to make the incision into the stomach.

The difficult part is to make the incision precisely where the stomach is closest to the abdominal wall so that no other organs are injured in the process. The problem is that, presumably due to peristalsis, the light keeps moving so the surgeon has to jump from point to point following the light. There's been many a heated discussion between the surgeon and the gastroenterologist (also know as a "GI") about the light moving all over the place and never holding still. This results in a few fits and starts on many patients so when they wake up it looks like a crazed slasher has attacked his abdomen. The surgeon blames the GI for not holding the scope still. The GI says he's doing his best but peristalsis is too powerful for the scope to resist moving. In private, a few candid GI's have admitted to moving the scope all over the place to piss off the surgeon. Sometimes they just don't like the surgeon but most of the time they do it out of resentment that they get only $150- for the procedure but the surgeon gets $450- for the same amount of time. The surgeons for their part admit that they really don't have to jump around after the light, they just do it to goad on the GI. A few even admit that the slash marks look suspiciously like their initials. The patient's well being doesn't actually enter into the conversation at any time. Insurance, yes; well being, no.

In any case, having a PEG placed is no bowl of cherries and you really don't want to get one if you don't need one. Some, like Mrs. Mangoe, need one. Once you have a PEG, you can pretty well kiss eating goodbye. No steak, no pie, no fruit, no nothing. Even your saliva can kill you. That's because everything goes down the wrong tube, that's to say, it goes into your lungs. This is followed by extreme shortness of breath, chest pain, high fevers and pneumonia followed shortly (if God is merciful) by death. If you are unlucky enough to linger, you get to go to the ICU, be intubated and have tubes come out of every natural and quite a few manmade orifices. You get to be serenaded by the ICU symphony of alarms and bells and nonstop activity day and night. You get to have 1000 watts lights shine in your face day and night. You get to be woken up for vital signs every four hours. My personal favorite is the rectal thermometer right after your ice water enema followed immediately by having every blanket in the building placed on top of you due to your 54* temperature. Does wonders for your 106* fever which they'd know about if they only had the humanity to take your temperature by mouth. All this leads to a condition called ICU psychosis which is God's second chance of showing you mercy since he didn't see fit to take you right off the bat. By being psychotic it allows your mind to neither feel nor care about the agony your body is being put through.

So you risk a lot if you try to eat but are physically incapable of it. And that leads us back to Mrs. Mangoe. She was not only incapable of swallowing but also incapable of feeding herself even if she could swallow. So enter her kind hearted niece, Mrs. Bea Goodall. Mrs. Goodall never finished high school and barely has the brains to finish a sentence. But she has a heart a mile wide to make up for her mental shortcomings. So when she saw the plight her dear aunt was in, always asking for food but never having it allowed, she finally relented and consented to smuggle some of her favorite food into her room. Oh, how it warmed Bea's heart to see the bright smile on Mrs. Mangoe's face when she showed her what she brought her. There they were, the object of a year and half lust: grapes! Big, juicy, succulent, cool, sweet grapes! Her favorite snack of all time.

"Oh thank you Bea! You're my favorite niece. You are the only person to ever bring me any food, although I've been begging for some lo these many months. Come, put one in my mouth before someone comes and takes them away." Implored Mrs. Mangoe.

"Would you like me to sit you up Auntie?" asked Bea.

"No, no, that won't be necessary. The nurses never do when they give me the tube feedings and it'll just waste time. Quick, let's eat!" exhorted Mrs. Mangoe.

So Bea, being the ever dutiful niece, places the first grape in her aunt's mouth. Quick as she could, she virtually inhales the grape and demands more. Almost as quick as Bea can place them in her mouth, Mrs. Mangoe disposes of them. After a dozen or so, Mrs.Mangoe starts to slow down, then stops altogether. And I'm not just talking stops eating, I'm talking stops everything! Breathing, heart pumping, moving in general. The only thing that moved was her eyes rolling up in her head, followed shortly thereafter with generalized seizures and then nothing again. With the same innate intellect of a former Governor who later became President even after having his security detail pimp to for him, Bea realized something was wrong. With the same exemplary memory of that former President's wife testifying under oath to a grand jury and her mind going completely blank, she remembered there's a call bell to call the nurse. Grabbing what she thinks is the call bell, Bea deftly activates the TV remote but gets distracted by a commercial regarding purchasing lots on the moon. She's returned to the here and now by the violent kicking of her aunt having another seizure and decided if the nurse isn't going to check on the call bell, she'll have to go find one herself. After turning the wrong way out of the room, Bea opens the outside door, thus activating the emergency alarm. Bea is now stuck outside the locked safety door. Fortunately, the noise from the door alarm is disturbing enough to awaken even the most lethargic of nurses and an aide decides to come down the hallway to investigate. As luck would have it, this aide is real nosey and always sneaks a peek in everyone's room, mostly to see if there's any left over food for her to steal as the life of a nurse's aide requires all the energy one could muster. At least that what she's been told to expect and has been stocking up on energy since her first day 20 years ago. She's stocked up so much energy that she can't fit through any but the double wide hall doors so her job is now hall monitor as the union won't let her be fired merely for grossing out the rest of the world. And, oh yes, not being able to do any useful work. Being too large to fit through the patient's doorway, she now subsists on food being thrown to her by the terrified patients in an effort to make her go away. Anyway, she sees Mrs. Mangoe is violently thrashing about and takes pity on her in that no one should ever have to work that hard. Lord knows she wouldn't. It also makes her look bad if the sick patients in for rehab are moving quicker than the help. So after turning off the door alarm and ambling back to the nurse's station, sneaking another peek at Mrs. Mangoe on her way back to make sure there's still something going on, she mentions as an aside to Nursey that Mrs. Mangoe seems to be agitated about something. Nursey, looking somewhat perplexed, as Mrs. Mangoe hasn't given her a lick of trouble for the entire time she's been there, does her New York "watch out for the muggers" brisk walk down the hall to see if the hall monitor is earning her keep. Taking one look at the violent seizures Mrs. Mangoe is having followed almost immediately by ceasing of all vital activities again, Nursey spurs into action. She pulls the emergency bell announcing "Code Blue" for all to hear and starts one man CPR.

Nursey first tries to clear Mrs. Mangoe's airway. She pulls out a mashed grape and nearly plotzes on the spot! Always the professional, Nursey pulls herself back together and starts chest compressions. One by one, with each compression, another intact grape flies out of Mrs. Mangoe's mouth. The first one hits Nursey in the cheek, she ducks for the next few. Finally help arrives and she assigns one to do mouth to mouth. The nurse assigned to mouth to mouth bends over and just as she covers Mrs. Mangoe's lips with her own, Nursey does a chest compressed jetting a grape right into the other nurse's mouth and down into her trachea. She rears up, holding her throat and making the most dreadful gasping noise you could imagine. I wander into the room, realize what's happening and reach in front of the nurse to perform a Heimlich maneuver. Before I do so, I reposition the nurse so she's facing directly at Nursey. Meanwhile an aide has taken over chest compressions for Nursey so she's now standing at the foot of the bed. Almost simultaneously, trying to time it to perfection, as soon as the substitute nurse starts the down stroke for the chest compressions, I give a mighty squeeze on the struggling nurse's abdomen. In a thing of unimaginable beauty, a grape from each of the victims are propelled through the air at high velocity and smack Nursey squarely on each cheek. A small scream then a loud thud were the last sounds we heard from Nursey for the rest of the code.

God was kind. Mrs. Mangoe had swallowed too many grapes and they were lodged too deeply to save her. At least she died happy, finally getting to eat her favorite food, even if it was her last meal.

Someone had to clean the vomit off of Nursey to help her maintain her professional stature as it couldn't be brought consciously to bear while she was unconscious.

Hours later Mrs. Goodall finally found her way to the front door where she was let in and taken back to Mrs. Mangoe's room to pick up her effects. "Where is dear auntie?" inquired Bea.

"She's at a better place." was all that the aide could say.

"Oh, that's nice, I'll have to see her there then." She turned and walked out to her car, looking for that better place but not quite remembering if she got the right directions. No problem, she thought, it's getting late so I'll just see her tomorrow.

After having so many grapes forced on her, Nursey thought she might actually be developing a taste for them after all.

Chapter 53: I Wish I Had Said That

I get into a lot of fights with people. I'm not particularly prejudiced against anyone. I'm happy to fight with anyone that I feel is a lesser being than me. Since that's just about everyone, I get into a lot of fights.

What do I fight about? Just about anything where I have an opinion and feel other people are wrong. I get into a lot of fights.

I remember one time I was arguing with a hospital pharmacist. He was clearly, almost by definition, wrong, as he disagreed with something I had ordered. So there I am, standing in the middle of the nursing station, dressed in my tennis clothes as I had just been called in off the courts for an emergency on a Sunday afternoon. I wasn't particularly happy to be there and here's this twerp of a pharmacist arguing with me over the use of a particular medicine. I was loathe to continue the argument and, having smelled alcohol on his breath, stated "You're drunk! Go home before I call the police and get you fired."

He started to seethe and responded with the classic putdown, "You put your pants on just like me, one leg at a time."

Not amused with his apparent ineffectual defense of his position I offered "If this was a dressing contest, you'd still lose by a mile. Now get out of here or else."

Defeated in the field of wits and the professional field of medicine, he tucked his tail between his legs and scurried off.

"Hello, Mr. Rife. I just wanted to let you know that I was threatened in your nursing station by your drunken pharmacist who was just about to poison my patient with the wrong medicine. I'll keep this between you and me if your new pharmacist introduces himself to me by five tomorrow. Oh, and sorry for disturbing you at church during your mother's funeral. Couldn't be helped." I hope the administrator knows which side his bread is buttered on. I don't want to waste any more time on a worthless pharmacist.

I turned to the nurses and started to explain myself but realized that communicating with the little people would be as much of a waste as continuing on with the pharmacist.

As I walked down the hall to rejoin the tennis match previously in progress, I heard the familiar howls of pain and horror from the various denizens of the back hallways. Those long forgotten former humans, now just living blobs of protoplasm waiting for the merciful end to come.

"Arrrrrgh!"

Ah, music to my ears. People are suffering. I started humming "I'm in the money" as I sauntered down the hall.

Chapter 54: Why Can't I Get A Good Night's Sleep?

Home has always been considered one's castle, a refuge from the madding crowd. Those sentiments obviously were established long before the invention of such modern miracles as the beeper, fax, e-mail, wireless web, cell phone and, of course, the telephone. No longer is home a place to relax but merely another stop on the physician's perpetual rounds.

To fight back against the invasion of my privacy, having hunted me down in my most remote sanctuary, I've found it somewhat satisfying to make rude and semi threatening comments from the anonymity of a telephone without having to worry about witnesses and personal confrontation. It's an impersonal way to make slanderous attacks on the high and low alike. A great equalizer in a world where physical stature would otherwise essentially predetermine whether or not a confrontation would occur in the first place and if so, who'll be the winner. Essentially, it replaces physical prowess with mental prowess as the sole determiner of the victor. Thus, the meek, that is to say, the small in stature, have inherited the earth. Thus, a 90 year old, 70 pound grandmother, can now bully and win in an argument with a 20 year old college football player working customer service over the summer. He can't see her and she can't see him. They have no idea where each other live. They can't put their hands around each other's neck. Therefore, the winner is determined by who can yell the loudest and who can out think and out mouth the other. Even I can win. So let's join the battle.

I get home on a typical night. Dinner's almost ready. The phone rings.

"Hi." I answer nicely for once, not yet primed for battle.

"Hi. I'm John, from 'Got You In A Clinch'. We have an exciting new credit card program where anyone can now have a credit card at a great APR! You've been selected for one of these great, low annual rate charge cards. You can also accumulate points towards a great rest home for your in-laws."

Now there's a great deal! Finally something worthwhile to redeem the points for, I think to myself.

"All you have to do is give me your social security number and your bank saving's account number and we can get you set up tonight." John continued.

I called over to my wife "Hey dear, I told you that they'd be offering us credit again real soon. The bankruptcies aren't even discharged yet and they don't even care that my civil rights haven't been restored yet. Is this a great country or what?" I resumed my attention to John and said "So John, how do I sign up? What do you need?" as enthusiastically as I could.

John, having heard what I literally yelled into the microphone to my wife was understandably a little taken aback. "Y-y-you having some legal difficulties?" he stammered out.

"Nah, whatever might have been wrong in the past is long since past. Nothing to worry about now. Let's get this form filled out right now. We need some stuff and we're going shopping right after we finish supper. Hell, it's probably cold already anyhow. We'll just go out to eat once we get off the phone now that we got ourselves some credit again. Now where were we? Oh, right, let's get the form filled out now. Mom's out warming up the car, she's been hankering for a few little trinkets to go with her formal wear. Haven't gotten her new jewelry in months. So shoot, what do you need to know?"

"I'm not so sure ..." John eeked out.

"What do you mean not so sure? You're the one who called me. Let's get on with it or the Better Business Bureau and the State Attorney will be making some not so subtle inquiries. What does it matter to you anyway? You get paid for signing me up. You weren't involved in selecting me to call. Go ahead and do your job. Hurry up, I'm getting hungry. Haven't had a decent meal in three years, two months and five days. That slammer food sucks. Now don't go ahead and get me mad at another person. It's been a long time since that happened and I've got a lot of pent up anger and I'm not going back in. They'll never take me alive!"

"Okay, okay." John surrendered. "What's your address?"

"I don't like giving that sort of information out to strangers. Never know how they're gonna use it. What's more, don't plan to stay in one place long enough to find out. How about you send the bills to general delivery at the post office and I'll be by to pick it up as soon as it gets there?"

"No, no. this isn't going to work. Sorry I bothered you folks on such a nice evening. Goodbye now." John escaped.

"Wait, before you go, how about you giving me your phone number in case I get an address? My caller ID wasn't able to pick your number up. Probably a technical glitch, you know how sensitive these things are. Just give me your home number so I can speak to you personally..."

Click. John was gone, too bad, I hadn't had a chance to torture him enough. Not nearly as much as he did me. Oh well, there'll be plenty more tonight to take out my pent up frustrations on, I'm on call tonight.

I didn't have to wait very long for my next victim. My beeper went off for the first admission of the long evening. Thirty admissions a night wasn't unusual. Fortunately, I didn't have to go in to see them, they could all be seen the next day. But 30 admissions meant 30 nurses that I could ply my trade on. Some were actually pretty good and efficient so they would usually get a bye. The rest were fresh meat to the man eater I became on the phone.

I dialed the number in my beeper. This time the answering service at least got the right area code even though the number was off. They almost always get at least one number wrong so you either had to have the correct numbers memorized for the 50 or so nursing homes my group attended or call back the answering service, let them know how incompetent they were and wait for the irate nurse to call back to find out why I hadn't returned her first call.

We'd been through a number of answering services over the years. It's amazing that they'd be required to pay minimum wages to subsimian life forms, but the law's the law. One memorable service was called "ding-a-ling". No kidding. They weren't the worst one we ever had but they always were close contender for that title. Their name made them easy targets for derision. Ding-bat came readily to mind.

Since I didn't remember the correct number for the SNF they paged me with, I was forced to call them up.

"Hello, I need to talk to Anna, the operator who just paged me."

"May I tell her your name?"

"No."

"I have to know your name."

"Why?"

"So I can tell her who's calling"

"Tell her the doctor she just paged with the wrong number is calling."

"That doesn't narrow the field very much, now does it?"

"As far as I can tell, it doesn't eliminate anybody."

"Well, I need a name." She insisted.

"Have you asked your parents if it isn't time they decided on one. I hear they come in handy in the business world."

"Smart aleck, I need your name."

"It's already taken, but if you are desperate enough, I'll sell it to you for a thousand bucks. Mind you, it comes with a fair bit of baggage. You might want to find yourself an unused one and start out fresh. Take it from me, it'll be better in the long run."

"Give me your name now or you won't get through."

"I don't think I'd get through to you no matter what I did. I've been wondering for some time now. Why do you call yourselves the ding-bat answering service? I was thinking a more appropriate name might be the 'stupid answering service', and as you get a little more experience, maybe the 'incredibly stupid answering service'."

"You can't talk to me like that!"

"Apparently I can and did."

"I've taken about all I care to from you. I'm putting on my supervisor!"

"Great. Now we're getting somewhere." A brief pause and another operator comes on.

"Hello doctor, if that's what you really are. Why are you upsetting my girls so badly?" demanded Jane, the supervisor.

"Actually, I thought I was doing a good job of upsetting them, if you were to ask me."

"You know what I mean. Why did you call us the stupid answering service? That wasn't very nice."

"Actually what I asked Anna was whether or not you were the stupid answering service or the incredibly stupid answering service. I tried to make no judgment between the two. I just thought the ding-bat answering service didn't aptly portray the image you were trying to project. I was just helping you with your marketing plan. And with the level of service your company provides, you better have a great marketing plan bringing in new business constantly as you'll need it just to stay even. Honestly, I doubt even the best marketer can overcome the implementation programs you're obviously trying in your operational area."

"You scum!" Click.

"You too." I said to the dead line. Okay, we'll wait for the angry second call.

A few calls later I find myself speaking to a nurse's aide saying the nurse can't speak right then, she was coding my patient. Everyone was trying to help her get the crash cart upright as it rammed into a wall after glancing off a patient's wheelchair and toppled over. I could hear a sweet symphony of call bells, door alarms, ambulance sirens and the code bell all seemingly synchronized as if it was some mad scientist's lab designed to make crazed animals out of normal people. I got to thinking that every time I heard a code bell go off, I know some patient has gotten his wings.

So I asked "Why did you call me if you didn't want to speak to me?" A reasonable question I thought.

"We do want to speak to you but everyone is busy?" replied the aide.

"So you're a nobody?" I asked innocently.

"Of course I'm a somebody, it's just that I'm not needed for the code." Replied the aide becoming somewhat indignant.

"A somebody who nobody needs. Not too good for the ego I would guess." I muttered barely audibly.

"I heard that!" she fumed.

"Heard what?" I goaded her on. "I wasn't speaking to you."

"Maybe not but you were speaking about me!"

"No I wasn't, but I was speaking."

"Look, what do you want?"

"Actually, I don't want anything. You called me, remember?"

"Well, I can see that was a mistake. Do me a favor and don't call back even if we beep you, okay?"

"Can I get your name so I can quote you on that to the head nurse?"

"No, go away." Click.

I guess I'll find out how things turned out if they give me a death certificate to sign in the morning.

A few calls later, I'm getting pretty cranked up. The volume of admissions is getting oppressive and the insipid nature of the nurses, usually from third world islands, is becoming unbearable.

"I have eight admissions for you." The nurse starts out. I can't decide whether I should shoot her or shoot me. I settle for verbal shots across the bow.

"Eight admissions seem like an awful lot. Could we send half back to the hospital until tomorrow?" I jokingly ask.

"We already sent three back because we didn't like their diagnoses. You're stuck with the other eight. Here we go: first one, lasix 40 mg daily, digoxin …"

"Wait a minute. You're giving me medicines without a diagnosis let alone patient name and other identifying information. Do you want me to divine that information or are you going to give the same things to everyone so it doesn't matter who they are or what they have?"

"Oh, you want their name?" the nurse asks innocently with an accent that barely makes the words intelligible in English.

"Yes, that would be helpful, plus a little clinical information like diagnoses and anything else you might think would be helpful." I said calmly.

"Okay, patient's name is Habinagudtime Mishinuwerhere. He has diabetes, heart attack, stroke, lung cancer, chicken pox, strep throat, canker sore,…"

"Wait a minute, wait a minute. Are you telling me he went to the hospital because of canker sores and chicken pox?" I asked incredulously.

"Not this time but I am reading all his diagnoses for you." She replied. I'm thinking why had god chosen to spare her island from a tsunami?

"Look, I only want to know what he went to the hospital with this time. I don't need to know that he once had a hangnail." Slow burn.

"I don't know why he went to the hospital this time. I only know what I read as his diagnoses." Was she doing this on purpose or was she really that obtuse.

"Tell you what, go ask the patient why he went to the hospital and what they told him was wrong. Okay?"

"Okay, I ask." I waited. Three more beeps while I'm doing so.

She comes back and says "Patient don't know why he went to the hospital except he was sick."

Grrrr. "Sick in what way?"

"I don't know. Do you want me to ask him?"

"YES!" ten – nine – eight …

Two more beeps.

"He says he was very sick but doesn't know with what."

"All I know is he's a lot healthier than you're going to be if you don't get me a diagnosis right now!"

"I get my supervisor."

Beep.

"Hello, I'm the nursing supervisor. Can I help you?"

"Maybe, we'll find out."

"What does that mean?" she sounded upset.

"It means that if you are responsible for training the nurse I was just speaking to, then I doubt you'll be able to help me. By the way, your home has won the daily award my company gives to a SNF every night."

"Oh, and what award is that?"

"Your company gets the award for lifting the largest rock to find a nurse under."

"Look, we have eight patients to verify the orders on. Let's get on with it and a little less of your lip."

Okay, a feisty one. "Let's have the first one then."

We plod on through the first patient. Again with the canker sores and chicken pox.

Oh my god, I've got seven more to go.

Scientifically, an IQ between 70 and 80 indicates someone is not educable. Between 60 and 70 not trainable. Below that, in descending order: idiot, moron and imbecile. Finally, between 0 and 10 there's a category reserved for foreign trained nurses.

And so it went throughout the evening. Making friends, influencing people. I remember reading that book by Dale Carnegie. The most important passage was contained in a postscript. A reporter was asking Mr. Carnegie what happened, if after all his tricks and techniques failed to sway the other person, what would he do. Mr. Carnegie replied that sometimes you just have to tell the other guy "to go to hell"! I understood immediately the wisdom of those words and have cut out all the middle men and gone straight to that bottom line. Under the rubicon that life's too short, either you get it right the first time or you don't get it at all.

Finally, just when I thought it was safe to try to sleep, I get a beep. I look at the clock. 2:38 AM. This better be important. Better be damn important. I called the number. Even though it was wrong on the beeper, this one I had memorized. Will need to remember to send strong e-mail in the morning to the answering service, cc all their other accounts. What am I talking about? It is the morning. Well, I mean later this morning, perhaps after the sun has risen.

"What?!?" I hoped they could hear the venom dripping.

"Doctor, one of your patients has pulled out his Foley. He's bleeding quite severely. We want to send him to the hospital but he refuses. What should we do?"

"Send him to the hospital? Hasn't he already suffered enough? What do you want me to do?"

"Tell him to go to the hospital. We've been trying for half an hour. We have the paramedics and police here but he still refuses."

"So how do you think I'll be able to make a difference? Tell him he's going to die if he doesn't go." Snzzzzz.

"We've told him that and he says that's alright with him. We can't keep him here. You have to try!"

"Okay, put him on." The phone changes hands. "Mr. Dummschitt, why won't you go to the hospital?"

"I've had enough of hospitals. I'm not going back. Ever!"

"You know you're going to bleed to death if you don't go?" Snzzzzzz. It's hard to care more about a patient than they do about themselves.

"I don't care if I die. I'm old, I've had enough."

"Fine. Just do me a favor. When you hang up the phone, give the nurse the names and phone numbers of all of your next of kin so you can call them up and tell them goodbye." Click. Goodbye, you courageous soldier.

Snzzzzzz.

The next morning I was met in the front lobby by the dean of nurses and her two assistants. "I want to know how you got the patient to go to the hospital when my nurses couldn't."

"Must be my charisma." I replied.

Chapter 55: Watch Out, I'm A Busy Man

I wasn't lucky enough to get to take care of Jamison but I hit it big with the arrival of Bobby Montlebaum on my service. Bobby, as his few friends called him, had as large and obnoxious a body to perfectly match his large and obnoxious personality. He had figured prominently in several class actions suits over the years, making him just short of a billionaire. Nevertheless, given the life expectancy of a typical lawyer nowadays and the fear of anyone near him being taken out at the same time, he couldn't find a single person to take care of him in his time of need. He had to rely on the court mandated medical facility unlucky enough to be the target of his suit in a frantic effort to get any care at all. So my nursing home was court ordered to take care of Mr. Montlebaum. The administrator gave interviews to all the media stating that the courts had coerced him into taking on unpleasant patients and he in no way condoned the prior activities of the plaintiff's bar as a whole or Mr. Montlebaum in particular. Nevertheless, once a patient is admitted, it is his responsibility to insure the best of care is afforded to all, without prejudice. He hoped this would put an end to the picketing that started outside of his facility against any lawyer being admitted there when there were decent people in need of care who would be turned away because Mr. Montlebaum forced his way in.

Given that background, it was unbelievably easy for Mr. Montlebaum's case to be assigned to me. No other doctor would go near him. Even I played a little hard to get. I made it clear from the start that I would be demanding some concessions from the administrator to take on this patient. In reality, I would have paid to be assigned as his doctor.

I got what I wanted, basically banal stuff like a parking spot near the entrance and free lunches but I didn't play hardball. I just wanted to make my life a little easier so I'd have more time to devote to my celebrity patient. In short order, Mr. Montlebaum would soon be wishing I was a busier man than I was and didn't take nearly the interest in him that I did.

I reviewed his chart. Apparently, Mr. Montlebaum was suffering from a rare case of idiopathic heart failure of relatively short duration. There was some sort of epidemic going round, probably viral, that afflicted a large number of important lawyers attending a closed guarded conference following the slaughter of tens of thousands of their comrades. The exact number hadn't yet been established as the amount of DNA needing to be matched was excessive. Interestingly enough, in addition to the lawyers, the only other people seemingly affected were a handful of kitchen help who cleaned up afterwards. The mystery was being diligently pursued by the CDC in Atlanta. The question of whether or not this was a poisoning couldn't be answered as all the evidence had long ago been disposed of, that is, all the plates were washed, all the food thrown out, and more importantly, all the booze drunk. Epidemiology was all the CDC workers had to go on and there wasn't much of that.

I entered his room which was decorated in a drab, dungeon like motif. It well matched the rest of the decaying, decades old buildings where we warehoused our old, unwanted citizens. Our "seasoned citizen" are being thrown out like so much refuse into the country's vermin infested rat holes known as nursing homes, waiting their turn to be placed in a proper six foot deep hole. These were the survivors by longevity but losers by their poor social and financial planning. They were both unloved and destitute. Not realizing they needed to be either nice when they were young so someone would care for them when they got old or shrewd enough to have saved enough money to be able to at least buy attention if not love, they had neither and suffered for their youthful failures by living long enough to have to be placed in a nursing home.

There really are things worse than death. Over the years I've invited many friends to let me show them what nursing homes were like. Most declined my invite, those who accepted lived to regret it, never looking upon me and my work quite the same. They tended to shy away from me from then on but did fund their IRA's to the max from then on, so they did learn something.

Having finished reviewing the chart, I walked over to my newest patient's room. I envisioned a still smoldering 666 emblazoned over the threshold, but no, it just said 522. Stepping through the doorway, I spied my patient in person for the first time. I did know what he looked like from the numerous newspaper interviews chronicling his plight and not a few web sites that had recently sprung up listing the newest sport targets in America: trial lawyers. Many had gone into hiding, some made a public repentance hoping to be spared. That just gave the shooting public a better target when they walked out of the TV studios.

He was rather large, I commented to myself, but not so much lengthwise as widthwise I observed. His skin was so pallid I could almost imagine him being the Pillsbury doughboy himself.

"Mr. Montlebaum, I am going to be your doctor here. Your regular doctor doesn't come to the nursing home so I see you in his stead. How are you feeling today?" said with all the sincerity of a spider to a fly as I handed him my card.

"How do you think I feel you quack?" he wheezed out from under his oxygen mask. "I'm 49 years old, a billionaire and am only able to find care by court order. The AMA probably assigned you to my case to torment me because you're the worst doctor in the world and they know I won't live long enough to sue you. Well, screw you! I already have papers filled out to sue you and this rat hole of a nursing home and now that I have your card, I can fill in the name of the defendant and at least get that started before I die."

"My, are we cheerful today. Well, I can say one thing for you, you've at least given me fair warning, although I knew it was your nature to do now what you've always done before, sue. So I came prepared, whether or not you were courteous enough to warn me. See this little syringe in my hand?"

I could see his eyes grow wider with a new dawning fear that perhaps for once he wasn't in charge and words and papers were going to be somewhat ineffectual to alter events which were about to unfold. "Y-y-y-yes, what are you going to do?"

His bravado was turning out to be a little false. At the first sign of adversity, he was beginning to crumble. Well, maybe being a cripple in a nursing home dependent on oxygen and others to move him might have softened him up a little for me. "I'm going to show you true malpractice. Not the bad outcomes that you've been calling malpractice for years that were, in fact, not really malpractice at all. No, this is malpractice, with the emphasis on malice. You know malice, that's your stock in trade, isn't it?"

All this talk was starting to upset him greatly. He made a number of increasingly feeble attempts to yell for help but with each such attempt his heart was getting weaker and weaker and he soon became so tired, his efforts crumbled under the pull of gravity on his substantial body.

"There, that's better." I said as he continued to pant but his flailing arms fell by his side. "There's really no reason to struggle, just lie back and accept the inevitable." I said reassuringly. "This, unfortunately, won't hurt, but don't feel disappointed, that'll come in a little while."

I lifted his rather corpulent right arm, the one with the heparin lock in it. He put up a vain attempt to set himself free but I'd have nothing of it. I didn't bother with an alcohol wipe, if he became septic, all the better. Inserting the syringe into the IV access port, I could see his agitation becoming more acute but in his weakened state, that translated to just panting heavier. The contents of the needle were common enough, simply some of the newer, faster acting insulin, Humalog. It's onset of action was within minutes and only lasted a couple of hours. By the time the nurses made their next rounds, he'd have been in and out of insulin shock and they'd be none the wiser for it. I'd diagnose a new stroke, most likely from a clot formed in his heart from the heart failure and his problem list would grow by one. That's if the nurses even noticed the change in his neurological status. Given the nurses own neurological status, them noticing the patient's change was at best a 50-50 situation.

I calculated the dose to bottom him out at a blood sugar of about 15 to last about half an hour. That wouldn't be enough to kill him but it would be enough to turn him into a quadriplegic and unable to talk. But importantly, he would regain consciousness and would be able to feel pain. How much pain and for how long he could stand it given his weakened heart was something I was planning to find out.

So it was that by the time I withdrew the needle, he was already starting to sweat and his heart was racing faster. These could be signs of a lowering blood sugar or stark terror, either one was fine with me.

I stayed with him until his eyes were just starting to glaze over. Leaning over, I whispered into his ear, "Good night, Mr. Montlebaum, you'll be seeing me in your dreams. And soon, that'll be all that you'll have. Be back tomorrow with a new toy for you to play with." I deftly pulled the suit papers from his now limp hand and left the room.

A new toy. Hmmm. What shall I start with? Nutcrackers (literally), electrical stimulators (set real high), blunt needles?? Decisions, decisions. Well, I'm sure I'll find something to amuse the both of us by tomorrow.

Chapter 56: Another Night Call

I'm on call tonight and I'm rapidly losing any semblance of human sympathy, largely because the nurses that work in SNF's are mutants. Here's a case in point (absolutely true story, recounted as close to verbatim as I can recall):

(Note: the sentiments enclosed in parentheses weren't actually said but boy do I wish they were.)

Nurse: Doctor, I'm calling to report lab results
Doctor: Are any of the labs critical that I need to know now or the patient will die?
N: I don't know
D: Okay, tell me the one which you think is worst
N: Chloride...
D (cutting her off): No, next
N: BUN 42
D: What was her last BUN?
N: She just got here so it's her first test
D: You're telling me she was born there so that she never had any tests before? You know I don't do pediatrics.
N: No, she came from the hospital

Glenn Allen

D: So you're saying that she made it through an entire hospitalization without any blood tests being ordered
N: I don't know
D: Well look through the chart
N: In other words, you are saying you want me to look through the chart
D: No, those aren't in other words, those are my exact words
N: Okay, I'll look through the chart. (Time passes) I don't see any labs
D: Try actually opening the chart and reading it
N: Oh, here are some. Let's see, BUN 43
D: So is she getting better or worse
N: I don't know
D: Okay, that was an unfair question. (It was based upon my assumption that you possessed a brain with an IQ at least in the simian range.) Let me rephrase the question. Concerning ourselves only with the two BUN values, comparing one to the other, does it seem it's rising or falling?
N: Um, let's see. It was 43, now it's 42.
D: Excellent, now is it better to be higher or lower?
N: For BUN, I think it might be better if it's lower.
D: Outstanding. So is it getting better or worse?
N: Worse, no wait, better, I think.
D: I'll accept that in an effort to save what little part of my sanity is remaining. Okay, let's move on. Any other lab that you want to tell me?
N: Yes, hematocrit, 97.
D: No, you're telling me the MCV. Try again, this time reading the value on the same line as the test.
N: I did, but I'll do it again. Let me put the straight edge against the paper and try again. Yup, 97.
D: I'll bet you my house against yours that it's not 97.
N: But I read it twice.
D: Maybe so, but try one more time, this time aiming for accuracy.
N: Okay, but I'm sure I did it right.
D: No, you didn't.
N: Ooops, you're right, it's 37.
D: Good, I'll be over in 30 minutes to pick up my new house keys.

N: What are you talking about?
D: I bet you our houses that you were wrong and I won. I want my house. You're not going to tell me that just because you didn't say okay when I made the bet that you aren't obligated to pay up are you?
N: Well you can't have my house.
D: Okay, but I'm going to tell all my friends about you and that you can't be trusted to honor a bet (or for that matter, take care of patients with your submammalian cranial capacity). Listen, it's clear that none of what you're going to tell me is anything that I need to know. Just fax it to the attending. Do you know her number?
N: No.
D: Great. Bye. (Click)

Another phone call:

Idiot (AKA: nurse): Ms Jones' finger is swollen.
Savant (no need for further elaboration): Can you tell me anything more about it that might be helpful to me in determining why it's swollen?
I: No.
S: That's nice. What would you like me to do about it?
I: You're the doctor, you tell me.
S: Okay, (holding hand to forehead and looking up to the stars for divine intervention), let me guess, the patient was eating and got carried away so that there are vicious teeth marks all over her hand because she couldn't tell where the fork ended and her hand started
I: No.
S: Okay, don't help me now, let me keep guessing - she fell out of bed a week ago and only now has regained consciousness to realize that her hand is broken and it's hurting real bad.
I: No, she didn't fall, she's not complaining of pain and I just noticed it today.
S: Aw geez, I asked you not to help me. Now I have to deal with facts and you know how much that upsets me when trying to diagnose people. Well, if you insist on cheating, let me ask - when exactly did you notice that her hand was swollen?
I: I told you, today.

S: Excellent! We're back in the game! No pesky reality checks to get in our way. So let me guess some more. But before I do that, let me use question #2 of my 20 questions. Do you see any redness or foreign bodies sticking out of her hand?
I: No.
S: Okay, that just about blows every other guess I have except for her getting her hand caught in the drain plug at the bottom of a pool? Is that it?
I: No.
S: Look, I'm going to have to give this some more thought. Tell you what; I'll call you back as soon as I'm been able to divine the answer. Don't call me anymore tonight as I'm already on my knees communing with the spirits and they get pissed if they're interrupted. If I don't get back to you tonight, call the attending after eight AM tomorrow and let her try her hand at guessing too. Two heads are better than one, but I doubt you'd know that as you're still working with only the quarter you were left with when they squeezed the rest out in that vice. Bye now.

Chapter 57: A Hospitalist's Hospital

I came back the next day to an empty bed in room 522. Mr. Montelbaum had been admitted last night to the hospital. He was found on rounds by the night charge nurse, unable to speak or move when she tried to wake him for his sleeping pill. That was over 12 hours after my visit. An exceptionally long time for neglect even under nursing home standards. That means they didn't feed him lunch or dinner. Didn't take him out of bed, go to physical therapy, take vital signs, wash, clean or perform any other service for him for an entire day. It also means he had no visitors or anyone who cared for him to call or enquire by any means. It means the judge who got him admitted under court order didn't care. He had no one. Too bad, I would have liked to see anyone who cared about him suffer too.

I had a good time last night reading over the suit papers he was preparing. There were generic defendants. Everyone who had seen him at anytime during his nursing home stay was to be sued, including the janitor and telephone operator. He was going to make this final hurrah his opus in massive court proceedings. Too bad I intervened. He'll never see his day in court.

I had come back with some special goodies to spur his misery on. It'll just have to wait until he returns from the hospital.

A few days later Mr. Montelbaum still hadn't returned from the hospital and I was getting worried that he might have died and I wasn't going to be able to finish him off myself. I called the hospital and spoke to his attending.

"Hi Carl, how's Mr. Montelbaum doing?"

"Not so good, it turns out. You know he's had a stroke?"

"Of course." I answered expectantly.

"Well, he has been lying in bed a couple of days and became impacted. So I ordered an enema. As the nurse was inserting the enema tip, he jerked and fell off the bed, breaking a hip. We took him to surgery, fixed the hip but he aspirated and developed a pneumonia. We had to place a tracheostomy tube and a feeding tube in through his abdomen to his stomach. He's also developed a few fairly deep sacral decubiti so we're having a hard time with him."

"Okay, just call me when you're shipping him back." And keep up the good work. A trach, PEG and bedsores! The trifecta! Yes!

That hospital is turning out to be the Hospitalist's Hospital.

Chapter 58: Soul Searching

After two months in the hospital, Mr. Montelbaum finally returned to the nursing home. The court ordered him to be transferred to hospice for terminal care.

I saw him the next day. He had lost almost 50 pounds and was actually looking in a lot better shape than he had for years. That is, if you ignored the yellow tinge to his skin from the liver failure, tubes in his neck, abdomen and bladder, the smell from the fetid bedsores covering his entire rear and the contractures that were starting to curl him up in a fetal position. Like I said, looking good!

There wasn't much more I could add to the situation. I had come to the nursing home that morning with my bag full of nasty surprises for Mr. Montelbaum, but there was little I could do to make a worthy contribution to his misery. Nature and the system seemed to have handled the situation for me.

Shortly after admission, he gasped his last breath and as his soul departed his body, heading for hot places down south. I had to sit and do a little soul searching of my own.

I had spent my life railing against the injustices done in the name of justice by those sworn to seek out and uphold justice. Although my accomplishments were substantial in at least eliminating many of the current practitioners of that black art perpetrated by the plaintiff's bar, had I made any fundamental changes in our legal system? The answer, at least until now, was no. There were no new laws passed limiting the right to sue without cause. There were no laws passed rescinding any previously passed laws. There was perhaps a temporary change in sentiment against unrestrained suits but a few lawyers had already started filing personal injury suits again, albeit quietly and none had resumed TV advertising. Nevertheless, I perceived only a temporary lull in the feeding frenzy know as personal injury law. The seas were closing in again on me after having been parted for only the briefest of times. Public sentiment was also turning against the lawlessness of my lawyer massacres. The liberals (mostly made up of lawyers, don't you know) were writing op-ed pieces saying that even though we might despise trial attorneys, what is going to stop me and my ilk from moving on to the next group we might disagree with. Since everyone is associated with some special interest group, the liberals were able to make their case that no one would be safe from attack unless everyone was. Law enforcement agencies were ordered by their lawyer politician masters to become more involved in routing out the terrorists. Lawyers must be allowed to do their work without fear. (Fear actually was their work, but that was left unsaid.)

We met as a group for the last time. Bulldog and Sandy and I had our fill of this endeavor. The only loose end we had was what to do with Detective Freed. We decided he should be found in his rented apartment, shot in the head with his own revolver. The note would read "I can't go on. My wife has left me, I can't live with myself for killing James B. Brown III. I feel responsible for the ensuing antilawyer pogroms that have swept the nation. May you and god forgive me."

"Sounds good to me. Let's handle this last task and we'll be on our way." I said.

The task was actually easier than we anticipated as Detective Freed had already finished off the job for us when we found him in his room. His note wasn't quite what we hoped for as it blamed unnamed others for masterminding the attacks but he was kind enough not to name names or any other details. Still, his note would have led to further investigations about his associates and we felt it best to let it end with him. The notes were switched and the police called.

Everything appeared tidy. We bade farewell and felt it best not to talk to each other for some time unless it became necessary.

Even now, several years later, I still contemplate our actions. The malpractice crises throughout the country have started to spiral out of control again. Virtually all industry has seen a withering attack of suits as the surviving lawyers became emboldened again and the hungry new ones out of law school saw a wide open field with so many of the old guard gone.

Was what we did worthwhile in the slightest? Was the pause in law suits and increase in national productivity just a cruel hoax? Have the spirits of Americans been irreparably broken? Had we raised them so high that they were just that more easily dashed on the rocks of despair of the waiting lawyers below them? Had I wasted my time trying to save people who didn't deserve to be saved?

Had my life been a total waste? Had I hated so long and so hard that I no longer could enjoy the good things around me? Was I headed for the same fate as Detective Freed but had been such a coward it's taken me this long to join him?

Wait a minute! Am I crazy? The hell I was! What I did was good and noble. I failed not in the undertaking but in stopping short of total victory!

I picked up the phone. "Sandy? Bulldog? I've got a job for you!"

Postscript

I was having dinner with my nephew, who, of course, like most of the rest of my family, is a lawyer. He had come in from a western city for several days for a golf clinic, having recently been made partner in a huge law firm and had more money than he knew what to do with. So we drive up to a fairly nice restaurant at the height of the dinner hour and the line was huge. In true lawyerly fashion (that is to say: an underhanded lying scoundrel), he told the maitre de who he was and that he had a reservation. Naturally, they couldn't find his name as he had made no reservation. At that point, he plied his well honed shtick and told them that the concierge at the world famous resort he was staying at obviously failed miserably in his job and he'd take it up immediately with his superior. Not wanting to get the concierge in trouble and in an effort to placate a clearly upset customer, the maitre de apologized for the clear breakdown in otherwise excellent communication with this world famous resort and seated us immediately. If I was any sort of man, I would have exposed the ruse immediately and walked out, probably leaving my nephew standing there to find his own way home. But, I wasn't and I sat down and enjoyed a good meal.

However, I wasn't about to let this drop and in effort to assuage my own guilt, I proceeded to pepper the entire meal with lawyer jokes, some of which follow. I admit that I made up none of them so if the copyright owners want to sue me, join the line.

Joke 1: Why do laboratory researchers prefer lawyers over rats? There are more lawyers than rats. There are no animal rights groups for lawyers. They don't get as attached to the lawyers as they do the rats. There are just some things rats won't do

Joke 2: What do you call 400 lawyers chained together at the bottom of the ocean? A good start.

Joke 3: A lawyer dies and goes to heaven. He's met by ST. Pete himself, ushered into a brand new limo and is driven to his new home. The home is a huge mansion on the top of a multiacre wooded estate. There's flowing streams, tennis courts and beautifully laid out paths throughout the grounds. Before they get out, ST. Pete asks if he would like to see the neighborhood before they tour the home. The lawyer says, sure and they drive around to the back streets where they encounter hovel after hovel. St. Pete starts to call out the names of his neighbors: "Here's Pope Pious XII, and there's Pope John I and there's Pope …"

"Wait a minute." the lawyer interrupts. "What gives? You have me living in this magnificent estate and all these Popes are living in shanties."

"Well," replies St. Pete, up here in heaven, Popes are a dime a dozen, but you're the first lawyer."

So throughout the entire dinner, I'm throwing out these zingers that I've found would make virtually anyone else guffaw but all I get from my nephew is a derisive "Ha".

I've run out of jokes and have all but admitted defeat.

My nephew changes the subject by asking me about medical shows on TV. Specifically, he wants to know if we really can resuscitate virtually everyone that comes through the door as he sees on the show ER.

I reply that TV shows are so unrealistic that they lead to unachievable expectations by the public and do a great disservice to the medical profession, leading, not unexpectedly, to more lawsuits whenever anyone suffers anything other than a perfect outcome. Then, I ask, "By the way, do you know how to resuscitate a lawyer?"

My nephew thinks about this for a minute and shrugs "No."

I respond, emphatically "Excellent."

This was so unexpected and caught him so off guard that he actually gave a genuine laugh.

I wasn't sure which gratified me more: that I could come up with an original joke on the spur of the moment or that I finally got my nephew to laugh. In either case: Victory!

Printed in the United States
116719LV00003B/102/A